educating
IRELAND

educating IRELAND

Schooling and Social Change, 1700–2000

Editors

DEIRDRE RAFTERY AND KARIN FISCHER

IRISH ACADEMIC PRESS

First published in 2014 by Irish Academic Press
8 Chapel Lane
Sallins
Co. Kildare
Ireland

www.iap.ie

This edition © 2014 Irish Academic Press. Chapter contents © contributors

British Library Cataloguing in Publication Data
An entry can be found on request

ISBN: 978-07165-3245-3 (cloth)
ISBN: 978-07165-3244-6 (paper)
ISBN: 978-07165-3246-0 (PDF)

Library of Congress Cataloging in Publication Data
An entry can be found on request

Inside design by www.sinedesign.net

Printed in Ireland by SPRINT-print Ltd

CONTENTS

LIST OF
CONTRIBUTORS

MARIE CLARKE is a senior lecturer in the School of Education, University College Dublin, where she was Head of School (2007–2011). She has published in leading international journals, on the history of education, higher education, development education and teacher education. She is a member of the Governing Authority, University College Dublin, and former President of the Irish Federation of University Teachers.

CLARA CULLEN is an Associate of UCD Humanities Institute. Recent publications include *The World Upturning: Elsie Henry's Irish Wartime Diaries, 1913–1919* (2012), and *His Grace is Displeased: Selected Correspondence of John Charles McQuaid* (2012), edited jointly with Margaret Ó hÓgartaigh. She won the Royal College of Physicians of Ireland History of Medicine prize in 2013.

TONY LYONS lectures in the History of Education at Mary Immaculate College, University of Limerick. He is the author of a number of book chapters and journal articles, and his book *The Education Work of Richard Lovell Edgeworth, Irish Educator and Inventor, 1744-1817* was published by Mellen Press in 2003.

BRIAN McCARTHY completed his PhD research in the history of education at University College Dublin in 2008, writing a thesis entitled 'A History of the Provision and Reform of Probationer Education and Training in the Garda Síochána, 1922-2007' in 2008. His first book, *The Civic Guard Mutiny*, was published by Mercier Press in 2012. He is a guidance counsellor in St. Peter's College, Dunboyne, County Meath, and is a tutor on the Graduate Diploma in Guidance Counselling with the University of Limerick.

CHRISTOPHER McCORMACK has written for scholarly journals including *Paedagogica Historica: International Journal of the History of Education*, and *Riocht na Midhe: Records of Meath Archaeological and Historical Society*. In 2010, he completed a PhD in the history of education at University College Dublin, on 'The Endowed Schools Commissions 1791–1894, as mediators of superior schooling'. A retired secondary schoolteacher, he is author of a book on the history of the Gilson Endowed School.

ANTONIA McMANUS, formerly of the School of Education, Trinity College, and of Hibernia College, is author of *The Irish Hedge School and Its Books, 1695–1831*. She has recently completed a new book, *Ministerial Legacy to Irish Education, 1919–1999*.

CATHERINE NOWLAN-ROEBUCK is a primary school teacher in a large Dublin school. At University College Dublin, she completed a PhD in the history of education which examined the involvement of the Presentation Sisters in Irish education during the nineteenth century. She has contributed to publications such as *History of Education*, and the forthcoming book *Education, Vocation and Care: Histories of Women Religious*, edited by Deirdre Raftery and Elizabeth Smyth.

EILÍS O'SULLIVAN is a member of the Faculty of Education, Mary Immaculate College, University of Limerick, where she lectures on the History and Policy of Education. She has presented research at international conferences based on her PhD, which examined educational provision by lay women of the middle and upper classes in early nineteenth century Ireland.

MARTINA RELIHAN obtained a PhD in the history of education from University College Dublin in 2008, for research that received an award from the Irish Research Council for the Humanities and Social Sciences (IRCHSS). She is a frequent visitor to Sarajevo, Bosnia Herzegovina where she is researching the country's educational system in the nineteenth century. Her work has appeared in many scholarly books and journals, and she is a regular contributor to Irish radio broadcasting.

CONTRIBUTING
EDITORS

DEIRDRE RAFTERY is Director of Research at the School of Education, University College Dublin, where she lectures and supervises research in the history of education. She was a Visiting Research Fellow at the University of Oxford, in 2010, and is a Life Member of Girton College, Cambridge. She has published many articles, book chapters and books, including *Women and Learning in English Writing, 1600–1900* (1997), and (jointly) *Female Education in Ireland, 1700–1900: Minerva or Madonna?* (2007); *Gender Balance and Gender Bias in Education: International Perspectives* (2011), and *History of Education: Themes and Perspectives* (2013). She was joint editor of *History of Education* (Routledge/Taylor & Francis), from 2009–2014, and is a member of the Executive Committee of the History of Education Society (UK) She was an IRC funded Visiting Scholar at La Trobe University, Melbourne, in 2014.

KARIN FISCHER lectures in Irish and British Studies at the University of Orléans, France and has also taught at Trinity College, Dublin and the University of Caen. She has since co-edited several books in the field of Irish studies and on issues of cultural diversity at an international level and published a wide range of book chapters or articles on education policy, school history and historiography, identity and inclusion in Ireland, North and South, from both historical and contemporary perspectives. An updated version of her book *École et religion – Hiérarchies identitaires et égalité citoyenne en République d'Irlande* (Presses Universitaires de Caen, 2011) is to be published by Manchester University Press in 2014 under the title *Schools and the Politics of Religion in the Republic of Ireland*. She is a member of the Corresponding Board of *History of Education* and of the Executive Board of the French journal *Études Irlandaises*.

ACKNOWLEDGEMENTS

The editors gratefully acknowledge the support of the following: the History of Education Society (UK); the National University of Ireland (Scholarly Publications Award); the University of Orléans, France (Scholarly Publications Award – RÉMÉLICE Research Centre); the staff of Irish Academic Press. Gratitude is also expressed to each of the submitting authors and to Catherine KilBride for her thoughtful contributions to the final manuscript, and proofing of the volume.

The cooperation of the following is also acknowledged: Alexandra College Dublin Archives; Cahir Archives, Butler-Charteris Hall; Colonial Office (UK); National Archives, UK; Dublin Diocesan Archives; Erasmus Smith Archives; Glucksman Library, University of Limerick; Harcourt Home Archives, Dublin; Kildare Place Society (KPS) Archives, Church of Ireland College of Education, Dublin (CICE); National Archives of Ireland; National Library of Ireland; Natural History Museum, Dublin; Public Records Office, Northern Ireland; Quaker Regional Archives, Cahir Heritage Society; South Presentation Convent Cork Archives; University College Dublin Library and Archives; Vocational Education Committee Archives.

Finally, we thank our families for their constant support and interest, especially our husbands, Peter Caprani and John Power, and our children, Leonard Caprani, and Juliette and Kathleen Power.

Deirdre Raftery and Karin Fischer

This book is dedicated with gratitude to two scholars who have inspired and influenced our work:

Susan M. Parkes, Trinity College Dublin
and
Paul Brennan, University of Paris III – Sorbonne Nouvelle

PREFACE

This book is a most welcome addition to scholarship in the history of education, bringing research on Irish society, schools, educators and education policy to an international audience. The volume brings together the work of leading scholars and early-career researchers, working on the eighteenth, nineteenth and twentieth centuries. Some chapters break new ground by drawing on research at archives that have not, heretofore, been examined in detail. Other chapters offer fresh insight into areas that have not been re-examined for decades.

In Part One, the unofficial system of eighteenth-century 'hedge schools' is examined by Antonia McManus; the history of education policy and change is served well by a study of 'superior schooling' by Christopher McCormack, and Tony Lyons provides a close examination of the legacy of Thomas Wyse. Part Two, with its focus on nineteenth-century education and society, opens with Eilís O'Sullivan's study of the provision of schooling for the poor by women of the upper ranks, giving a new perspective on women's education enterprise in Ireland. There is also a chapter on the unique educational role of the Museum of Irish Industry, by Clara Cullen; an analysis of the contribution of the Presentation Sisters to schooling, by Catherine Nowlan-Roebuck; and Deirdre Raftery's study of the little-known world of governesses in Irish homes. Part Three of the book looks at education policy and change in the twentieth century. Martina Relihan's research explores engagements between the Church of Ireland and the State, about the Irish language and education after the founding of the Irish Free State; Brian McCarthy provides welcome insight into the education and training of the Garda Síochána from the Free State period up to the 1980s; Marie Clarke analyses developments in education policy and the role of Vocational Education Committees in the 1960s and Karin Fischer also engages with policy and change through her work on education in the 1980s in Northern Ireland.

What emerges is an important book, rich with reflective and analytical research, that deepens our knowledge of Irish education and illuminates our understanding of key areas of change in the world of education in Ireland over three centuries.

Professor Jane Martin, University of Birmingham
President, History of Education Society (UK), 2010–2013

1

PART ONE
EDUCATION POLICY AND PRACTICE IN THE LONG EIGHTEENTH AND NINETEENTH CENTURIES

1 THE IRISH HEDGE SCHOOL AND SOCIAL CHANGE

ANTONIA McMANUS

The hedge schools of Ireland originated in the sixteenth century with the suppression of the monastic schools by King Henry VIII. They are also mentioned in the Cromwellian Records of 1655, but they developed rapidly following the passing of the Penal Laws of 1695, which proscribed Catholic education and prohibited parents from sending their children abroad to be educated.[1] Teachers taught surreptitiously for the next eighty-seven years, and their favourite location was, as folklore has it, on the sunny side of a hedge. When the Penal Laws were repealed in 1782, they still retained the name 'hedge schools', although teaching was conducted in a variety of buildings, including chapels. This chapter examines how hedge schools effected social change in Ireland, while also noting ways in which they responded to such change.

IRISH HEDGE SCHOOLS

Past writers on hedge schools were former students of Professor Timothy J. Corcoran S.J., Professor of Education at University College Dublin (UCD). He was the first academic to give serious attention to the history of hedge schools. He did so in two positive accounts published in 1916[2] and 1928.[3] One of his students, P.J. Dowling, wrote *The Hedge Schools of Ireland*[4] in 1932 and it was re-printed up to the late 1960s. Two other students of Professor Corcoran's, the Rev. Martin Brenan, future Professor of Education at St. Patrick's College, Maynooth, and Philip O'Connell, sometime Principal of the Central Technical School in Clonmel, Co. Tipperary, produced books on hedge schools in 1935 and 1942 respectively.[5] All of these accounts lauded hedge schools and their masters but tended to discount or dismiss the views of hedge school critics. In her study, Mary E. Daly observed that '...[m]ost accounts, such as that of Dowling and O'Connell, seem excessively eulogistic.'[6]

This chapter is informed by recent research[7] which acknowledges the achievements of hedge schools for over a century but which takes cognisance of the shortcomings of hedge schoolmasters and the limitations of a hedge school education.

Hedge schools were fee-paying schools, run mainly but not exclusively by male teachers and they immediately won the strong support of parents, even when proscribed by law. The 1731 inquiry conducted by the House of Lords committee into 'The Present State of Popery' revealed a surprisingly high number of hedge schools in Dublin, Mayo, Armagh and Cork.[8] The report referred to the fact that there were more Catholic schools in operation but they proved impossible to identify as they were illegal. Their popularity continued to grow in the post-penal era. In his diocesan report of 1790 Bishop Patrick Plunkett of Co. Meath noted 240 hedge schools in his diocese.[9] In 1807 Dr. Coppinger, Bishop of Cloyne and Ross, drew up a list of 316 hedge schools in his diocese. Both sets of figures revealed an average of about six hedge schools in every parish, a number which was confirmed in the general survey conducted nationwide in 1824 for the Irish commissioners of education, who were conducting their inquiry into Irish education.[10]

The many reasons for the popularity of the hedge schools reflected aspects of Irish social history. For example, there was a long tradition of learning in Ireland which dated back to the coming of Christianity in the fifth century and the establishment of the monastic schools, and indeed to the much older tradition of the Bardic schools, which lasted until 1641. People were well aware that they were 'the residuary legatees of a civilisation that was more than 1,000 years old.'[11] In supporting hedge schools, the Irish demonstrated that they would fight for the education of their children with a tenacity born of desperation. Secondly, there were few alternatives open to them. The state-sponsored parish, diocesan, royal and charter schools promoted a different culture and religion, so too did the plethora of bible society schools or education societies of the late eighteenth and early nineteenth centuries.[12] Some of these schools were avowedly anti-Catholic and all of them eventually became proselytising in intent. The Catholic parish schools of 1731 placed their emphasis on propagating the faith and the small number of schools of religious orders and lay people came nowhere near satisfying national demand.

These reasons alone hardly account for the longevity of hedge schools. Their popularity was due in large measure to the democratic principles upon which they were founded. They were schools 'of the people, for the people, by the people.' Parents could select the hedge schools to which to send their children, and they decided the curriculum to be taught. They supplied reading books and they were also entitled to three lessons of individual instruction for their children each day. In this partnership of parents and masters, the former were in a commanding position as they paid fees to the master, who charged per subject per quarter. As poverty was endemic the masters accepted payment in kind and home produce was bartered for a hedge school education. Parents made what one observer called 'meritorious sacrifice of earnings ... for the education of their children'[13] at a time when a shilling represented a full day's wage for a well-paid farm labourer.[14]

Lord Palmerston observed with admiration the sacrifices made by his Irish-speaking tenants in Co. Sligo in 1808, commenting on how many parents built very modest hedge schools for the masters to ensure an education for their children:

> The thirst for education is so great that there are now three or four schools upon the estate. The people join in engaging some itinerant master: they run him up a miserable mud hut in the roadside, and the boys pay him half a crown or some five shillings a quarter.[15]

By the 1820s, the population had risen to six-and-a-half million, and hedge schoolmasters responded imaginatively to the demand for education by providing evening classes from 6pm to 11pm. This also allowed them to accommodate students whose services were required at home during the day. On occasions, parents took the law into their own hands in a desperate bid to secure a hedge schoolmaster for their parish by kidnapping one from another parish. According to contemporary writers this practice was a common one.[16] William Carleton, the nineteenth-century novelist who had conducted a hedge school for a period, explained why he believed such a practice was resorted to. He said:

> The country was densely inhabited, the rising population exceedingly numerous ... the old and middle-aged heads of families were activated by a simple wish, inseparable from Irishmen, to have their children

educated: and the young men, by a determination to have a properly qualified person to conduct their night classes.[17]

Hedge schoolmasters provided their own teacher training. Hedge schools were, in every sense, schools 'of the people' as 'Poor Scholars' or student teachers underwent a long and arduous training under hedge schoolmasters of repute. The earliest reference to the 'Poor Scholar'[18] is to be found in an English translation of an Irish poem, entitled 'The Poor Scholar's Blessing', written around the middle of the eighteenth century. Lady Chatterton met Poor Scholars during her tour of Ireland in 1838,[19] but 'The Poor Scholar appears to have passed out of existence before 1850',[20] in the wake of the Great Famine of 1846–47. This century-old tradition involved the issuing of a challenge by the Poor Scholar to his teacher. The 'challenge was generally couched in rhyme and either sent by the hands of a common friend, or posted upon the chapel-door.' If the student was defeated he continued on in his local hedge school, but if he succeeded he would seek out a more learned teacher. The Poor Scholar would issue many such challenges over two years, before finally settling in his profession. During this time he would travel considerable distances to reputable hedge schools. Fortunately, education was held in such high esteem that the hospitality of the people and the professional services of the masters were offered gratuitously to him. Carleton discovered that 'his satchel of books was a passport to the hearts of the people.' Having a Poor Scholar in his school enhanced the master's reputation and gave him added status.[21] In fact the master enjoyed enormous professional status in Irish society. The antiquarian and folklorist Crofton Croker estimated that 'next to the lord of the manor, the parson and the priest' the hedge schoolmaster was 'the most important personage in the parish.'[22]

The professional status of the master was usually determined by his reputation for erudition and his success as a teacher. It was crucial for his reputation that he should impress parents and according to Carleton he was forced to engage in ludicrous pedantry in their presence. He would speak in words which were truly sesquipedalian, which were 'dark and difficult to understand,' and which were usually interspersed with Latin quotations.[23] His future in the profession depended on this performance as Richard Lovell Edgeworth stated in a letter to the lord primate in the early nineteenth century, 'the best teacher … soon attracts all the scholars, and the inferior master is soon obliged to give way.'[24] This meant that the master lived with a profound sense of insecurity as he competed against at least five other teachers in his parish and he never knew when a rival was going to set up in opposition to him. There was therefore no room for modesty in the teaching profession, and from the outset masters would boast about their accomplishments in 'flaming advertisements' detailing an impressive list of subjects mastered.

When Richard MacElligott promoted his school at Crosby Row in Limerick city, he advertised in the *Limerick Chronicle* as follows: 'Richard MacElligott … [has] completed a plan which reduces the Greek and Latin languages to the level of the tenderest capacities'.[25]

It was common practice for masters to refer to themselves as 'professors' or 'philomaths' in their advertisements. If they excelled in any branch of learning parents would confer honorary titles upon them such as 'The Bright Star in Mathematical Learning' or 'The Great O'Brien par excellence'.[26]

In terms of education, the masters served the people well. They ensured that the most up-to-date textbooks were in use, such as *The Child's New Play Thing*, *Reading Made Easy*, *The Universal Spelling Book*, and that the older arithmetic books by Elias Voster and John Gough were superseded by Paul Deighan's *A Complete Treatise on Arithmetic*, which included book-keeping. Three Limerick hedge schoolmasters went so far as to publish a 'recommendatory letter' in the *Limerick Gazette* of 2 February 1813 suggesting that parents should purchase the newly-published arithmetic by Deighan. Arithmetic was a subject in which the masters excelled, credit for which was given by their strongest critics, as well as by their staunchest allies: the parents. Perhaps unsurprisingly, the leading mathematician of the age was James McCullough, a past pupil of a hedge school in Glenellie, Co. Tyrone, who went on to become a Professor of Mathematics in Trinity College in 1836, at the age of twenty-five.[27]

Latin and Greek formed an important part of the hedge school curriculum. This didn't meet with the approval of Sir Robert Peel, who as Home Secretary (1822–27) expressed the view in the House of Commons in 1826, that he didn't wish to see children educated like the 'young peasants of Kerry' who 'run about in rags with a Cicero or a Virgil under their arms'.[28] This was, after all, an age which promoted the utilitarian philosophy of Jeremy Bentham (1748–1832), which emphasised 'useful learning as opposed to the decadent and illiberal liberal education'.[29] There was a deeply held conviction by some political leaders, contemporary writers, and evangelical educators that the poor should not be educated above their station in life. It was one that was not shared by hedge schoolmasters. In some instances, however, the teaching of the classics was done to meet the practical needs of students who wished to gain entry to the Church, the army, trade or service on the continent.[30]

Up until 1793, when the first Irish seminaries were founded at St. Kieran's College, Kilkenny and St. Patrick's College, Carlow, Irish students who wished to study for the priesthood in the Irish Colleges on the continent, relied almost exclusively on the native schools for instruction in the classics to meet their entry requirements. According to the private report of Dr. Curtis, the rector of the Irish College at Salamanca, for the year 1789, the academic standard of entrants from Ireland was generally high and students came from twenty-six different counties.[31] Considering that the Irish College had been incorporated with the University of Salamanca in 1608, the qualifications for entrance must in many cases have been of corresponding standard.

Hedge schoolmasters satisfied the wishes of parents who desired social advancement for their children by teaching them English. English was the language of commerce, fair and market place. It was the language of the landlord and the tithe proctor and of the courts. English was necessary for the Irish who emigrated and it also came to dominate Church service by the late eighteenth century. Some people may have been influenced by the advice offered by Swift when he told them: 'It would be a noble achievement to abolish the Irish language so far as to oblige all the natives to speak only English on every occasion of business in shops, markets, fairs and other places of dealings.'[32] A more potent influence was that of Daniel O'Connell, 'the most important and most conspicuous man of his time and country' whose name was 'mightier in its appeal in Ireland than any other name.'[33] O'Connell was a declared Benthamite when it came to the Irish language. Although a fluent Irish speaker, he declared dispassionately that he was 'sufficiently utilitarian not to regret its abandonment' and added: 'The superior ability of the English tongue, as the medium of all modern communications is so great, that I can witness without a sigh the gradual disuse of Irish.'[34]

Another factor which may have precipitated the decline of the language was the use to which it was put by Protestant proselytising education societies. As a number of these education societies issued their religious tracts in Irish, the language itself came to be associated with proselytism in the minds of some people. However, as almost every Irish poet of the eighteenth century was also a hedge schoolmaster we can safely assume that they didn't support parents' views on the Irish language. We know that in 1754 they convened a court of poetry, in the old Bardic tradition, to discuss the revival of the Irish language, realising 'that what little remained of Irish was sure to vanish utterly unless they took steps towards its revival.'[35]

Despite their reservations the masters co-operated with parents by teaching their children English from textbooks and an eclectic mix of reading books. It was clear from the Report of the Commissioners of Education (1825) which listed books read in the hedge schools of Counties Donegal, Kildare, Galway and Kerry, representing the four provinces of Ireland, that Irish was on the wane.[36] Even taking into account how few Irish books were published at this time, it is remarkable that only six Irish books were listed, all of which were religious books and catechisms. Of the 299 books listed under the heading Works of Entertainment, Histories, Tales, fourteen caused offence to concerned church clergymen of all denominations, bible society proprietors, members of the establishment and landed classes. These were mainly imaginative works, romantic fiction, innocuous criminal biographies with a moral corollary and stories of royal concubines who came to a sorry end. The list contained such classics of English literature as Milton's *Paradise Lost*, Goldsmith's *Deserted Village*, Chesterfield's *Accomplished Gentleman* and Dr. Johnson's *Classical Essays*.

Many of the hedge school reading books were pirated versions of English originals, as a thriving re-print industry (1748–1800) developed in Ireland, due to an oversight in the Copyright Act of 1709, which excluded Ireland from its provisions. It is evident from the printers' lists and advertisements for the eighteenth and nineteenth centuries, and from the Report of the Commissioners of Education (1825) that the perennial favourites for young readers were *The Story of Guy Earl of Warwick*, the *History of Fortunatus* and *The Story of St. George and the Dragon* – stories guaranteed to appeal to the imagination of the child. But this ran counter to the philosophical thinking of both liberal and conservative groups in society. John Locke, the late seventeenth-century radical philosopher, viewed fairy tales as 'perfectly useless trumpery,'[37] and Rousseau believed that 'children required the naked truth,'[38] while Sarah Trimmer, the evangelical writer, denounced *The Story of Cinderella* as 'a compendium of vice' and condemned *Robinson Crusoe* as a dangerous book which led to an early taste for a rambling life.[39]

But it took Irish parents and the hedge schoolmasters to appreciate the importance of stimulating and nurturing the imaginative life of the child. All attempts to replace or suppress these books in Ireland failed. The national education commissioners only succeeded in replacing the hedge school books with their own books by making them compulsory reading in all but name. In fact it took six years of effort before the commissioners savoured success and they only achieved this by providing their own lesson books free of charge to schools and by making teachers' promotion conditional on their passing an examination on their contents.

One of the most important subjects taught in hedge schools was religion. The Report of the Commissioners of Education (1825) listed ninety-two books under the heading Religious Works and Tracts as well as eleven Roman Catholic catechisms, four of which were in Irish. Uniquely for the period, the hedge schools provided a non-denominational education, which was a remarkable achievement in a country described by Bishop James Doyle of the diocese of Kildare and Leighlin as 'infuriated by sectarian zeal.'[40] The 1825 Commissioners' list also included four catechisms of the Established Church by Stopford, Mann, Marriott and Lewis together with a Presbyterian catechism by Shorter. The hedge schools in fact offered an impressive range of subjects which included arithmetic, surveying/land measuring, book-keeping, astronomy, science, history and geography, Latin, Greek, English, and Irish Dancing. The quality of the curriculum in any hedge school depended on the ability of the master, which ranged from bare literacy to inflated pedantry to genuine scholarly achievement, and on the capacity of parents to pay.

It should also be remembered that the majority of the youth population did not attend schools of any kind, as revealed in the 1821 census.[41] It is calculated that 'at best just over 32% of the age cohort 5-15 years were found in attendance at schools of any sort in 1824.'[42] But is should be noted that hedge schools catered for all age groups, and proof of high levels of literacy are evident, particularly for the late eighteenth century. In the 1790s there were fifty printers in Dublin alone, thirty-four provincial presses and at least forty newspapers.[43] The strength of the Dublin and rural book-selling and publishing industry is borne out by the surge in devotional literature sales in the late eighteenth century.[44]

THE SOCIAL STATUS OF THE HEDGE SCHOOLMASTER

The hedge schoolmaster was a central figure in the life of the community and his social status was therefore considerable. According to Carleton he was 'the master of ceremonies at all wakes and funerals.'[45] He served his community in a multiplicity of roles, sometimes out of a sense of civic duty but more often still out of economic necessity. He was the village scribe employed by the unlettered. He was also the 'cheap attorney of the neighbourhood,'[46] who carried out an immense amount of legal work. Most of the masters were engaged in transcribing the manuscripts while others still were forced to work as part-time labourers 'for a subsistence.'[47] David Manson, the Belfast hedge schoolmaster was also a brewer, while Amhlaoibh Ó Súilleabháin who taught with his father John at the crossroads in Callan, Co. Kilkenny also conducted a drapery business. Other teachers in this area found ready employment as clerks in the collieries.[48] The master was also the village surveyor, a service considered vital in the community. James Bicheno writing about the Irish economy in 1830 was bemused by this requirement of the Irish people, considering how little land they themselves had to measure.[49]

Of all the roles that schoolmasters played in society, that of entertainer was among the most important. The poet/hedge schoolmasters were held in the affections of the Irish people because they entertained them with their songs and poetry. Seán Ó Coileán, the lyrical poet from Clonakilty, Co. Cork, was known to his people as 'The Silver Tongue of Munster'[50] and Eoghan Rua Ó Súilleabhain from Kerry was known affectionately as 'Eoghan an Bhéil Bhinn', Eoghan of the Sweet Mouth.[51] They were revered in Irish society because they raised the morale of an impoverished people burdened with rack rents, tithes and priests' dues, and because they lifted the spirits of a people who endured intermittent famines.

Even though a strong bond had been forged between the priests and the majority of the Catholic population in penal times, following the repeal of the Penal Laws in 1782, that close relationship was fractured for a period. This was mainly due to the Catholic Church's denunciation of agrarian agitation and its subsequent excommunication of Whiteboys and members of other secret societies of the eighteenth century. The hedge schoolmasters were 'of the people' and shared the same political and cultural outlook as the people; they not only supported the secret societies but in some instances played a leading organisational role in them. According to Crofton Croker, the hedge schoolmaster was: '… frequently the promoter of insurrectional tumults: he plans the nocturnal operations of the disaffected: writes their threatening proclamations.'[52]

The Catholic prelates strongly disapproved of the United Irishmen's rebellion of 1798, which was based on what they considered to be dangerous French principles. Many of them had been trained on the continent and they knew 'well how dangerous revolution could be, and how ineffectual the church usually was when it tried to control social agitation.'[53] The people didn't follow the guidance offered by their spiritual leaders on this occasion either and neither did some of the hedge schoolmasters, who had either direct or indirect involvement in the Rising. A notable feature was the calibre of master who got involved – without exception they had attained distinction in the teaching profession. Richard MacElligott was an eminent Celtic scholar from Limerick, who was arrested in 1798. The Belmullet, Co. Mayo poet, linguist and hedge schoolmaster, Riocárd Báiréad, was imprisoned for his membership of this movement and James Baggott, the renowned Limerick mathematician, known as The Great O'Baggott, was a personal friend of Lord Edward FitzGerald, one of the leaders of the rebellion. They would have been familiar with the radical writings of Thomas Paine, Rousseau and William Godwin, some of which were in wide circulation at the time. It seems highly unlikely that there was widespread involvement of hedge schoolmasters in illegal movements as most masters would have wished to avoid the risk of being hanged, excommunicated or banished from their parishes.

After the 1798 rebellion, the priests gained in popularity with the people once more, but this was to be short-lived. The reason for this was that the ruling classes grew suspicious of the priests, suspecting some of them of having sympathy with their revolutionary parishioners. Several priests were killed and their houses were attacked by Orangemen and militia. But due to circumstances beyond their control priests were destined to be isolated from the people yet again in the nineteenth century. They were forbidden, by a church which was undergoing reform, from attending weddings, banquets, station dinners, horse-races, theatres, public houses, or other places of amusement. The easy familiarity once enjoyed by the people with their priests was now gone, especially after priests were directed to adopt a distinctive clerical dress, which 'provided the outward symbol, as well as being an effective guarantor, of the new social distance between the pastor and his flock.'[54]

The tightening of ecclesiastical discipline also meant that the priests were precluded from attending such quasi-religious celebrations as the 'pattern'. This was the festival day of a saint to whom a well or a shrine was dedicated, a day on which thousands of people assembled for religious devotions at a holy site but which sometimes degenerated into a scene of 'dancing, drinking, roaring and singing.'[55] Irreverent behaviour at the traditional 'merry wake' held following a death was hardly likely to meet with church approval either, as the normal amusements of an Irish social gathering were also to be found at the wake-house. There was dancing, story-telling, singing, excessive drinking and match-making.[56] However, there was nothing precluding hedge schoolmasters from participating in these quasi-religious festivities because, as an anonymous pamphleteer of the nineteenth century explained, the hedge schoolmasters were 'imbued with the same prejudices, influenced by the same feelings, subject to the same habits'[57] as the people among whom they lived.

THE CATHOLIC CHURCH AND THE HEDGE SCHOOLMASTER

There is clear evidence that a symbiotic relationship often existed between the parish priest and the hedge schoolmaster, whereby the local chapel often served the purpose of a hedge school. The parish priest, who had a general duty of supervision of religious instruction in hedge schools, had the right to visit to ensure that children knew their catechism and that the teachers taught it. He also had a duty to ensure that the master was a man of good moral life.[58] The masters needed the approval of the parish priest if they wished to survive in the competitive teaching profession. No doubt this coloured the decision of many masters to fill the honorary role of parish clerk in order to ingratiate themselves with priests. Hedge schoolmasters also played a key role in the Catholic revival movement known as the Confraternity of Christian Doctrine. This involved attending chapel every Sunday to instruct the children in catechism. Dr. Doyle, Bishop of Kildare and Leighlin, proudly boasted: 'I am sure that that there is no part of Ireland in which Sunday schools are more diligently attended than in my diocese.'[59]

The Catholic Church had little option but to avail itself of the professional services of the masters in their missionary work because of the shortage of priests and the simultaneous growth in population. The population had risen by 80 per cent between 1731 and 1800 but the number of priests only rose by 12 per cent. There were 1,587 Catholics to every one priest in 1731, compared to 2,627 Catholics at the end of the century.[60]

This mutually beneficial relationship between priests and hedge schoolmasters was brought to an abrupt end in the 1820s due to the political struggle for control of Irish education which took place between 1820 and 1831. A main participant in this conflict was the Society for Promoting the Education of the Poor of Ireland, also known as the Kildare Place Society (KPS). The KPS was set up in 1811 to provide elementary education for the poor of Ireland, by adopting what it called its 'leading principle' which was: '…to afford the same facilities for education to all classes of professing Christians without any attempt to interfere with the peculiar religious opinions of any'.[61]

In all schools under its auspices a strict rule had to be observed that the bible was to be read to the children 'without note or comment' and no other religious instruction was to be allowed.[62] When the Society sought government financial support in 1816 'this was readily forthcoming.' It received annual grants ranging from £6,000 in 1816 to £30,000 in 1831.[63]

However, the Society came under suspicion in the 1820s and allegations were made that it had reneged on its 'leading principle' of non-interference with the religious beliefs of children. Claims were also made that the Society had granted financial assistance to schools already in receipt of funding from two proselytising societies, the London Hibernian Society and the Association for Discountenancing Vice and Promoting the Knowledge and Practice of the Christian Religion, thereby breaking two of its own rules. But the most serious challenge to the future of the Society came from a politician, Daniel O'Connell, who was a member of the KPS. He attended their annual general meeting in 1819, and again in 1820, to lodge a protest against their Bible-reading rule, which he alleged was discriminatory against Catholic children. He expressed his approval of the 'leading principle' but he claimed that the former cancelled out the latter. He withdrew from the Society when the decision to retain the rule was upheld by majority vote.[64] On 25 February 1820, O'Connell addressed a letter to the Catholic prelates which was published the following day in the *Dublin Weekly Register*, in which he accused the KPS of pretending to afford equal educational opportunities to all children, when their real aim was proselytism. He advised the bishops to establish a 'National Association for Education' lest they leave themselves open to charges of hostility to the education of the poor.

O'Connell's political ambition was not to achieve state aid for Catholic education, but to achieve Catholic Emancipation. He recognised that, without the co-operation of the Catholic Church, this was less likely to be achieved. He needed to find a cause which would draw the Church into politics and ultimately into the Catholic Emancipation campaign itself. He had now found such a cause. The bishops accepted O'Connell's advice and promptly established a society in January 1821 which was intended to be the Catholic equivalent of the Kildare Place Society, called the Irish National Society for Promoting the Education of the Poor. Both Catholic prelates and influential laymen founded this society in the hope of altering the distribution of the Kildare Place funds to permit Catholic control of funds for the education of Catholic children, or that they might at least obtain a share of the public money accruing to the education societies. Six months later the Society had only managed to establish one non-denominational school for boys at No. 4 Lower Abbey Street, Dublin, in contrast to the rapidly expanding KPS.

Without state funding, the society couldn't hope to survive. Bishop James Doyle, who was to become the leading Catholic Church spokesman on education, requested Sir Henry Parnell MP to present a petition to the House of Commons on behalf of the hierarchy and laity, for funding for the education of the Irish poor. Before presenting the petition to parliament on 18 May 1821, Parnell requested a report from Doyle on the state of Catholic education in Ireland. In 1824 when the nationwide survey was conducted, parochial returns were sent to Catholic and Protestant church clergymen eliciting information on the schools in their parishes. Right through the returns for Bishop Doyle's diocese of Kildare and Leighlin, the hedge schoolmasters were described as 'of excellent character,' 'of moral character,' 'of good character.'[65] It was clear from an analysis of the returns that 64 per cent of Catholic male teachers were competent to give further instruction beyond the basic numeracy and literacy level. It is reasonable to suggest that in 1821, when Doyle wrote his report, he was well aware of the professional competency of hedge schoolmasters, but under the circumstances he couldn't afford to paint a picture of them as worthy educators. He alleged that:

> ...nine-tenths of the farmers' children and all those of the better
> classes receive education of a very imperfect kind, and imparted
> in a very defective way, by men, in many instances, incompetent
> to teach.[66]

The petition was unsuccessful but Doyle drew up a manuscript in the autumn of 1821 entitled *Thoughts on the Education of the Poor in Ireland*, which he submitted to the Chief Secretary Charles Grant for the government's consideration. In it he attributed the lack of a sound religious education to the growth of secret oath-bound societies in the country.[67] There was no foundation whatever to his statement regarding the lack of a sound religious education in the hedge schools. The parochial returns for his own diocese showed that there were twenty-five different religion books in use as well as twenty-six doctrinal and devotional books, not to mention the impressive number of Sunday Schools conducted by hedge schoolmasters.[68]

Doyle's reference to the growth in secret oath-bound societies in the 1820s sits uncomfortably with the facts. The main secret society at this time was the deeply sectarian revolutionary society of Ribbonmen, founded around 1811, in which hedge schoolmasters had little or no involvement. Carleton wrongly claimed that there was scarcely a hedge schoolmaster in Ireland who did not 'hold articles ... that is, who was not a ribbon-lodge master.'[69] But his own experience of the Ribbonmen was confined to the Ulster borderlands, and then only for a limited period around 1813. A more reliable source of information would be the list of Dublin Ribbonmen for 1821 contained in the diary of the notorious chief of police for Dublin, Major Sirr. Of the seventy-six names listed in his diary, only one was a hedge schoolmaster. According to the list of Ribbonmen suspects for 1842 in the Public Records Office in London, no hedge schoolmaster was involved.[70] It is far more likely that the hedge schoolmasters supported the campaign for Catholic Emancipation which was renewed again in 1823 with the formation of the Catholic Association. One of the main reasons for the success of the campaign was the participation of the clergy, who were *ex officio* members of the Catholic Association right from the outset.[71]

There can be little doubt that the Catholic Association used the education issue to grow closer to the Catholic Church. In the House of Commons on 29 March 1824, John Henry North, a founder member of the KPS, claimed in his maiden speech that until the establishment of the Society 'the whole country, in regard to education, was in a state of thick and palpable darkness,' and that 'the Catholic priests never undertook the task of instructing them.'[72] The Catholic Association invited the clergy to refute North's speech. Letters poured into the Association's Capel Street rooms and the first to respond was the redoubtable Doyle. In his reply he gave the clergy full credit for keeping the light of education alive during the dark days of the penal laws. Arguably, he overstated the contribution of the clergy to Irish education, and indeed he admitted in a letter published in the *Carlow Morning Post* that his priests were 'overwhelmed with other duties of their calling.'[73] Official figures confirm that it was the hedge schools which kept the light of education alive as they increased in number from 4,000 hedge schools in 1807 to over 9,000 in 1824.[74]

THE IRISH EDUCATION INQUIRY, 1824–1827

Petitioning parliament for grant aid for Catholic education ceased while the 1824 Commission of Inquiry into Irish education was in progress. Like their predecessors in 1806, the 1824 commissioners found instruction in the hedge schools to be 'extremely limited' and the masters in general to be 'ill-qualified' and the books to be 'an evil which still requires a remedy.'[75] Martin Brenan has argued that the commission was inequitable because of the negligible amount of time allotted to discussion of the indigenous schools and Catholic educational establishments, compared to the disproportionate amount given over with the discussion of the schools and societies of the Established Church. He noted that in a report consisting of 102 folio pages, only three were devoted to the organisation of Catholic education, and of the 881 pages of appendices giving evidence on oath, only thirty-six were given to Catholic apologists.[76]

It would appear that at least three of the five commissioners were prejudiced against hedge schools and their masters. The charges they made against them were based on anecdotal evidence or on mere hearsay. For example, the Catholic commissioner and Treasury Remembrancer, Anthony Richard Blake, testified before the select committee of the House of Lords in 1837 that the character of the masters '… appeared particularly bad … they were described as very mischievous people, they were supposed to be persons engaged in writing inflammatory letters and notices'.[77]

However, his evidence was based on 'Communications with gentlemen as I went through the country'.[78] James Glassford, a Scottish advocate who toured Ireland three times between 1824 and 1826, and who was a well-known supporter of the London Hibernian Society, was also negatively disposed towards the masters. In a letter to the Earl of Roden he wrote:

> … in that poorest class, formerly called hedge schools, we do not look for an intelligent system of instruction: the teacher is himself too ignorant, or if naturally endowed, has not the ability to exercise the minds of his pupils.[79]

Charles Grant, a Scotsman who had been Chief Secretary for Ireland from 1818 to 1821 believed:

> The hedge schools … were schools in which the lowest state of morals was observed, in which the most immoral books were admitted and in which intellectual education was at the lowest possible scale.[80]

The 1825 education inquiry also had the effect of exposing the failure of the Kildare Place Society to implement non-denominational education but the government was not prepared to withdraw funding from it, until matters were brought to a head in 1831. Doyle persisted tenaciously with his written petitions to parliament on behalf of the hierarchy, even as Catholic Emancipation was in the process of being achieved in 1829.

By November 1830 a Whig government had taken over power and this proved fortuitous for the Catholic education campaign. Lord Edward Stanley became the Irish Chief Secretary and he approached the education question with an open mind. In January 1831 Doyle took the initiative to inform Stanley of the educational needs of his own diocese. He referred to the exclusive education provided by the KPS and the 'bad system' of education supplied by the hedge schools. But he took heart from the fact that they had been 'more successful in correcting or removing a bad system of education than in the establishment of a good one.' He added: 'We have within these few years suppressed numberless hedge schools and united, often within the place of worship, the children theretofore dispersed.'[81]

He suggested to Stanley that since Catholics outnumbered Protestants eight to one in his diocese alone, and as a large expenditure would be required to maintain 'Catholic' schools, it would be better to devise an education system uniting the children of the different religious persuasions in the same schools. This recommendation was taken directly from the educational plans revealed confidentially to Doyle by Spring Rice, chairman of the 1828 Select Committee on Education, plans which were to become the blueprint for national education. Stanley received these recommendations favourably and asked for his further suggestions, which Doyle supplied, using the same source.[82]

On 9 September 1831, the Catholic Church won a major victory when Stanley set out his proposals for the national education system of Ireland in the House of Commons. In so doing he referred to the failure of the KPS to provide an education for all, the failure of the government to take action when it was obvious that the Society could never become a national one, while allowing education 'to remain in hands unqualified for the task.'[83] The Catholic prelates had won the power struggle for the control of education and Doyle took particular satisfaction in the proposed scheme for the training of teachers and he looked forward to the displacement by them of the independent hedge schoolmaster. On 26 December 1831, he wrote to the clergy in his diocese:

> The rule which requires that all teachers henceforth to be employed be provided from some model school, with a certificate of their competency, will aid us in a work of great difficulty, to wit, that of suppressing hedge schools…[84]

CONCLUSION

The hedge schools dominated Irish education for over 136 years due mainly to the democratic principles upon which they were founded. They fulfilled the needs of society on a number of levels – educational, social and political.

They ensured that children of all denominations were educated, and in many cases to a high standard. They exposed children to a range of English reading books, including many classics of English literature. They broke with convention by introducing them to works of fantasy and fairy lore and by providing instruction in Latin and Greek. Evidence of high standards of achievement in English, the classics and mathematics is to be found in the records of the Irish Colleges and in the achievements of past pupils. Despite many challenges that faced the masters, it is difficult not to agree with Mary E. Daly when she commented that: 'There is little doubt that in dismissing hedge schools as insignificant institutions the commissioners of 1824 seriously erred.'[85] The masters served their people well on the social level as they played a central role in all community activities. They raised the morale of the people, who rewarded them with their deep affection.

Politically, the hedge schools promoted major social change in the nineteenth century by supporting Daniel O'Connell's Catholic Emancipation campaign and by educating people sufficiently to do likewise. Ironically, it was O'Connell's support for the Church's education campaign which marked the beginning of the end for the hedge schools. But the single most important contribution hedge schoolmasters made towards social change in Ireland in the nineteenth century was in the provision of continuous education, thereby ensuring that strong foundations had been laid for the successful introduction of a national system of education in 1831.

NOTES

1.   An Act to restrain foreign education (7 William 111 c.4 [1695]). An Act to prevent the further growth of popery (2 Anne c.6 [1703]).

2.   T. Corcoran, *State Policy in Irish Education, 1513–1816, Selected Texts* (Dublin: Fallon, Longmans, Green, 1916).

3.   T. Corcoran, *Education Systems in Ireland from the Close of the Middle Ages* (Dublin: UCD, 1928).

4.   P.J. Dowling, *The Hedge Schools of Ireland* (Dublin: Talbot Press, 1935).

5.   Martin Brenan, *Schools of Kildare and Leighlin* A.D. *1775-1835* (Dublin: M.H. Gill & Son, 1935); Philip O'Connell, *The Schools and Scholars of Breiffne* (Dublin: Browne and Nolan, 1942).

6. Mary E. Daly, 'The Development of the National School System 1831–1840' in A. Cosgrave and D. McCartney (eds), *Studies in Irish History* (Dublin: UCD Press, 1979), 162.

7. Antonia McManus, *The Irish Hedge School and Its Books, 1695–1831* (Dublin: Four Courts Press, 2002).

8. Report of the State of Popery in Ireland, 1731.

9. P.J. Corish, *The Irish Catholic Experience A Historical Survey* (Dublin: Gill and Macmillan, 1985), 164.

10. *Second Report of the Commissioners of Irish Education Inquiry* (Abstract of Returns in 1824, from the Protestant and Roman Catholic Clergy in Ireland, of the State of Education, in their respective Reaches), 1826-7 (12), x-ii, 1.

11. Daniel Corkery, *The Hidden Ireland* (Dublin: Gill and Macmillan, 1984), 41.

12. Áine Hyland and Kenneth Milne (eds), *Irish Educational Documents, Vol. 1* (Dublin: CICE, 1987). Susan M. Parkes, *A Guide to Sources For The History Of Irish Education 1780-1922* (Dublin: Four Courts Press, 2010); Kenneth Milne, *The Irish Charter Schools 1730-1830* (Dublin: Four Courts Press, 1997); Susan M. Parkes, *Kildare Place: A History of the Church of Ireland Training College and College of Education, 1811-2011* (Dublin: CICE, 2011); Dáire Keogh, *Edmund Rice and The First Christian Brothers* (Dublin: Four Courts Press, 2008).

13. John C. Curwen, *Observations on the State of Ireland* (London: Baldwin, Cradock and Joy, 1818), 388–389.

14. Mr and Mrs Samuel Carter Hall, *Ireland, its Scenery, Character* (London: Hall, Virtue & Co., 1855), 260.

15. Alice Stopford Green, 'Irish National Tradition,' in *History* (July 1917), 28.

16. See, for example, Carter Hall, *Ireland Its Scenery*, 260. The people of Connemara kidnapped a teacher and detained him until he had trained a replacement. When he was free to leave, he had no desire to leave people to whom he had become attached.

17. William Carleton, 'The Hedge School', in William Carleton, *Traits and Stories of the Irish Peasantry* (London: Garland, 1979), 287–288.

18. Mrs Morgan John O'Connell, *The Last Colonel of The Irish Brigade Count O'Connell and Old Irish Life At Home And Abroad 1745-1833*, Vol. 1 (London: K. Paul, Trench, Trubner & Co. Ltd., 1892), 57–60.

19. Lady Chatterton, *Rambles In The South of Ireland During The Year 1838, Vol. 1* (London: Saunders, 1839), 22–23.

20. O'Connell, *The Schools and Scholars of Breiffne*, 405.

21. Carleton, '*The Hedge School*', 273–274.

22. Thomas Crofton Croker, *Researches in the South of Ireland* (London: John Murray, 1824), 326.

23. Ibid., 275.

24. *Fourteenth Report of the Commissioners of the Board of Education in Ireland, 0* H.C. 1812-1813 (21) V. Appendix No. 3, 238.

25. Robert Herbert, 'Four Limerick Hedge Schoolmasters,' *Irish Monthly* (1944): 48–53.

26. McManus, *The Irish Hedge School*, 120–122.

27. D. Kennedy, 'Education and the People' in R.B. McDowell (ed.), *Social Life in Ireland 1800-4*, (Cork: Mercier Press, 1976), 57–58.

28. Timothy Corcoran, 'Education Policy After the Union,' *Irish Monthly* (1932), 690.

29. Stanley Curtis and Myrtle Boultwood, *An Introductory History of English Education Since 1800* (London: University Tutorial Press, 1960), 51.

30. William Lecky, *History of Ireland in the Eighteenth Century* (London: Longmans Green, 1913), 206.

31. Dr. P. Curtis, 'Students of the Irish College, Salamanca,' in *Archivium Hibernicum* (1915), 55.

32. Herbert Davis, *Jonathan Swift Irish Tracts* (Oxford: Blackwell, 1971), 89.

33. Michael McDonagh, *Daniel O'Connell* (Dublin: Talbot Press, 1929), xv–xvi.

34. Daniel Corkery, *Imeachtaí na Teanga Gaeilge* (Cork: Mercier Press, 1956), 114.

35. John Caerwyn Williams and Patrick Ford, *The Irish Literary Tradition* (Cardiff: University of Wales Press, 1992), 226.

36. First Report of the Commissioners of Irish Education Inquiry 1825 (400), xii, i, Appendix. No. 221.

37. John Locke, *Some Thoughts Concerning Education* (Dublin: Will Forest, 1928), 228.

38. Jean-Jacques Rousseau, *Emilius and Sophia* (Dublin: Potts and Chamberlane, 1779), 166–173.

39. Reginald Churchill, *The Concise Cambridge History of English Literature* (Cambridge: Cambridge University Press, 1970), 512.

40. J.K.L., *Letters on the State of Education in Ireland and on Bible Societies addressed to a friend in England* (Dublin: Richard Coyne, 1824), 16. Cited in Thomas McGrath, *Politics, Interdenominational Relations and Education* (Dublin: Four Courts Press, 1999), 185.

41. Joseph Lee, 'On the accuracy of the pre-famine Irish censuses', in J.M. Golstrom and L.A. Clarkson (eds), *Irish Population, Economy and Society: essays in honour of the late K.H. Connell* (Oxford: Clarendon, 1981), 37; 40–6. The figures of this census were generally regarded as an underestimation but Lee's research suggested that the underestimation was not as great as had been previously assumed. Cited in Harold Hislop, 'The Kildare Place Society, 1811-1831. An Irish Experiment in Popular Education' (Unpublished Ph.D Thesis, University of Dublin, Trinity College, 1990), 738.

42. Hislop, 'The Kildare Place Society, 1811–1831', 738–739.

43. Jim Smyth, *The Men of No Property: Irish Radicals and Popular Politics in the Late Eighteenth Century* (London: Macmillan Press, 1992),162.

44. Kevin Whelan, *The Tree of Liberty* (Cork: Cork University Press, 1996), 63.

45. Carleton, 'The Hedge School', 322.

46. *Thoughts and Suggestions on the Education of the Peasantry of Ireland* (London: T. Cadwell, 1820), 12.

47. Hely Dutton, *A Statistical Survey of the County of Clare* (Dublin: Graisberry & Campbell, 1808), 236.

48. William Tighe, *Statistical Observations Relative to the County of Kilkenny made in the Years 1800 and 1801* (Dublin: Graisberry & Campbell, 1802), 514.

49. James Bicheno, *Ireland and Its Economy* (London: John Murray, 1830), 285.

50. Corkery, *The Hidden Ireland*, 279.

51. Ibid., 214.

52. Crofton Croker, *Researches in the South of Ireland*, 328–329.

53. Desmond Bowen, *The Protestant Crusade in Ireland 1800–1870* (Dublin: Gill and Macmillan, 1978), 3.

54. Seán Connolly, ' "Ag Déanamh Commanding": Elite Responses to Popular Culture 1660–1850,' in J.S. Donnelly and Kerby A. Miller (eds), *Irish Popular Culture 1650-1850*, (Dublin: Irish Academic Press, 1998), 23.

55. Crofton Croker, *Researches in the South of Ireland*, 280–281.

56. Seán Ó Súilleabháin, *Irish Wake Amusements* (Cork: Mercier Press, 1967), 146–154.

57. *Thoughts and Suggestions on the Education of the Peasantry of Ireland*, 12.

58. Corish, *The Irish Catholic Experience*, 43–45.

59. Brenan, *Schools of Kildare and Leighlin*, 43–45.

60. Seán Connolly, *Priests and People in Pre-Famine Ireland 1780–1845* (Dublin: Four Courts Press, 2001), 32–33.

61. Regulations of the Society for Promoting the Education of the Poor in Ireland (SPEPI) Fourth Annual Report, 1816.

62. Susan Parkes, *Kildare Place: A History of the Church of Ireland Training College, 1811–1969* (Dublin: CICE, 1984), 17–18.

63. John Coolahan, *Irish Education: Its History and Structure* (Dublin: Institute of Public Administration, 1981), 11.

64. Henry Kingsmill Moore, *An Unwritten Chapter in the History of Education, Being the History of the Society For Promoting the Education of the Poor of Ireland, generally known as the Kildare Place Society* (London: Macmillan & Co., 1904), 75.

65. Brenan, *Schools of Kildare and Leighlin*, 61–62.

66. McGrath, Politics, *Interdenominational Relations and Education*, 164.

67. Ibid., 165.

68. Brenan, *Schools of Kildare and Leighlin*, 67–68.

69. William Carleton, *The Autobiography of William Carleton* (London: McGibbon & Kee, 1968), 2.

70. Michael Beames, 'The Ribbon Societies: Lower Class Nationalism in Pre-Famine Ireland' in Charles Philpin (ed.), *Nationalism and Popular Protest in Ireland* (Cambridge: Cambridge University Press, 1987), 254.

71. Dáire Keogh, *Edmund Rice* (Dublin: Four Courts Press, 1996), 72–73.

72. The Parliamentary Debates: T.C. Hansard New Series vol. X, col. 1480, 29 March 1824.

73. McGrath, *Politics, Interdenominational Relations and Education*, 158.

74. Parkes, *A Guide To Sources*, 21.

75. *First Report of the Commissioners of Irish Education Inquiry 1825* (400), xii, i, 44.

76. Brenan, *Schools of Kildare and Leighlin*, 8.

77. *Report of the Select Committee appointed to Inquire into the Progress and Operation of the New Plan of Education in Ireland* H.C. 1837 (485), ix, 53–54.

78. Ibid.

79. James Glassford, *Letter to Rt. Hon. Earl of Roden On the present State of Irish Education* (London, 1829), 20.

80. *Report of the Select Committee of the House of Lords on the Plan of Education in Ireland, with Minutes of Evidence* H.C. 1837, 1, 560.

81. W.J. Fitzpatrick, *The Life, Times and Correspondence of the Right Hon Rev. Dr. Doyle, Bishop of Kildare and Leighlin* (Dublin: James Duffy, 1861), 254.

82. McGrath, *Politics, Interdenominational Relations and Education*, 221–222.
83. *Hansard's Parliamentary Debates: Third Series* Vol. vi, col. 1252, 9 September 1831.
84. Patrick Dowling, *A History of Irish Education: A Study in Conflicting Loyalties* (Cork: Mercier Press, 1971), 117–118.
85. Daly, 'The Development of the National School System 1831–1840', 162.

2 SUPERIOR SCHOOLING: THE LEGACY OF THE ENDOWED SCHOOLS COMMISSIONS (1791–1894) TO IRISH EDUCATION

CHRISTOPHER McCORMACK

This chapter examines endowed superior schooling[1], associated with the Tudor/ Jacobite colonial project that, with the flight of the Earls (1607), had replaced the old Gaelic order in Ireland. In the wake of the Tudor conquests custody of the colony was entrusted to the Protestant gentry, Irish Church clergy, and Trinity College Dublin as the intellectual centre of what became known as the Irish Ascendancy. Tudor education policy was directed towards securing the mass conversion of the overwhelmingly Catholic population to the reformed Protestant faith as part of the colonial assimilative process, and the Irish Church-State relationship was crucial to the success of that process.

The Irish Church, as the established Protestant Church, was franchised to deliver education to the entire population, the vast majority of which was Catholic. Tudor monarchs, recognising the 'use of education as a tool for social change'[2] established a complete network of scholastic institutions. These included parish schools[3], diocesan grammar schools[4] and Trinity College, designed to prevent students having recourse to 'foreign [Catholic] universities'[5] The Tudor grammar school became the commonly accepted institutional form of superior schooling, and all schools in receipt of government or private funding were known as 'endowed schools'. Endowments took the form of a land grant, a fixed rental income, or legacy funds, willed to the benefiting institution. Trustees were appointed to apply the endowment funds in accordance with the wishes of the donor, and trusteeship governance was an essential feature of endowed schools.

Endowed schools constituted less than 10 per cent of all schools (the vast majority were privately-run institutions), yet they were uniquely important. As endowed institutions they were the subject of frequent inquiry by the Endowed Schools Commissions, and were almost a 'pilot' system of education. While only endowed schools came within the remit of the endowed commissions, all schools vicariously enjoyed the fruits of such inquiry.

Each wave of colonial thrust in Ireland had its associated endowed schools. There was close synchronicity between colonial plantation, original trust, scholastic institution and provincial location. The Munster plantation had its Earl of Cork schools; the Ulster plantation its Royal Schools; the Cromwellian plantation its Erasmus Smith Schools; the Williamite plantation its endowed schools at Midleton, Kilkenny and Clonmel.

By the end of the seventeenth century, in excess of three quarters of land holdings had changed hands. Geographically the colonisation project was complete. Cultural colonisation, however, was by no means complete. The Protestant reformation had failed to take root, and education was harnessed to address the Catholic masses. To meet the cultural colonisation deficit an alliance of landed gentry and Protestant clergymen, headed by the Lord Primate, launched a new type of schooling – the charity Charter Schools.[6] These were unashamedly proselytising institutions. The aim of government policy was to confine Catholic schooling to Protestant institutions, conducted by Protestant schoolmasters, and simultaneously to prevent Catholics from travelling abroad for schooling. Penal Laws[7] were enacted to effect this project. Catholics established their own celebrated hedge schools in defiance, and, as seen in Chapter One, the hedge school curriculum embraced elementary, classical and mercantile options.

By the end of the eighteenth century there was in existence, at least theoretically, a diverse web of schooling institutions. The role of the Endowed Schools Commissions[8] was to exploit these institutions in such a manner as to maintain colonial rule in conditions of rapid social change. In the process they elaborated a system of superior schooling considered here in terms of school governance, curriculum, access, and teaching provision. The Commission of Irish Education Inquiry (1788–91) was first in the field of such educational inquiry.

THE COMMISSION OF IRISH EDUCATION INQUIRY, 1788–91: THE GRAMMAR SCHOOL AND THE EDUCATION OF THE ASCENDANCY ELITE

The second half of the eighteenth century was a period of relative peace and prosperity that belied a deep-seated intellectual unease in Ireland. There was much Protestant opposition to the relaxation of the Penal Laws.[9] The same anxiety about the state of education was exhibited in the torrent of education plans that was such a feature of the period.[10] It conditioned the work of the Commission of Irish Education Inquiry and its findings which appeared in the *Report of the Commission of Irish Education Inquiry* (1791).

The Report (1791) was essentially an exercise in school governance. It was unique in making the first inventory of existing endowed schools, cataloguing their glaring abuses; abuses centred on the schools with large land tracts, such as the Ulster Royal Schools. Abuse typically concerned the leasing of school lands at prices well below their market values, thus diverting public funds to private gain. At the Dungannon Royal School, for example, the master, Dr Murray, had the school lands undervalued at £570; he leased them to his brother, on his own behalf, at this value, who in turn let the lands to tenants at a value of £976, thus securing the rent surplus to the master.

The Ascendancy unease was reflected in the opposing prescriptions advocated for curriculum reform in the contemporary literature. There was much criticism then, as subsequently, of the dominance of the classics in grammar schools. Hutchinson, Trinity College provost, sought in his 'Outlines of a Plan for a Great School' to improve the teaching of classics. Thomas Sheridan, in contrast, castigated the 'total neglect of our own tongue'.[11] At issue was the 'relative status of Latin and English', which had the capacity to strike 'at the heart of the established assumptions regarding the nature of curriculum'.[12]

Of the diocesan grammar schools, the *Report* noted that in many dioceses the schoolhouses 'are ruinous, and the mastership of the scholars mere sinecures'.[13] Orde's *Plan* to address the deficiency, which the *Report* endorsed, made provision for five institutional tiers of schooling provision, two of which – the Professional Academy and the Collegiate or Great School – represented the utilitarian and liberal traditions of superior schooling; their respective roles in schooling engaged the educational mind for much of the ensuing century.

The *Report* was concerned with access to schooling. Originally the old Tudor grammar schools were 'Free Schools'. The Ulster Royal Schools were also designated 'Free Schools'. In order to maintain some semblance of the idea of free schooling, the *Report* made provision for limited access to these institutions from the lower tiers of schooling through an elaborate system of scholarships, which depended largely on the goodwill of government, or the generosity of other endowed institutions.

The success of the colonial education project depended on teacher provision. The master's existence was a precarious one that depended upon 'a rather tenuous set of agreements'[14] entered into with the parents. One master graphically described the profession as the refuge for 'the ruined man of fortune, the reduced citizen, the unsuccessful physician, the exploded lawyer, the hooted actor, and the decrepit soldier'.[15]

The *Report* was least forthcoming on the question of teaching provision. The master of the endowed grammar school was frequently a graduate clergyman, and, as such, considered a trained teacher. The vast majority of private grammar schools, however, were conducted by lay masters, most of whom were not graduates. Orde's *Plan*, while acknowledging that aspiring masters 'should be chosen with great care and circumspection,'[16] made little provision for their professional training.

Training, as such, was based on the master-apprentice system. Aspiring masters had to advertise themselves through their publications. One master noted that the gentlemen who 'examined' him certified, among other things, that he had 'written and published many pieces';[17] another described how his *Essay* constituted 'the best criterion for scrutinising his merit' as an 'experienced teacher'.[18]

The *Report of the Commission of Irish Education Inquiry* (1791) was never implemented and was overtaken by political events. The rebellion (1798) requisitioned the Act of Union of Great Britain and Ireland (1800). The *Report*, which addressed issues of governance, curriculum, access and teacher supply, was a pioneering piece of work. It established a paradigm of inquiry that would be repeated many times in the ensuing century. It officially catalogued the existing stock of endowed schools. The *Report* elaborated a system of superior schooling in the liberal and utilitarian traditions that, when freed from the Established Church principles in which they were embedded, would pave the way for the development of a curriculum inspired by what was best in both.

THE WYSE SELECT COMMITTEE (1835–38):
THE ACADEMY: SCHOOLING THE MIDDLE CLASS

The decades that followed the Act of Union experienced considerable social change. Between 1821 and 1841 the population, essentially the Catholic population, had increased by more than one million.[19] The Catholic middle class had grown in wealth and influence. Catholic Emancipation (1829) granted a limited franchise and enabled Catholics to enter the post-Union parliament in London. Of 568,964 pupils in receipt of elementary schooling (1826), no fewer than 403,774 were in Hedge/Pay Schools.[20]

The Irish Church-State relationship came under renewed pressure. The failure, with a few notable exceptions, of the Incorporated Society's Charter Schools, and the schools of the Kildare Place Society, through loss in public confidence, led in the 1830s to the withdrawal of the parliamentary grants from both societies.

In contrast, the Catholic Church-State relationship was emerging as the significant one. The shift in the power balance between the churches threw the Irish Church-Catholic Church relationship into enhanced relief. Ó Canainn has noted that now 'the goal of the two churches was control of Catholic education'.[21] As the demand for an education acceptable to Catholics was addressed in the provision of a system of national schooling (1831), the gap between the Irish Church's ostensible role as national education provider, and the actual paucity of Irish Church schools on the ground, was exposed. The Whig 1830s administration drastically reduced the number of Irish Church bishoprics in line with the Church's reduced role in education provision.

The Wyse Select Committee inherited this legacy of social change in a power shift from Protestant to Catholic, and from upper to middle class. It served to mediate schooling in such a manner as to secure the hegemony of the middle class upon which the security of the colony was premised. In practical terms, this entailed revisiting the existing stock of endowed schools and redeploying their funds, examining their structures of governance, expanding their curriculum, and developing a teaching profession that would secure delivery of the reforms. In the process, however, the Select Committee had to confront the opposition of those reactionary interests determined to maintain the existing social class *status quo*.

The Wyse Select Committee received evidence from a range of informed opinion that included politicians, educators, heads of schools, and the secretary of the Commissioners of Education in Ireland (1813–1926).[22] The committee's brief was to inquire into how 'Academical Education may be improved, extended, and permanently maintained in Ireland'.[23] It assumed the rationalisation of the existing stock of endowed schools. The academy was the institution central to it. Its recommendations embraced issues of governance, curriculum, access and teaching provision.

The Wyse brief was ambitious and national. The plan envisaged that 'there should be in each county in Ireland one Academy[24] at least, combining classical and scientific instruction'.[25] Wyse hoped that existing endowments could be incorporated into the broader system of superior schooling. His plan of governance envisaged three tiers of control – the existing Board of National Education as central board, a local board under the control of the Grand Jury, and a School Board – bringing all levels of education provision into organic unity. In seeking the co-operation of the Board of Commissioners of Education in Ireland for his plan, Wyse asked its Secretary, W.C. Quin, if it were desirable that there should be erected an Academy in each county. Quin acknowledged its desirability in principle. He strenuously resisted, however, the application of Royal School funds to this project, 'if such application would alter the character of those schools'[26] as Protestant foundations.

Wyse inherited from the *Report* (1791) a curriculum that embodied both liberal and utilitarian traditions. His task was to rescue it from the Established Church principles in which it was embedded. The mixed system under which the National Board (1831) operated, by which students were brought together for secular instruction, but separated for religious teaching, suggested a way forward.

Wyse was particularly impressed by the comprehensive curriculum of the Presbyterian Belfast Academical Institution. Questioning Dr Hincks as to the kind of education 'most useful to the middle classes', Hincks, himself a classicist, replied 'a general scientific education'.[27] Hoping to extend the almost exclusively classics curriculum of the diocesan endowed schools, Wyse inquired if the Act establishing the Board empowered it to prescribe 'a particular course of education not classical'. Quin replied that since 'the Act of William declared that these shall be classical schools, it might be a legal question'[28] whether the Board had the power to do so. The conservative Board relied on legal precedent[29] in its resistance to curriculum change.

The *Report* recommended combining 'classical and scientific instruction'[30] within each academy. General and specialised courses would be provided in both disciplines and all students would be exposed to a general course in both, before embarking on a specialist study of either discipline. It recommended the academy as the institution most 'suited to promote the objects of education, social harmony and economy'[31] – an object always uppermost in the minds of the commissioners as mediators of superior schooling.

Securing broad schooling access was essential to the success of the Wyse Plan. The endowed grammar schools were characteristically designated 'free schools'. Wyse sought to broaden access. Of the endowed schools, Wyse observed they 'were given to all classes and persuasions of the nation'.[32] The reality was different. Wyse complained that 'education, like everything else, was converted to a mere instrument of Protestant ascendancy'.[33]

Wyse questioned Quin whether the schools might not be made more generally applicable to all classes of the community. Quin replied that he did not think that 'these schools should be made applicable to all classes'.[34] He believed that 'an influx from the middle classes'[35] would result in the withdrawal of 'the sons of resident gentlemen from those schools'.[36] The Wyse Select Committee articulated a form of schooling appropriate to the middle class. It did not dispense with rank ideology. Ideology was, however, based on stratification that privileged the middle class over that of the gentry, upon which the Ascendancy hegemony had heretofore been premised, and from which there was a reluctance to depart.

On the issue of teaching provision, evidence to the Wyse Select Committee represented a refinement of the thinking of the late eighteenth century schoolmasters. The evidence of Dr Bryce of the Belfast Academy was particularly insightful. Bryce (1828) observed that the 'one fatal defect' of the system was 'the omission of all provision for the regular professional education of teachers'.[37] In what was a most radical idea at a time when the national school system had not as yet been introduced, Bryce 'proposed to erect Teaching into a fourth learned profession, by establishing a Professor of the Art in every University'.[38]

Bryce recognised the low status of the teaching profession but attributed this to 'the present defective state of the science of education'.[39] He pointed out that 'the great thing that is wanted … is a large body of well qualified teachers.'[40] He advocated 'an association of teachers of all ranks and grades'.[41] He would give it 'a corporate character';[42] rather in the nature of a Teaching Council, it would set 'standards of entry to the profession'.[43]

The Select Committee recommended the establishment of a Central Polytechnic College in Dublin[44] as a professional school for Teachers.[45] The Wyse Select Committee *Report* did not respond to the Bryce suggestion for an association 'having a corporate character'.[46] To do so would have been politically risky. In the event the reforms implicit in the Wyse Select Committee *Report* required strengthening the role of the Central Board, which a strong association of teachers could have inhibited.

The Wyse Select Committee *Report* was, however, for its time bold and imaginative. Though in many respects utopian in tone, in content, methodology and the razor intellectual sharpness of its analysis it constituted the basic educational document of the century and represented the essential point of reference to which future educationalists would doubtless refer.

THE KILDARE COMMISSION (1854–58): THE GRAMMAR SCHOOL, THE ACADEMY AND SCHOOLING THE CLASSES

The two decades that separated the Wyse Select Committee (1838) and the Kildare Commission (1858) were a period of rapid change. The Great Famine (1845–48) deprived Ireland of two million inhabitants. It led to the decline in the landed classes that constituted the backbone of classical grammar schooling. The successful operation of the National Board at elementary level in enhancing literacy levels, created the appetite for superior schooling. The historian Joe Lee has equated modernisation with 'the growth of equality of opportunity', and designated the period 1848–1918 as constituting 'the modernisation of Irish Society'.[47]

The period corresponded with a broader disillusionment with classical schooling as answering the needs of the age. In England respectable middle-class pressure elicited Endowed Commissions of Inquiry into the ancient universities and grammar schools. Irish endowed schools likewise had to address the *nova ordo* that emerged with the introduction of competitive examinations for 'the public service'.[48] Table 1 demonstrates the inadequacy of superior schooling provision – endowed and non-endowed – to address the challenge.

Table 1. Population and Superior Schooling Provision (1841–91)

	1841	1851	1861	1871	1881	1891
Population	8,175,124	6,552,385	5,798,967	5,412,377	5,174,836	4,704,750
No. at superior schools	27,391	18,502	21,674	21,255	20,405	35,306

Sources: Censuses of Ireland (1841–1901), and J. Godkin, *Education in Ireland* (London: Saunders, 1862).

The Kildare Commission, like the Wyse Select Committee, declared that the grammar schools were 'founded, mainly, for the benefit of the middle rank of society'[49] upon which the security of the colony was premised. It took stock of the schools within its remit. It classified them into exclusive and non-exclusive schools. The exclusive schools were those confined to the Church of Ireland, such as the Erasmus Smith and Incorporated Society foundations. These the Commission proposed placing under the governance of the Incorporated Society. The Commission was really interested in developing what was left – what it termed non-exclusive schools – which included Royal Schools, Diocesan Schools and Schools of Private Foundation, that is, those in the governance of the Board of the Commissioners of Education. The *Report* recommended the establishment of a new non-denominational board – the Board of Endowed Schools – to replace it. The hope was that the new board would thus be free from the denominational constraints of the old one, and thus better equipped to adapt schooling to the needs of the age.

The temper of the age required a more comprehensive curriculum. Memorials[50] addressed to the Kildare Commission called for education 'of a generally useful kind' that would 'accommodate schools to the needs of [the] times'.[51] Witnesses deplored the 'great want of Intermediate schools'.[52] The bounteously endowed Royal Schools were the focus of attack. Memorialists, citing the Wyse Select Committee *Report*, claimed that 'the course of education now pursued … is what is termed classical, fitted only for the higher classes of society'.[53] The Lord Primate replied that 'such it had always been',[54] that the Royal Schools were 'intended to prepare a body of students for Trinity College'.[55]

Ringwood, master of the Dungannon Royal School, was more attuned to the temper of the age. In a series of letters addressed to the Commissioners of Education in Ireland, of which the Lord Primate was an *ex officio* member, Ringwood attacked the exclusively classics-based syllabus on which the Royal Scholarships tenable at Trinity College were based. He questioned why the course prescribed for Royal Exhibitions (scholarships) should be directed towards 'classical fellowships' and exclude competition for those 'connected with science'.[56]

The University Commission's *Report* (1853) into Dublin University recommended that its Matriculation examination should include those subjects 'which properly enter into a sound *School* Education',[57] which was then adopted by the board of the university. Somewhat reluctantly, the Commissioners of Education in Ireland adopted a similar course.

Access to schooling remained an issue. A number of factors limited access to the endowed schools. One such, as noted, was the excessively narrow classics curriculum; another impediment was the denominational issue; and of course, the availability of free schooling. On this issue the Kildare Commission drew the attention of the Commissioners of Education in Ireland to their statutory duty as regards 'the rights of pupils to free admission'.[58] The Kildare Commissioners were, however, forced to admit that, as the 'the right of free admission being unlimited, is practically defeated … a minimum number of free places should be fixed by statute'.[59]

On teacher training the Kildare Commission advanced little fresh thinking. The *Report* relied heavily on the master/apprentice model. It noted that teacher training was not sufficiently informed by 'the science of education and the art of teaching'.[60] While appealing to 'the forty normal schools of Prussia', the Commissioners appeared blissfully unaware of the Bryce recommendations to the Wyse Select Committee twenty years previously. In an age of gentlemanly amateurism, there was a deep-seated reluctance on the part of government to educate the professional. The Commissioners were distancing themselves from a system of teacher training with which they were neither intellectually nor psychologically at ease.

The Kildare Commission failed to produce a unanimous *Report*. The Anglican Commission member argued that the Royal Schools were Irish Church schools; the Catholic Commission member refused to accept the principle of mixed schooling on which the *Report* was premised. Press coverage of the *Report* was strident and partisan and reflected the divisions within the Commission. Despite repeated calls for legislation to implement the findings of the *Report*, none followed. Mixed, united, neutral, or promiscuous superior schooling had failed. What bore the appearance of two pieces of stand-alone legislation flowed from it – the Church Disestablishment Act (1869), and the Intermediate Education Act (1878). Henceforward educational policy would address education denominationally. Social class access to endowments would be extended within a denominational framework, and school governance would be denominationalised – privatised in fact.

THE ROSSE COMMISSION (1878–81): THE INTERMEDIATE SCHOOL AND EDUCATION FOR THE MASSES

The Church Disestablishment Act (1869), the Intermediate Education Act (1879), and the Rosse Commission (1879–81) were mutually interactive measures. The Church Act formalised denominational schooling; the Intermediate Act was a device to fund it in a manner that the Whig administration could accept; the Rosse Commission endorsed Intermediate schooling. In its public hearings it sought to assess the supply of and demand for it. All three were lay, secular measures that possessed a distinctly democratic orientation. Disestablishment stripped the Irish Church of its funds and deprived it of its state role in schooling. The Diocesan Schools were disendowed and, with three notable exceptions, ceased to function. Disestablishment had the effect of concentrating the Irish Church mind in managing its Anglican schooling nationwide. The Intermediate Education Act and the Endowed Schools Commissions, particularly the final Commission, assisted significantly in this project. The Irish Church turned to its existing stock of schools that were not affected by Disestablishment. These included eighteenth-century hospitals, such as King's Hospital, and Wilson's Hospital and asylums such as Pleasants Asylum. In a process of superiorisation[61] these institutions advanced from charity to superior schools (see Appendix A).

The public hearings of the Rosse Commission (1878–81) coincided with the first two examinations of the Intermediate Board. Evidence to the Commission reflected intense public interest in education. The Commission endorsed Intermediate schooling and advanced school governance on the principle of subscription. Local Committees established new Intermediate schools. Other foundations, such as Bangor Endowed and Prior Endowed, embraced the Intermediate examination. These exist today, either as prestigious schools in their own right or as schools in new configurations, such as Raphoe Royal and Prior Endowed.

The Intermediate Act provided for the payment by results achieved in a number of curriculum subjects, and payable to the school manager. It supplemented the income of schools, particularly those that presented a large number of candidates. Heretofore the classics curriculum reigned supreme. Dr Mahaffy, school inspector for the Rosse Commission, argued that the extended canon of Intermediate subjects diluted the position of classics and mathematics. Royal Schools resented the perceived loss in prestige that resulted. When a witness to the Enniskillen Royal School hearing remonstrated at the prospect of Portora being turned into an Intermediate school, the Rosse Commissioner smartly reminded him that 'Portora is an Intermediate school at present', that they 'give intermediate education there'.[62]

Intermediate schooling was a Protestant – largely Presbyterian – project, and it was an urban phenomenon. Not surprisingly, while the Intermediate Act stimulated access to schooling, it also exposed latent tensions in Irish society surrounding class, religion, gender, and the urban/rural divide.[63] An *Irish Times* leader-writer, described how, in that 'intellectual tilt and tournament' that was the first Intermediate Examination (1879), 'every locality and social caste in the country entered the lists'.[64] For the majority, intermediate education meant the education addressed to the middle class. However, the Irish Christian Brothers refused to accept this definition. For them 'intermediate' meant secondary education, or an education higher than elementary, and not 'higher' as befitting a 'higher social class'.[65] The advocacy of scholarships for bright boys whose parents were poor kept alive the idea of free schooling in the popular imagination. The examination thus made 'access to the Universities possible' for a minority of 'poor but clever students'.[66]

The effect of the Irish Church Act (1869) was to formalise denominational pluralism. The effect of the Intermediate Education Act (1878) was the creation of a broad canon of curriculum specialisms and a clearer demarcation of school type. On the one hand, it tended to fragment the teaching profession; on the other hand, it created a loose form of networks and associations, that, while allowing teachers to specialise within particular teaching areas, afforded opportunities for inter-organisational co-operation.

Table 2. Pupil and Teacher Numbers at Superior Schools, 1861 and 1881[67]

	Pupils	Teachers	Heads	Ass.ts	Lay/ Cleric	Ass.ts
1861	21,674	1,355	729	626	376	250
1881	20,405	1,275	488	787	472	315
1901	35,306	2,207	490	1717	1030	687
1910*		2,241	490	1751	945	806

Source: General Report of Census of Ireland 1881, Part II, (Dublin: Alex Thom, 1882): 67 [Online: 83]; General Report of Census of Ireland 1901, Part II, 1902 [Cd 1190], 65; *John Coolahan, The ASTI and Post-Primary Education in Ireland, 15.

While there was a decrease in the number of schools, and a corresponding increase in the number of assistants, the number of pupils remained relatively stable (See Table 2). This was a consequence of the growth in size of schools that were conducted mainly by religious orders.

Coolahan has observed that the Intermediate Education Act 'did nothing to lay the foundations of a secondary teaching profession'.[68] The Act, however, has to be distinguished from its operation. Once in operation, a schooling-dynamic was created which tended to lessen the isolation of the teacher. This was a particular problem, as neither teachers nor pupils had 'any thought of, or direct concern for, what was going on in other schools'.[69] The Irish Church Act (1869) posed particular problems of uncertainty for teachers. Irish Church schoolmasters in response, established the Irish Schoolmasters' Association (1869). The Catholic Headmasters' Association (1878) was designed to exercise a monitoring brief on the operation of the Intermediate Act. The Central Association of Irish Schoolmistresses (CAISM), was founded in 1882 in response to the attempt by the Intermediate Board to conduct the examination of girls 'on a different principle from boys'.[70] The CAISM recognised that this could devalue the education of girls.

It can be concluded that the Rosse Commission assisted the advancement of the teaching profession. For example, Mahaffy highlighted the plight of the assistant master, a position offering so few attractions that few 'able and gentlemanly men can be expected to embrace it'.[71] Additionally, the fact that the commissioners addressed their questionnaires to the headmasters, not the governors, assisted in establishing the status of teachers as professionals in their own right.

THE ENDOWMENT SCHOOLS (IRELAND) COMMISSION (1855–94): CONSTRUCTING SCHEMES OF GOVERNANCE

The Church Disestablishment Act made provision for the establishment of the General Synod of the Church of Ireland. It also provided for the participation of laymen in its synod or parliament. The synod was vital to the reorganisation of Anglican schooling in the wake of the Act. It became the centre of energy around which the Irish Church organised itself educationally. In this work the Church was assisted in great measure by the Endowed Schools (Ireland) Commission (1885–94).

The work of this commission was essentially one of governance. The commission drafted a large number of schemes of governance for Endowed Schools which came under its remit, and for other schools which sought what was described as 'Consent Schemes'. These schemes still constitute the basic instruments of governance for these schools. scheme 34, in respect of the Ulster Royal Schools Trust, was its most important scheme. The scheme defined conditions under which schools could share in the endowments of the Royal School trust, and provided for a system of scholarships. Catholic schools, for the first time, were able to share in these endowments.

Two further Schemes – Scheme 147 and Scheme 210 – were vital to the reorganisation of Anglican schooling. Scheme 147 concerned the Dioceses of Dublin, Glendalough and Kildare, and it enabled the Irish Church to apply its endowments more efficiently in the respective dioceses; it became the model scheme of governance for other dioceses. Scheme 210 concerned the Incorporated Society for Promoting Protestant Schools in Ireland, and it was equally important to Anglican schooling. The Society's Charter of Incorporation (1733) enabled it over time to incorporate existing charity school trusts, such as the Connolly, Pococke, Primrose and Foy foundations. These constituted a nucleus for the development of a more general system of Anglican superior schooling.

Middle-class schooling, upon which colonial governance was premised, and of which the Endowed Schools Commissions were the mediators, depended for its success on the availability of a body of trained professional teachers. As early as 1828, the educationist R.J. Bryce noted that 'the one fatal defect' was the lack of 'regular professional education of teachers'.[72] In an address to the National Association for the Promotion of Social Science, more than three decades later, he declared that 'a race of properly qualified teachers is the one thing wanting'.[73] The Wyse *Report* (1838) highlighted the need to educate, train and certify teachers, thus constituting the essential requirements for teacher registration. Several decades later, the Palles Commission (1898) reporting on the operation of the Intermediate Board was pressed to introduce a system of teacher registration. Coolahan has noted that its failure to do so was 'an extraordinary case of evasion'.[74] A mechanism for teacher registration in Ireland was not established until 1917.

CONCLUSION

Education always occurs within a political context, and for Ireland that context was a colonial one, and the Endowed Schools were essential to the colonial project. A series of Endowed Schools Commissions mediated superior schooling in the management of consensus for colonial rule. Through this process of mediation they managed to cushion the aftershocks of such seismic political shifts as Catholic Emancipation (1829) and Church Disestablishment (1869), thereby preventing the rupture of the political Union of Great Britain and Ireland. Achieving this objective involved the ongoing adjustment of schooling in response to political and social change. In the process, the Endowed School Commissions developed a system of superior schooling considered in this chapter in terms of governance, curriculum, access and teaching provision.

Trusteeship governance was a central feature of endowed schools. While some school trustees did not always live up to the high expectations of their office, generally the regular coming together of a small group of trustees to discuss the affairs of the school brought to bear on the office a not inconsiderable degree of application and intellect. This led to a high degree of networking between governors, as certain *ex officio* governors were members of a myriad of school boards. The networking and the sharing of information not only benefited schools individually but contributed to the science of school governance more generally.

Many of the old endowed schools are today highly prestigious institutions, some of which owe their existence to the Schemes of governance provided for them by the Endowed Commission 1885–94.[75] The schemes proved adaptable instruments in enabling schools to rationalise in accordance with changing educational needs. The relatively seamless merging of nineteenth- and twentieth-century schooling in Ireland provides eloquent testimony to the success of the process. Responding to social change, Endowed Schools Commissions steered curriculum development from dominance of classics, to science and literature, to 'intermediate' schooling, which in the following centuries became the dominant schooling paradigm. All schools, from humble charity institutions to prestigious grammar schools, were assimilated within its robust rubric.

Theoretically the old Tudor Grammar schools were 'Free Schools'. From the earliest, however, they progressively became the preserve of the middle class. The Commissions, however, endeavoured to maintain in the endowed schools a modicum of free places. The actual provision in the final Commission for scholarships for the 'bright boy' and 'bright girl' kept alive in the public imagination the idea of free education until such time – a century-and-a-half later – when the country was ready to express a more generous national impulse *via* the provision of state-funded 'free' second-level education.

Inspired by the writing of late-eighteenth century schoolmasters, the Wyse Select Committee (1835–38) theorised the requirements of a teaching profession that included a sound education, examination and certification, and an established a University chair of education. It contained all the elements essential to teacher registration. That these ideas were not developed by subsequent commissions reflected the power of the upper ranks, who feared that the growth of the professional classes would alter the 'relations of society'[76] in a late Victorian class-based society.

The legacy of the Endowed Schools Commissions to Irish education has been considerable. The Commissioners – classically-trained gentlemen – were the products of the Victorian class-based society they sought to reform. They were, however, by no means held captive by it. Curious, observant, patient, meticulous, indefatigable, possessing an eye for detail, they demonstrated a capacity to marshal a considerable body of statistical detail, and to apply it to a succession of enquiries, that was such a feature in an age of *laissez faire*. And they were unpaid.

Their mode of inquiry – the public courts – called witnesses to account for the management of the educational institutions entrusted to their charge. An instrument of transparency, the public court generated an interest in education in the public imagination, as it reflected and propelled educational change for more than a century. Against considerable opposition from vested interests, the Commissioners mediated superior schooling, considered here in terms of school governance, curriculum development, access, and teaching provision. It is arguable that educationalists today tend to take these educational elements as discrete entities, without adverting to their historical antecedents, which confer on them their vital energy and constitute their priceless archive.

NOTES

1. The term 'superior school' was first employed by the Census Commissioners (1841). The Commissioners defined 'superior schooling … to include all schools in which any foreign language is taught': *Report of the Commissioners Appointed to take the Census for Year 1841*, 1843, (504), xxxviii [Online, 38]. All Census Commissions subsequent to 1841 adopted the term, and constructed their tables of participation levels in the system by reference to it. The term became synonymous with 'grammar' or 'secondary' education.

2. Raymond Gillespie, 'Church, State and Early Education in Early Modern Ireland', in Maurice O' Connell, (ed.), *Daniel O'Connell, Education, Church and State: Proceedings of the Annual Daniel O'Connell Workshop* (Dublin: Institute of Public Administration, 1992), 56.

3. [28 Henry VIII, c. 15] An Act for the English order, habit and language, 1537, in Hyland and Milne (eds), *Irish Educational Documents*, Vol. 1, (Dublin: C.I.C.E., 1987), 38.

4. [12 Elizabeth I] An Act for the Erection of Free Schools, 1570, in Hyland and Milne, (eds), 39–40.

5. Bodleian Library, Smith MSS, Vol. 20, Queen Elizabeth's letters on behalf of the College of Dublin, dated Dec. AD 1591, in Hyland and Milne, (eds), 42.

6. Kenneth Milne, *The Irish Charter Schools 1730–1830* (Dublin: Four Courts Press, 1997), Appendix A, 337-344. The Charter incorporating the Society enjoined the Society 'to teach the children of the popish and other natives … in the principles of the Protestant religion … and to teach them to write, and to instruct them in arithmetic and such other parts of learning … and to bring them up in virtue and industry; and to cause them to be instructed in husbandry and housewifery … or in such like manual occupations, as the said Society shall think proper'.

7. [7 William, III c. 4] An Act to Restrain Foreign Education (1695) in Hyland and Milne, *Irish Educational Documents* Vol.1, 46.

8. For a fuller treatment of the subject, see Christopher F. Mc Cormack, 'The Endowed Schools Commissions 1791-1894, as mediators of superior schooling in Ireland', (unpublished PhD thesis, University College Dublin, 2010).

9. Richard, Bishop of Cloyne, *The Present State of the Church of Ireland* (Dublin: W. Sleater, jnr,, 1787). The bishop, arguing the essential unity of the civil and religious arms of state governance, feared the fracture of the Irish Church-State relationship that would result from relaxation of the Penal Laws.

10. Thomas Orde, *Mr. Orde's Plan for an Improved System of Education in Ireland* (Dublin: W. Porter, 1787); J.H. Hutchinson, 'Outlines of a Plan for a Great School', 1785, NLI, Bolton Papers, MS 15884 (1); Anthony King, *Thoughts on the Expediency of Adopting a System of National Education* (Dublin: George Bonham, 1793); Thomas Stearne Tighe, *A Letter Addressed to Mr. Orde upon the Education of the People* (Dublin: P. Byrne,

1787); John O'Donovan, *Thoughts on the Necessity and Means of Educating the Poor of Ireland* (Dublin: R.E. Mercier, 1795); J. Carey, *Sketch of a Plan for the Reformation of the Grammar Schools of Dublin* (Dublin: G. Perrin, 1787).

11. Thomas Sheridan, *A Rhetorical Grammar of the English Language* (Dublin: Price, 1781), xi.

12. Philip J. O'Connell, 'Thomas Sheridan and the Education of Young Gentlemen in the Eighteenth Century: with Particular Reference to Ireland', (unpublished MEd. thesis, University College Dublin,1994), 41.

13. *Report of the Commission of Irish Education Inquiry 1791* in *Report of the Kildare Commission into the Endowed Schools 1858*, [2336-I][2336-II][1336-III][2336-IV], (Dublin: Alex. Thom, 1858), 344 [Online: 1675].

14. Philip J. O'Connell, 'Thomas Sheridan', 32.

15. Patrick Carolan, *An Essay on the Present State of Schools in Ireland* (Dublin: R. Gibson, 1806), 8; J.S. Dodd, *Essay on Education with a New Plan of an Academy* (Cork: Eugene Swiney, 1770).

16. Thomas Orde, *Plan*, 68.

17. J.S. Dodd, *Essay*, Preface.

18. Patrick Carolan, *An Essay*, Preface.

19. *General Report of Census of Ireland 1911*, Table 2, Comparative View of Houses and Population of Ireland ... 1821–1911. London: H.M.S.O., 1912, 724.

20. *Second Report of the Commissioners of Irish Education Inquiry*, Roman Catholic Returns, [12], 28 November 1826, 4–18, [Online, 4-18].

21. Seamus Ó Canainn, 'The Education Inquiry 1824-26 in its Social and Political Context', *Irish Educational Studies*, Vol. 3, No. 2, 1983, 17.

22. The Board of the Commissioners of Education in Ireland (1813–1926) was the longest standing of all educational boards. It became the incarnation of the Board of Control suggested in *The Report of the Commission of Irish Education Inquiry* (1791). It was an all Protestant board. The board was established to exercise control over the endowments and operations of the endowed schools under its remit. They included the Schools of Royal Foundation, Schools of Private Foundation and the Diocesan Schools. Important endowments like the Erasmus Smith Trust and the Incorporated Society Trust secured exemption from its remit. The Commissioners of Education in Ireland are to be sharply distinguished from the Endowed Schools Commissions to which all endowed schools were answerable. Unlike the Endowed Schools Commissions, which were established at particular intervals for the purpose of particular inquiries, the Commissioners of Education in Ireland were a permanent board.

23. *Report from the Select Committee on Education* H.C. (701), 1838, 64 [Online: 64].

24. The Academy was a Presbyterian institution, established in the wake of relaxation in the Penal Laws. Wyse was impressed by many aspects of this institution, particularly its broad curriculum that included classics, mathematics, science and modern languages.

25. *Report* 1838, 65 [Online: 65].

26. *Report of the Select Committee on Education*, H.C. (630), 1835, Q. 1752, 151 [Online: 157].

27. *Report* 1835, Q. 213, 20 [Online: 26].

28. *Report* 1835, Q. 1487, 137 [Online: 143].

29. The celebrated Lord Eldon judgment (1805) supported the Leeds Grammar School

classics headmaster in his refusal to extend the classics curriculum to include a commercial stream.

30. *Report* 1838, 65 [Online: 65].
31. Ibid.
32. Thomas Wyse *Speech on Moving for Leave to bring in a Bill for the Establishment of a Board of National Education* (Dublin: John Milliken, 1835), 71.
33. Ibid., 73.
34. *Report* 1835, Q. 1718, 149 [Online, 155].
35. Ibid., Q. 1737, 150 [Online, 156].
36. Ibid., Q. 1739, 150 [Online, 156].
37. Bryce, *Sketch of a Plan for a System of National Education for Ireland* (London: George Cowie, 1828), Preface.
38. Ibid.
39. Ibid.
40. *Report* 1835, Q. 1261, 115 [Online, 121].
41. Ibid., Q. 1281, 121 [Online, 127].
42. Ibid., Q. 1283, 121 [Online, 127].
43. Ibid., Q. 1284, 122 [Online, 128].
44. *Report* 1838, 78 [Online, 78].
45. Ibid.
46. *Report* 1835, Q. 1283, 121 [Online, 127].
47. Joseph Lee, *The Modernisation of Irish Society 1848–1918* (Dublin: Gill and Macmillan, 1973), Preface.
48. *Report of the Commission* 1858, 248[Online: 256].
49. *Report*, 256 [Online: 264].
50. Documents No.I, Intermediate Education, *Report of the Commission*, 1858, 295–6 [Online, 1636–7].51. *Report*, 1858, Q. 10522, 559 [Online, 913].
52. Ibid., Q. 10515, 556 [Online, 910].
53. *Report*, Q. 11742, 638 [Online: 992].
54. *Report*, Q. 9370, 471-5 [Online: 82–59].
55. Ibid.
56. R.H. Ringwood, *A Second Letter*, 21 December 1853, (Dublin: Hodges & Smith, 1854), 17–19, NLI, Ms. 18654.
57. *Dublin University Commission* (Dublin: Alexander Thom, 1853), 65 [Online, 70]. Italics as used in *Report*.
58. *Report*, 1858, 241 [Online, 249].
59. *Report*, 1858, 276 [Online, 284].
60. *Report*, 1858, 251 [Online, 259].
61. For a fuller treatment of the superiorisation process, see Christopher McCormack, '"Straw bonnets" to superior schooling: the "failure" of the charity school movement in the context of nineteenth-century Ireland: a reappraisal', *Paedagogica Historica: International Journal of the History of Education* (London: Routledge, 2012), http://dx.doi.org/10.1080/00309230.2012.671835 (accessed 10 February 2014).
62. *Report of the Commission* 1881, Q15994, 528 [Online, 1072].
63. While this chapter deals principally with education for boys, for a study of intermediate

education and girls, see Deirdre Raftery and Susan M. Parkes, *Female Education in Ireland, 1700–1900: Minerva or Madonna?* (Dublin and Portland OR.: Irish Academic Press, 2007).

64. T.J. Mc Elligott, *Secondary Education in Ireland 1870–1921* (Dublin: Irish Academic Press, 1981), 44–5.

65. A Christian Brother, *Edmund Ignatius Rice and the Christian Brothers* (Dublin: M.H. Gill, 1926), 481.

66. Jones, *Intermediate Education in Ireland: Review and Prospect* (Belfast: J.A. Murphy, 1902), 1–2.

67. In Table 2 the number of 'Teachers' has been estimated. The Committee of Irish Catholics for the year 1870 tabulated Catholic educational institutions at 47 Colleges and Schools – the Catholic system of superior schooling at the time – with a total of 320 teachers and 5,178 pupils. This return produced a pupil/teacher ratio of approximately 16:1. This ratio has been applied to the total superior school population. On the basis of this ratio for the year 1881, there were 1,275 teachers in the system. School 'Heads' correspond to the number of schools on the basis of one head per school. 'Assistants' were derived by subtraction of 'Heads' from total. The Lay/Cleric ratio was fixed rather arbitrarily at 3:2.

68. John Coolahan, *The ASTI and Post-Primary Education in Ireland 1909–84* (Dublin: Cumann na Meánmhúinteoirí, Éire, 1984), 5.

69. C.M. Byrne, 'The Irish Intermediate Education Act', *Irish Ecclesiastical Directory* (Dublin: John F. Fowler, 1915), 127.

70. Resolution II, 4 February 1881, Minutes of the Intermediate Board 1878-86, N/A, Ms. 2000/98/1, 169.

71. *Report* 1881, 255 [Online, 261].

72. Bryce, *Sketch*, Preface.

73. R.J. Bryce, 'Fallacies', *Transactions of the National Association for the Promotion of Social Science*, 1860 (London: George W. Parker, 1861), 365.

74. Coolahan, *The ASTI*, 8.

75. Raymond Wilkinson, 'The Educational Endowments (Ireland) Act 1885 as part of nineteenth-century educational reform', *Irish Educational Studies*, Vol. 3, No. 2, 1983, 105. Wilkinson noted that it 'is unlikely that schools such as the Royal Schools would have long survived had the Commission never sat', 113.

76. The Rt.Hon. Lord Norton, 'Address delivered at the opening of the Social Science Congress at Cheltenham, 23 October 1878', (London, 1878), 4.

3 THOMAS WYSE AND NON-DENOMINATIONAL EDUCATION IN IRELAND, 1830–1845

TONY LYONS

As seen in Chapters One and Two, in eighteenth-century Ireland there were many forms of schooling. Education was provided by a small number of Protestant endowed schools, along with an even smaller number of Royal Schools. There were also some 'official' schools, otherwise known as English Schools in Ireland, but these had very limited success.[1] During that same century there emerged a matrix of clandestine, illegal Hedge Schools or Pay Schools.[2] These served the majority of the population, including both Catholics and Presbyterians. Towards the end of the century two new types of schools began to surface – the Societies Schools, catering for both Catholics and Protestants, and the other type were schools established by the Catholic religious orders, more of which later. University education was provided for by the University of Dublin, with its single college, Trinity College. It was a bastion of education for Church of Ireland students, with a smattering of some Catholics and some Presbyterians.

Therefore, by the beginning of the nineteenth century, Ireland was served by a motley collection of schools of varying hues. This chapter deals with the issue of the religious and political questions within Irish education debate both in Ireland and at Westminster at the time, with a specific focus on Thomas Wyse's ideas and contribution. Crucial to the establishment of a national school system in 1831 were the circumstances, and in particular the increasing power of the Catholic Church in the 1820s, culminating in political freedom for Catholics within the terms of the Emancipation Act in 1829. Key figures to emerge during the 1820s were Daniel O'Connell, Thomas Spring Rice, a Protestant MP favouring Catholic rights, and Thomas Wyse, a wealthy Catholic landowner from Waterford who supported O'Connell during the latter half of the 1820s in the struggle for emancipation.

Following emancipation in 1829, Wyse turned his attention almost exclusively to education and devoted his energies as MP, first for Tipperary and later for Waterford, to the evolving education debate in Ireland and at Westminster over the next fifteen years. As we shall see, aside from his public political negotiations at Westminster on the question of education, Wyse was also a literary commentator on education issues and used several mouthpieces to publicise his version of education's role in society. Allied to the foregoing was his specific role on parliamentary committees debating and reporting on education. Essentially, Wyse proposed a non-denominational national system of education for Ireland, incorporating primary, secondary, university, and adult education levels, with legislative underpinnings. Over the previous half century several attempts had already been made to introduce a satisfactory education system in Ireland: the debate had gone on for decades, beginning with Sir Thomas Orde's Plan in 1787, continuing with Richard Lovell Edgeworth's Plan in 1799,[3] going through the various Commissioners' Reports, Select Committees' Reports, the last of which before the introduction of the national system was in 1828. Common to all these endeavours was systematisation, and in terms of post-Union politics, there began to emerge ideas on socialisation and politicisation, with education now gradually being viewed as an agent of control in each of these matters.[4]

It could be argued that Thomas Wyse has not received a great deal of attention from the viewpoint of published historiography. One exception to this is the 1937 volume *Irish Education: A Historical Survey* by James Johnston Auchmuty.[5] As the title suggests, this book deals with Irish education history on a very broad canvas, but one third of the book is devoted to Wyse and his contribution to the history of education in Ireland. The imbalance was qualified by Auchmuty's startling claim that 'Wyse was by far the most important figure in the whole history of Irish education.' Auchmuty also produced a biography of Wyse, in which he devoted some 10 per cent of the book to education.[6] Richard P.J. Batterberry's pamphlet *Sir Thomas Wyse 1791–1862: An Advocate of a 'Mixed Education' Policy over Ireland* (1939),[7] offers a critique of the two Auchmuty books, writing that Wyse was pre-eminently a great educationalist, who had taken up politics. Referring to Wyse's efforts regarding the mixed education ideal, Batterberry states that it was 'a policy of very special merit, personal, national, religious.' William J. Bradley completed a PhD thesis in 1945, 'Sir Thomas Wyse, Irish Pioneer in Education Reform',[8] while a second doctoral thesis, 'The Educational Aims and Activities of Sir Thomas Wyse (1791–1862)' by John Cosgrove, appeared in 1975.[9] Both of these works add to the Wyse canon from a general viewpoint, but each one only briefly treats of the issue of mixed education.

Other work on Wyse appears in Angela Clifford's *'Godless Colleges' and Mixed Education in Ireland* (1992),[10] which includes a copy of a 1901 pamphlet by Winifrede M. Wyse. Of greater significance is David Alvey's 1991 book, *Irish Education: The Case for Secular Reform*, while D.H. Akenson's monumental work, *The Irish Education Experiment: The National System of Education in the Nineteenth Century* (1970) is still the chief reference point for education historians of the national school system.[11] In the book Akenson refers to Wyse as a 'gadfly', a thorn in the side of those charged with social reform and Wyse also receives fair treatment from Akenson regarding his role in the introduction of the 1831 system. Worthy of consideration also is Denis G. Paz, *The Politics of Working-Class Education in Britain 1830–50* (1980).[12] The book offers an interesting and valuable debate on mixed and popular education and acknowledges Wyse as a proponent of education reform.

More recently, Gillian Smith's study, 'Thomas Wyse (1791–1862) and the Origins of an Irish System of National Education' (2002),[13] provides a discussion on the state of education in Ireland in the first half of the nineteenth century. She deals with the debates surrounding the introduction of the national system in 1831 and establishes Wyse as a forceful and persistent figure, who was the 'Member for Education' within the negotiations. By the time the introduction of the national system of education was announced by E.G. Stanley, Chief Secretary for Ireland, in 1831, there was virtually nothing new in this venture. A plan for education in Ireland had been in the air for decades before 1831, and indeed the content of the two Stanley letters[14] reflects the core elements of a plan put forward by Thomas Wyse the previous year. This chapter endeavours to establish Wyse's contribution to what emerged in the 1830s and to define his understanding of mixed education.

WYSE, POLITICS AND EDUCATION

The Wyses were well known in political and administrative circles both in Ireland and overseas. The family claimed descent from Andrew Wyse, a Devon man, who came to Ireland during the reign of Henry II, having been granted lands in Waterford.[15] During the Reformation the family remained loyal to Catholicism and this strong attachment remained unbroken for centuries to come. Young Thomas Wyse was educated at the well-known Jesuit school at Stonyhurst in Lancashire, where he was sent at the age of nine. Later, at age nineteen, he returned to Ireland to study at Trinity College, Dublin.[16] He excelled as a student, and became well-versed in oratorical skills, as well as being renowned as a linguist.[17] During his European tour, beginning in 1816, he spent part of his time in Italy, and there in 1821 he married Laetitia Bonaparte, niece of Napoleon. Upon inheriting the Waterford estates, Thomas Wyse and his young bride came to Ireland in 1825. Between then and 1829 he devoted his considerable energies to the cause of Catholic Emancipation and in the process became a strong supporter of Daniel O'Connell. However, the two men clashed on the nature of the 'mixed' education principle, O'Connell being somewhat ultramontane, that is, referring to Rome as the ultimate arbiter in matters concerning education and social teaching,[18] and Wyse viewing education as a device for social improvement, unfettered by religious entanglements.

Wyse was a liberal, a social and political reformer, and he became very much a supporter of legislative attempts to introduce some element of improvement in the lives of people at all social levels.[19] 'In common with a small but increasing number of enlightened liberals, [he] believed that education should not be restricted to the privileged classes, that every person had a right to an education, irrespective of religion or class, and that the state had a responsibility to provide this education'.[20] For Wyse, democracy and education went hand in hand, and as O'Connell might be referred to as the architect of political democracy, the appellation of architect of educational democracy can be ascribed to Wyse. There were elements of upward social mobility in his thinking when he claimed that 'education, which ought to be a preparatory discipline for all … must also contain within itself the vivifying and active means of improving all'.[21] Though he wished the poor to have their lot improved through education, he did not have any desire to upset the prevailing *status quo* with regard to the relative positions among the upper classes, the middle classes, and the lower orders. His aim with education reform was to provide for an educational uplift for all classes. His philosophy was a utilitarian one, invoking the principle of the greatest happiness of the greatest number.[22] He believed that everybody had a right to education and that all Irish citizens should have an equal opportunity.[23] As a supporter of the British Whig (Liberal) government he threw his energies into educational reform and was instrumental in the setting up of the National School system of 1831 in Ireland. Between 1830 and 1845, Wyse was chiefly concerned with education issues in Ireland. As we shall see, on many occasions and through many mouthpieces, he proposed the idea of non-denominational education, not only at primary school level, but also at secondary level, both of which should be State-financed. He also advocated the establishment of a second university for Ireland, one of a non-denominational nature with an emphasis on economic and industrial development, loosely based on the University of London model.[24] The University of London (1828) became the blueprint for what became known as the 'redbrick' universities. This was a new trend as opposed to the traditional European/British model of *studium generale*. Science, along with other utilitarian disciplines, formed the foundation of a new emphasis in university education.[25] Increasingly, universities were to cater for the needs of industrialisation, and Wyse was a supporter of such institutions.[26]

The outstanding education issue in Ireland at the time was the role religion would play in an increasingly complex education landscape. Wyse made great strides in addressing this problem through the 'mixed' education or 'united' education principle. The key to a resolution lay in direct state involvement in which all creeds would be treated equally. The idea of a national education system was prevalent nowhere in the world of the day, with the possible exception of the United States.[27] The British and the French were decades away from anything resembling national systems. Following an Education Act in England in 1870 a system of national education was introduced in England and Wales. France, on the other hand, had to wait another ten years before something similar was introduced. In Ireland the post-Union political landscape was ripe for the introduction of any system of education that would bring a sense of political and religious unity to the island.[28]

Successive Irish Ascendancy parliaments of the eighteenth century offered no sense of this unity, and Catholic representation did not exist within their ranks. Officially recognised schools in the eighteenth century provided education opportunities for a minority Protestant population. That, coupled with penal legislation, left the majority population, along with some elements of Presbyterianism, somewhat sidelined and left to their own illegal devices in the provision of popular education.[29]

EDUCATION CHANGE AND THE INVOLVEMENT OF THE CHURCHES

The end of the eighteenth century witnessed the ushering in of 'a vigorous new element'[30] in Irish education. A variety of Protestant proselytising, societies emerged, establishing a matrix of schools throughout Ireland. These schools followed in the footsteps of an earlier manifestation – the Charter Schools – which began in 1733. The earliest of the societies, with the lofty and unwieldy title of 'Association for Discountenancing Vice and Promoting the Knowledge and Practice of the Christian Religion', was founded in 1792.[31] This society, along with the 'London Hibernian Society',[32] was overtly proselytising both in theory and in practice. The schools established by these societies received State subventions and were frowned upon by Catholic authorities, as there was the perception that some element of proselytisation was taking place in these schools. The schools catered for both Protestant and Catholic children. With the increase in Catholic political power in the 1820s, state support for these societies was withdrawn, as by now a climate of Catholic Emancipation had welled up to such an extent that official State sponsorship of the societies and their schools had become contentious.[33]

One Society founded in 1811 appeared to be different from the others: the 'Society for Promoting the Education of the Poor of Ireland', better known as The Kildare Place Society because of the location of its headquarters in Dublin. It was non-denominational and was supported by Protestants as well as Catholics, including Daniel O'Connell.[34] This religiously neutral society received no government aid until 1815 when it was granted £7,000, increasing to £30,000 in 1830. Its schools hoped to avoid any controversial doctrinal issues by reading the bible without note or comment. This approach was almost on a par with government thinking at the time.[35] It was also *ad idem* with official policy on the education of the poor. From 1812/13 onwards there was to be no attempt 'to influence or disturb the peculiar religious tenets of any sect or description of 'christian'[36]. Along with being successful in establishing over 1600 schools and initiating teacher training in Ireland, this society was also to the forefront in supporting the principle of religious neutrality in its schools until the early 1820s, when it became ensnared in controversy over the issue of favouritism towards Protestant schools. It was not able to avoid grant-aiding some schools 'under the auspices of the Protestant proselytising agencies'.[37] Following demands by Catholic authorities for an inquiry into the activities of the society and the withdrawal of Daniel O'Connell from the Board, the beginning of the end was nigh, and the practice of public funding of education through agencies such as the Kildare Place Society would soon come to an end. 'This was reflected in the findings of the government inquiry which reported in 1828, where its recommendation of combined literary but separate religious instruction was a clear precursor of the principle on which the national school system of 1831 was to be predicated'.[38]

Coterminous with the growth of the Protestant Societies from the 1790s to the 1820s, Catholic religious orders such as the Ursulines, the Presentation Sisters, and the Christian Brothers established a number of schools for poor boys and girls. These were voluntary efforts which materialised gradually at the time the Penal Laws[39] were being repealed. Following the Relief Acts of 1782, 1792 and 1793 a number of schools and colleges came into existence. Honoria (Nano) Nagle had anticipated the reliefs and had introduced the Ursuline Sisters into Ireland as early as 1771, and, as will be seen in Chapter Seven, she established the Presentation Order in 1775. These were followed by the Christian Brothers, founded by Edmund Rice in 1802, and the Mercy Sisters, founded by Catherine McAuley in 1828. Although the Christian Brothers' work was largely confined to providing elementary education for poor boys, they also conducted advanced classes of an intermediate type for some of their pupils. The provision for education under the auspices of the various religious orders made slow progress in the early years. However, during the course of the nineteenth century rapid advances were made.[40]

WYSE AND 'MIXED EDUCATION'

The 1820s proved to be a very eventful decade: official State policy towards assisting proselytising agencies came to an end;[41] Catholic leaders such as bishops, along with lay support from Thomas Spring Rice,[42] Daniel O'Connell, and in the latter half of the decade, Thomas Wyse, emerged as a powerful group bringing pressure to bear upon Westminster to introduce both political and religious reform.

As noted earlier, upon his return from the continent in 1825, Wyse gave unstinting support to O'Connell, and to the 'Catholic Association', in the struggle for Emancipation. 'He was one of O'Connell's chief lieutenants in marshalling the first great mass movements of the century, a movement which achieved Catholic Emancipation but which was as much an expression of the emerging liberal philosophy as a specifically religious crusade'.[43] However, this relationship was to deteriorate rapidly in the 1830s when O'Connell clashed with those who supported the 'mixed' education principle.[44] Wyse, on the other hand, was an ardent champion of this principle, and spent fifteen years of his political life proposing, defending, revisiting the 'mixed' or 'united' education idea using a variety of vehicles, including the House of Commons at Westminster, committees, pamphlets, speeches, reports, and at least one major book, *Education Reform* (1836).[45] Over this fifteen-year period, Wyse earned the title 'Member for Education' from fellow MPs for his exertions in the cause of a national system of education for Ireland.[46]

Before urging his plans for Irish education reform upon the British Government, Wyse made efforts to establish what the views of key individuals were on the matter, attaching particular value to the views of Catholic prelates. These bishops, at a meeting held in Dublin in 1826, had adopted the liberal attitude evidenced in the Catholic Association and in the Society of Friends of Civil and Religious Freedom.[47] The resolutions adopted on that occasion permitted the co-education of Catholic and Protestant pupils in the same schools 'provided sufficient care be taken to protect the religion of the Roman Catholic children and to furnish them with adequate religious instruction.'[48] Should the majority of the children attending a school be of the Roman Catholic faith then the headmaster should be a Roman Catholic, but no exception was taken to children attending schools where Protestant children were in the majority and with a Protestant teacher headmaster, provided of course that the above-mentioned safeguards were respected.[49] One of the most liberal of the Catholic prelates was James Doyle, Bishop of Kildare and Leighlin,[50] who was a supporter of Wyse and his plan for non-denominational education for Ireland, *ab initio*.[51]

Wyse, in promoting non-sectarian education for Ireland, was mindful of the historical baggage associated with education provision. In a reference to the eighteenth century he stated:

> All education soon got infected with a political and sectarian spirit; it was an attack on one side, a defence on another – a battle fought in every school, under every hedge, for the minds and feelings of the country.[52]

Furthermore, he elaborated:

The great object of education being to make men happy, and in order to do that, useful and good, Religious [*sic*] education should be the first of all; but it should not be of such a nature, nor given in such a manner, nor by such persons, nor at such times, nor in such places, as to neutralize its good effects, or to produce such bad effects as religious discords.[53]

Thomas Wyse was first and foremost a promoter of an education system for Ireland where Catholics and Protestants would be educated together. The object of education provision in the early 1830s 'is to prepare future Citizens for a common country.'[54] The Wyse understanding of national education extended from primary to secondary, to university and to supplementary[55] education. In order to achieve a semblance of national education, legislation was required and Wyse was very cognisant of the fact that without proper legislation[56] the initiative introduced by Lord Stanley in 1831 could well fail. In the nineteenth century, there was a paucity of legislation regarding the primary sector. The national system of 1831 was introduced without any Bill being passed. Wyse introduced a Bill in 1831 'to advance the education of the people' but withdrew it in favour of Stanley's more expedient method of sidestepping long parliamentary debates. The Stanley provision of 1831 relied solely on a letter (two versions) requesting the Duke of Leinster to act as Chairman of the National Board. In direct response to this initiative, Wyse wrote in 1836:

I still ... retain the opinion I then expressed, and I am happy to find myself borne out by so considerable a portion of public opinion in Ireland, that the measure will be always feeble and incomplete, till it shall be embodied into the law of the land.[57]

Subsequent events would suggest that Wyse was quite correct in his concerns and the 'experiment' of 1831 would in time founder on the rocks of denominational conflict.[58]

On the question of denominationalism, the liberal Catholic bishop James Doyle of Kildare and Leighlin advised Lord Stanley to 'educate all children without social distinctions, in a system where religion was left solely to the respective clergymen, and where a board of commissioners acceptable to all denominations would have power to devise their own rules and regulations.'[59] The sentiment expressed here echoed an earlier contribution by Thomas

Spring Rice MP for Limerick,[60] and it also matched the liberal and inclusive philosophy of Wyse regarding educational equality for Ireland. Wyse expressed this philosophy on many occasions and notably in July 1831 in a speech to the House of Commons where he reiterated his conviction that education reform was essential because of the exclusive and sectarian composition of existing institutions.[61] He argued:

> ... education in Ireland, up to now – and we may begin from the Reformation if we think proper – has all along been a mere matter of religious and political partisanship. I am, then, for a National system of education in Ireland, in this large and noble sense; and did the House allow me, I should be prepared to show, that such a system is the only one which can tend to quench our dissensions....[62]

Wyse wished for a permanent system of education which would be truly national, a system that would lead to political and social harmony as well as technical progress, and most of all, would encompass some level of religious tolerance. In his efforts throughout the 1830s to bring a legislative framework to the 'mixed' education principle in Ireland, Wyse had considerable support among parliamentary colleagues at Westminster as well as some Catholic prelates in Ireland, including Archbishop Murray of Dublin, who had been a supporter of the 'mixed' education principle since Stanley's pronouncements in 1831. He also, however, had enemies, some of them implacable, a case in point being Archbishop McHale of Tuam.[63] McHale was especially suspicious of foreign influences as is evident from the following comment by Winifred Wyse, niece of Thomas Wyse, in a pamphlet published in 1901:

> The suspicion that atheism of the eighteenth century lurked in all systems of foreign education, even those sanctioned by Rome, was the dominating note of his otherwise great mind ... The Bishop moreover would not brook comparison with any other country; Ireland for the Irish, to its greatest extreme, was his motto from first to last. Hence he took instant umbrage at Mr. Wyse's eulogy of the Prussian system, publicly: "We have heard enough about foreigners, and don't wish to hear any more of them".[64]

Other contemporary views of Wyse were perhaps more personal judgements rather than party political understandings. John O'Connell, son of the Liberator, was a stern critic of his because he steadfastly refused to give unqualified allegiance to the Liberator and to the Repeal Movement. Wyse was a unionist although he spoke vigorously against bad government, enforced tithes and coercive Acts.[65] John O'Connell expressed a malicious contempt for Wyse: 'Thomas Wyse is indeed a very clever fellow, very. He has a great deal of eloquent fluency and a highly educated mind; but he bewilders himself sometimes with his philosophical theories; in fact, he metaphysicalises himself into balderdash'.[66]

The main political difficulty for Wyse, apart from the fact that education legislation found itself on a lower rung on the political agenda than other matters, intrinsic to the subject matter of his Bills, was that he advocated a system of 'mixed' education. This aroused much apprehension within the ranks of the Catholic prelates, some of whom opposed non-denominational education. Undeterred, Wyse devoted his waking hours to this cause in Ireland. For Wyse, sectarianism perpetuated a great social evil and this concern was the kernel of all his efforts. He was convinced that the teaching of religion was at the heart of true education but by that he did not mean the sectarianism that bedevilled the education of his time. In *Education Reform*, he wrote:

In these countries, but especially in Ireland, where forgetfulness of sectarian distinctions, and brotherly union of all persuasions is so desirable, for the cause of a common country, as well as of a common Christianity, any arrangement which tends to perpetuate these distinctions, or to preclude this union, is undoubtedly to be deprecated. To class our national schools under partial designations of Protestant and Catholic and Presbyterian is a contradiction. By becoming sectarian they cease to be national. By thus parcelling out our people in lots, by thus keeping them "parqués", in their respective pasturages we recognise a sort of inherent incompatibility; we tell the child that it is in his nature and in his duty to live apart and hostile; we grow Protestants and we grow Catholics for future conflicts; and lest … they should seek in religion, only that in which all agree, we take care to point their attention to that in which each differs. We convert into a law of hate, what Heaven gave us as a law of love and degrade seminaries for the universal mind of a country into rival garrisons for a faction. Half our animosities arise from ignorance of each other...[67]

Keenly aware of one of the biggest difficulties besmirching education, he thus advocated a non-denominational system which would offer secular instruction on normal schooldays as a means of overcoming the endless disputes among Church leaders over their rights and privileges. Religious instruction would be provided on an appointed day of the week, under local arrangements.

It was Wyse's desire and ultimate goal that a genuine national system of education include primary, intermediate, university, and adult education. On 22 June 1835, it was ordered that:

> ... a Select Committee be appointed to examine into the State, Funds, and Management of the Diocesan, Royal and other Schools of Public Foundation in Ireland, as also into the System of Education pursued therein, with a view to increasing their utility and to enquire how far it may be practicable and expedient, and in what Manner, and from what Resources, to improve, extend and permanently maintain Academical Education in that Country, and to Report their opinion to the House.[68]

Other similar committees were re-appointed in 1836, and 1837. During the existence of the three committees, Wyse acted as chairman. The report of 1836 produced a detailed plan for intermediate (second-level) and higher education for Ireland. It concerned itself in particular with the existing endowed schools which should be reorganised and expanded to provide a basis for a countrywide system of day second-level schools or academies. These schools would offer a non-denominational education similar to the *de jure* ideology within the national school system.[69] In the Report for the training of second-level teachers, proposals were also made by Wyse for structured salaries as well as for pension rights for second-level teachers.[70] However, in a climate of *laissez faire* policy the government stood by and did nothing: the major Churches declined to offer any support, as some were already becoming suspicious of mixed education within the national system.[71]

From the reports of the 'Wyse' Committees, the whole network of intermediate schools generally received a sweeping condemnation with very few exceptions.[72] To alleviate the shortcomings at intermediate and higher education levels, the 1838 Report recommended a gradation of schools: every parish should have an elementary school, each county a second-level school, and above these there should be provincial academies which might or might not have the constitution of, or be subordinate to, universities.[73] The Report also addressed one of Wyse's personal interests for the education of middle-class Ireland, supplementary or adult education whereby such education could be afforded by visits to museums, libraries, botanical gardens, art galleries, all of which had been hitherto supported by societies and individuals.[74] As with many other reports from Royal Commissions and Select Committees the government turned a blind eye to the Wyse recommendations.

Concerning university education *per se*, Wyse had been a long-term supporter of the reform of foundations such as the Universities of Oxford and Cambridge, and the University of Dublin.[75] He was present at the foundation of a rival institution, London University (1828), dubbed by the establishment of Church and State alike as the 'Godless College of Gower Street'.[76] Following on his 1837 Report on foundation schools, Wyse wrote to the government in 1841 stressing the need for provincial colleges of higher education.[77] Wyse was concerned with the sectarian nature of Trinity College, Dublin, which discriminated against Catholics in its privileges and appointments.[78] During the early 1840s, he undertook a campaign to have either full and equal status for Catholic students attending Trinity, or a second university which would cater for Catholics. He was not entirely in favour of the latter as it would reinforce segregation between Protestant and Catholic Ireland.[79] In 1845, a compromise was in the offing when the Prime Minister, Sir Robert Peel, introduced a Colleges Bill for Ireland thereby enabling the provision of colleges in Cork, Galway, and Belfast.[80] Problems emerged immediately and the Catholic Church, with its newly-appointed Archbishop of Armagh, Paul Cullen, condemned these institutions as 'Godless Colleges' at the Synod of Thurles in 1850.[81] Shots were fired across the bow even before they opened their doors in 1849. The next sixty years would prove to be very fractious in the politics of Irish university education. Catholic prelates under the stewardship of Archbishop Cullen would forge ahead with providing a Catholic University in St. Stephen's Green in Dublin. The first Rector appointed here was John Henry Newman, and following his departure in 1858 the fortunes of Newman's College ebbed and flowed.[82]

CONCLUSION

It was understood by the 1850s that the 'mixed' education principle would founder eventually: university education did not embrace the Wyse philosophy of non-denominationalism, especially when Cullen's influence came to bear upon it. The possibility of 'united' education within the intermediate sector received little credence from the State, and virtually no support from the Churches; by the 1850s the national school system was also creaking under the weight of sectarian divisions, and when Thomas Wyse lost his parliamentary seat in 1847, it was time for him to call it a day. His appointment as British Minister to Greece and his departure for Athens in 1848 brought down the curtain on the 'Member for Education' and his labours for a national system of education for Ireland which would have the support of all creeds.

It was one of the features of Wyse's thought that he insisted upon a 'package deal' education system. Every single brick within the proposed system should be viewed with reference to the entire edifice. Thus it was that in the years following the report of the Select Committee in 1838 he repeatedly pointed out that all the government's efforts to provide elementary and secondary education would come to nothing if the system were not crowned by an adequate university education.[83]

The basic tenet of Wyse's proclamations at primary, intermediate, and university levels was that squabbles over some curriculum content, administration issues, texts, and so on paled into insignificance when one considered the internecine religious exchanges that bedevilled Irish education. He turned to a secular solution, or something very much like it. He wanted a national system that was good and permanent, that catered for every person in the country and that provided religion as an essential part of education but on a separate basis from the other subjects of the curriculum. Before Wyse made public his 1830 plan, he had negotiated with Stanley, as well as with some prelates, the basic outline of Ireland's future primary education principles and practices. Under the Wyse plan, and what Stanley introduced in Westminster in September 1831, secular instruction would take place on four or five days a week and religious instruction would take place on one or two days a week, depending on local arrangements. Teachers were not meant to be associated with the teaching of religion: clergy from respective flocks were meant to teach religion in the school outside of normal school hours or elsewhere under local arrangements. While this principle, *de jure*, held sway for decades, by 1900 most schools *de facto* had become denominational.[84]

By the time Wyse left for Greece in 1848 to take up his position as British Minister, a considerable portion of his plans for Irish education had been put in place. By the time of his death in Athens in 1862, however, Irish education was becoming increasingly denominational. The Wyse plan of 1830 was now suffocating under the tidal wave of opposition to the 'mixed' education ideal, and an emerging force, led by Cardinal Cullen, was to exert a long-lasting influence on the future of education in Ireland.

NOTES

1. Norman Atkinson, *Irish Education: a history of educational institutions* (Dublin: Allen Figgis, 1969), Chapter 3.
2. These schools never became part of a system, and they mushroomed throughout the country as a result of penal legislation denying education to Catholics who made up the majority of the population. Presbyterians were also denied certain education rights and they too developed a network of Pay Schools. During the first half of the eighteenth century the Penal Laws were enforced to some degree, but from the 1740s onwards a blind eye was turned towards these surreptitious centres of education, and during the 1780s and 1790s the laws proscribing education rights for certain religious groups were repealed. See Antonia McManus, *The Irish Hedge School and its Books, 1695–1831* (Dublin: Four Courts Press, 2002).
3. Tony Lyons, *The Education Work of Richard Lovell Edgeworth, Irish Educator and Inventor, 1744–1817* (New Jersey: Mellen Press, 2003).
4. John Coolahan, 'Imperialism and the Irish National School System' in James A. Mangan (ed.), *'Benefits Bestowed'? Education and British Imperialism* (Oxford: Routledge, 2012; first published: Manchester University Press, 1988), 76–93.
5. James Johnston Auchmuty, *Irish Education: A Historical Survey* (Dublin: Hodges Figgis, 1937).
6. James Johnston Auchmuty, *Sir Thomas Wyse, 1791–1862: the life and career of an educator and diplomat* (London: King & Sons, 1939).
7. Richard P.J. Batterberry, *Sir Thomas Wyse 1791–1862: an advocate of a 'mixed education' policy over Ireland* (Dublin: Browne and Nolan Ltd, 1939).
8. William J. Bradley, 'Sir Thomas Wyse, Irish Pioneer in Education Reform' (unpublished PhD Thesis, Trinity College, Dublin, 1945).
9. John Cosgrove, 'The Educational Aims and Activities of Sir Thomas Wyse 1791–1862' (unpublished PhD thesis, University of Manchester, 1975).
10. Angela Clifford, *'Godless Colleges' and Mixed Education in Ireland: extracts from speeches and writings of Thomas Wyse, Daniel O'Connell, Thomas Davis, Charles Gavan Duffy, Frank Hugh O'Donnell and others* (Belfast: Athol Books, 1992).
11. Donald H. Akenson, *The Irish Education Experiment: The National System of Education in the Nineteenth Century* (London and Toronto: Routledge and Kegan Paul/University of Toronto Press, 1970).
12. Denis G. Paz, *The Politics of Working-Class Education in Britain 1830–50* (Manchester: Manchester University Press, 1980).

13. Gillian Smith, 'Thomas Wyse (1791–1862) and the Origins of an Irish System of National Education', *Decies, Journal of the Waterford Archaeological and Historical Society* No. 58 (2002): 29–39.

14. Stanley invited the Duke of Leinster, by letters, to act as chairman of the new National Board.

15. Olga Bonaparte-Wyse, *The Issue of Bonaparte-Wyse: Waterford's Imperial Relations* (Waterford: Waterford Museum of Treasures, 2004), XV-XVI.

16. Trinity College, Dublin was established by Queen Elizabeth I as a bastion of Established Church (Church of Ireland) scholarship. However, in 1794 certain regulations were removed, which gave freedom to Catholics to enter as students. Catholics had never been barred from the college, but some rites prevented Catholic bishops from allowing young men of that religion becoming students there. See Norman Atkinson, *Irish Education: a History of Educational Institutions* (Dublin: Allen Figgis, 1969), Ch. 6.

17. He could translate German, could speak French and Italian fluently, knew Dutch, and he was also a renowned classical scholar. He was able to expand his knowledge of some of these languages and interests during his long tour of Europe from 1816 onwards, expressing a particular affinity with Greek art and literature. See Auchmuty, *Sir Thomas Wyse, 1791–1862.*

18. Smith, 'Thomas Wyse (1791–1862) and the Origins of an Irish System of National Education', 29–39. See also Auchmuty, *Sir Thomas Wyse,* Chapter 9 (The Breach with O'Connell).

19. James Coleman, 'A Forgotten Waterford Worthy', *Journal of the Waterford and South-East of Ireland Archaeological Society* Vol. 7/8 (1904/5): 143–155.

20. Smith, 'Thomas Wyse (1791-1862)', 25.

21. Auchmuty, *Irish Education,* 69–70.

22. Thomas Wyse, *Education Reform Vol. 1* (London: Longman & Co., 1836), 350.

23. Ibid., 350–354.

24. John Coolahan, *Irish Education: History and Structure* (Dublin: Institute of Public Administration, 1987), 108–109.

25. Ibid.

26. Ibid.

27. Auchmuty, *Sir Thomas Wyse 1791–1862,* 148.

28. John Coolahan, 'Primary Education as a Political Issue in O'Connell's Time', in Maurice R. O'Connell (ed.), *O'Connell: Education, Church and State* (Dublin: Institute of Public Administration, 1992), 87–96.

29. Along with McManus, cited above, see Tony Lyons, 'Popular Education in Rural Ireland 1700–1850' in Claudia Gerdenitsch and Johanna Hopfner (eds), *Erziehung und Bildung in ländlichen Regionen* (Frankfurt am Main: Peter Lang, 2011), 105-117.

30. Martina Relihan, 'The Nineteenth-Century National School System in Ireland: An Egalitarian Concept?' *History of Education Researcher* No. 78 (2006): 86.

31. Helen R. Clayton, 'Societies Formed to Educate the Poor in Ireland in the Late Eighteenth and Early Nineteenth Centuries' (unpublished PhD thesis, University of Dublin, 1980), 18–67.

32. Other Protestant Societies to emerge at the end of the eighteenth and beginning of the nineteenth centuries were the Baptist Society for Promoting the Gospel in Ireland, as well as the Sunday School Society for Ireland.

33. Alvey, *Irish Education: The Case for Secular Reform,* 114–116.

34. For a general history of the Society, see Henry Kingsmill Moore, *An Unwritten Chapter in the History of Education, Being the History of the Society for the Education of the Poor of Ireland, generally known as the Kilkdare Place Society 1811-1831* (London: Macmillan and Company, 1904). This book was reprinted by Nabu Public Domain Reprints, Breingsville, PA, USA (2010). See also Carol Revington, 'The Kildare Place Society: Its Principles and Policy' (Unpublished MEd thesis, University of Dublin, 1981).

35. Coolahan, *Irish Education,* 11.

36. Fourteenth Report of the Commissioners of the Board of Education in Ireland, H.C. 1812-13 (21) V, 221 (see Coolahan, *Irish Education*, 11).
37. Relihan, 87.
38. Ibid.
39. A series of Penal Laws was enacted by the Irish parliament from 1695 onwards. These laws, along with other matters, forbade the Catholic population from going to school, or teaching in school, but they were entitled to attend schools which were not associated with the Dissenters, that is, those who did not subscribe to the tenets of the Church of Ireland. These dissenting denominations included Presbyterians, as well as Catholics. Until approximately 1735 these laws were enforced to some extent, but after that time a blind eye was usually turned towards Catholics attending schools established by their own flock. The eighteenth century witnessed the emergence of a network of Hedge Schools or Pay Schools as a consequence of this proscription and these schools continued to expand during the second half of the eighteenth and early nineteenth centuries. By the mid-1820s an estimated 9,000 such schools existed throughout the country. See McManus, *The Irish Hedge School and its Books*. Also, Diarmaid Ó Muirithe, *A Seat Behind the Coachman* (Dublin: Roberts Wholesale Books, n.d.), 92–117.
40. Clayton, 18–67.
41. Alvey, 114–116.
42. Spring Rice was MP for Limerick, but not Catholic, though he was a supporter of political equality for Catholics.
43. Seán Petit, 'Thomas Wyse and the Issues of His Times', *Old Waterford Society Journal* 6 (1974/5): 6.
44. See Smith, 'Thomas Wyse (1791-1862)', 29.
45. Thomas Wyse, *Education Reform Volume 1: or the Necessity of a National System of Education* (London: Longman, Rees, Orme, Brown, Green and Longman, 1836). Wyse had planned to publish Volume 2, but it never saw the light of day. See Akenson, *The Irish Education Experiment*, 108–118.
46. Ibid., 108.
47. Auchmuty, *Irish Education*, 73.
48. Auchmuty, *Sir Thomas Wyse*, 150-1. See Alvey, 115.
49. Thomas Wyse, *Notes on Education Reform in Ireland During the First Half of the Nineteenth Century* (Waterford: C.P. Redmond and Co., 1901), 7–9. Edited by Winifred Wyse, Thomas's niece, this volume includes speeches and letters from his unpublished Memoirs.
50. He was affectionately known as JKL and signed many of his letters and publications in such a fashion.
51. See Atkinson, *Irish Education*, Chapter 5. See also Akenson, *The Irish Education Experiment*, 108–115.
52. Wyse, *Education Reform*, 18.
53. Ibid., 56.
54. Ibid.
55. In modern terms he was referring to adult education provision.
56. The title of the proposed Wyse Bill ran as follows: *Bill for the establishment and maintenance of parochial schools and the advancement of the education of the people,* H.C. 1831 (286), i, 491. Wyse made a second attempt in 1835: *Bill for the establishment of national education and the advancement of elementary education in Ireland,* H.C. 1835 (285), i, 407. Neither of the two Bills got to the Statute Books. For a discussion on education legislation in the 1830s and 40s, see Susan M. Parkes, *A Guide to Sources for the History of Irish Education 1780-1922* (Dublin: Four Courts Press, 2010), 124–130.
57. Wyse, *Education Reform*, 65.
58. See Akenson, *The Irish Education Experiment*, Chapter 5.
59. McManus, *The Irish Hedge School and its Books*, 66. See also Relihan, 'The Nineteenth-Century National School System', 89.

60. Ibid.
61. Smith, 27.
62. Ibid.
63. Auchmuty, *An Irish Education*, 90.
64. Quoted in Bonaparte-Wyse, *The Issue of Bonaparte-Wyse*, 54.
65. Auchmuty, *Sir Thomas Wyse*, 186–190. See also Batterberry, *Sir Thomas Wyse 1791–1862*.
66. Quoted in Cosgrove, 'The Educational Aims and Activities of Sir Thomas Wyse 1791–1862', 125.
67. Wyse, *Education Reform*, 265–6.
68. Auchmuty, *Sir Thomas Wyse*, 164.
69. Áine Hyland and Kenneth Milne (eds), *Irish Educational Documents, Vol. 1* (Dublin: Church of Ireland College of Education, 1987), 196.
70. Coolahan, *Irish Education: History and Structure*, 58.
71. Ibid.
72. See O'Connell, *O'Connell: Education, Church and State*, Chapters 2 and 8; and Alvey, 124-28. See also Smith, *Thomas Wyse*, 23–41.
73. Auchmuty, *Sir Thomas Wyse*, 165. Sir Thomas Orde, Chief-Secretary for Ireland, had already produced a graduated plan for Irish education as early as 1787. There was very little new in the Wyse proposals of nearly a half century later.
74. Ibid. The Report recommended that support for such endeavours should come from a joint arrangement between local authorities and the Central Board of Education. Supplementary education was very unlikely to have any degree of success when the Royal Dublin Society and the Mechanics' Institutes had achieved limited success within the realm of adult education. See Kieran R. Byrne, 'Mechanics' Institutes in Ireland, 1825–1850', in *Proceedings of the Educational Studies of Ireland Conference: Dublin, 1979* (Galway: Officinia Typographica/Galway University Press, [1979]), 32–48.
75. The University of Dublin has one college, Trinity College.
76. Coolahan, *Irish Education: History and Structure*, 108.
77. Parkes, *A Guide to Sources*, 82.
78. The situation was eased somewhat in 1794, when certain rites and oaths were removed from the regulations. This allowed Catholics have easier access to the university, including Wyse and his close friend Richard Lalor Sheil (1791–1851). Sheil was a barrister, a successful playwright, an MP and diplomat; he was a defender of liberal Protestant opinion and opponent of Daniel O'Connell. While access to Trinity College was eased, scholarships were still restricted to members of the Established Church.
79. Smith, 'Thomas Wyse', 35–41.
80. Coolahan, *Irish Education: History and Structure*, 114. These three colleges were known as Queens' Colleges, their status being raised collectively to Queen's University in 1850.
81. Clifford, *'Godless Colleges' and Mixed Education in Ireland*, 7–15. The Irish University Question was a long-standing saga going back to the end of the eighteenth century and it was not to witness an agreeable solution until the Irish Universities Act was passed in 1908. In 1908 the National University of Ireland was formed, embracing the three Colleges in Cork, Galway, and Dublin, and later, St. Patrick's College Maynooth. The College in Belfast was upgraded to full university status.
82. Clifford, *'Godless Colleges' and Mixed Education in Ireland*, 13.
83. Cosgrove, 'The Educational Aims and Activities of Sir Thomas Wyse (1791–1862)', 186–197.
84. Tony Lyons, 'The Catholic Church and Primary Education in Ireland: An Historical Perspective', in Eugene Duffy (ed.), *Catholic Primary Education: Facing New Challenges* (Dublin: The Columba Press, 2012), 73–90.

2

PART TWO
EDUCATION AND IRISH
SOCIETY IN THE NINETEENTH
CENTURY

4 IRISH WOMEN AND ELEMENTARY EDUCATION FOR THE POOR IN EARLY NINETEENTH-CENTURY IRELAND

EILÍS O'SULLIVAN

'...to give the people habits of industry, and consequently to promote their comfort and happiness...'[1]

In Leadbeater's *The Landlord's Friend* (1813), the fictional Ladies Charlotte and Seraphina discuss the latter's charity school and library. Lady Charlotte remarks to her friend:

> It is certain that if your attention to your tenants was universally followed, we need never dread civil discord. Lord Hardwicke, I remember, said that the Rebellion in Ireland could not have occurred had every county possessed a Mrs Peter La Touche.[2]

Elizabeth Vicars married Peter La Touche in 1788. Elizabeth founded an orphanage for poor girls near her home in Delgany, Co. Wicklow and opened a day school in the village. She went on to become vice-president of Dublin's Female Orphan House, which opened in 1790.[3] Philip, 3rd Earl of Hardwicke, became Lord Lieutenant of Ireland (1801–1806) after the 1798 Rebellion and after the Act of Union came into effect. It is unlikely that Elizabeth could have fulfilled Hardwicke's conviction, single-handedly preventing agrarian unrest or rebellion. However, at a time when women's endeavours often went unnoticed, his faith in the placatory effects of the benevolence of Elizabeth La Touche was significant. She was indeed possessed of impressive organisational skills, allied to kindly philanthropic effort. Among women of the Ascendancy, the upper classes in Ireland, Elizabeth La Touche was not unique. By the beginning of the nineteenth century, there were other women of 'capernosity and function'[4] throughout Ireland who exhibited considerable altruism and who became involved with the provision of elementary education for poor children. Their number was to grow over the next quarter of a century, so that by 1825 each county in Ireland could claim to have charitable women like Elizabeth who established and helped to support schools for the impoverished children of their localities. Many of these women were actively involved with the schools they founded and were willing to use their status and powerful connections to promote the needs of those schools. They visited the schools, encouraged the children and corresponded with education societies and other benefactors on behalf of the schools and of their teachers. Women of the Ascendancy were not alone in becoming involved with this form of philanthropic endeavour. Females of more modest means also provided for the education of poor children.[5]

Much has been written about Ireland's education systems and their attendant legislation.[6] However, until relatively recently less attention has been paid to women's role in the educational history of Ireland, impressive and extensive though that has been.[7] Existing literature contains few references to lay Irish women of the middle and upper classes or to their involvement in the provision of education at the beginning of the nineteenth century.[8] Why this should be so is debatable but gender, ethnicity, religion and/or class may have made the women less attractive subjects for researchers who worked generally within traditional patriarchal and politically and religiously polarised systems.

This chapter will outline the involvement of lay women with the provision of education for poor children, especially girls, at the beginning of the nineteenth century. In the main, it will draw on family papers, and the archives of voluntary societies such as Kildare Place Society (hereafter KPS),[9] and parliamentary and other reports. In consulting such primary sources the objective was not to re-visit information previously accentuated but to focus particularly on data about female school patrons and the teachers and pupils in their schools. Many of the sources consulted while researching this chapter have long been in the public domain. However, the sources are viewed in a way not previously done so that the educational involvement and motivation of women are underscored. There are, as yet, no publications detailing specifically the involvement of lay women in the provision of education in Ireland at the beginning of the nineteenth century. Nevertheless, some secondary sources were consulted while researching this chapter. These comprise contemporary publications (books, pamphlets, newspapers and works of fiction, especially those by female authors), researchers' private papers and modern publications, including local histories and biographies. Other sources include semi-structured interviews with local historians.

The chapter will begin by briefly setting the women in their time and social context. It will then move on to a consideration of the schools supported by the women and of the type of education offered therein. This part of the chapter will refer to the *Second Report of the Commissioners of Irish Education Inquiry*, 1826–27, and in particular to Appendix 22. The Commission of Irish Education Inquiry was one of a series of parliamentary commissions established during the late eighteenth and early nineteenth centuries to investigate educational provision in Ireland. This commission produced nine reports in total. The Second Report, Appendix 22, contains particulars of schools, teachers, pupils and patrons in each of the thirty-two counties of Ireland.

The chapter will conclude with an examination of the women's motivation in supporting schools for poor children, considering whether the women's involvement pointed more towards a perpetuation of social order than towards social change. Children's lives and their futures were altered, to a greater or lesser degree, by the women's involvement with local schools. In some cases, not only the children themselves but their families and the wider community were affected. The women certainly planned some of these effects. However, it must be questioned whether they intended the changes to shore up and preserve the society and structures they knew and approved or whether they imagined the changes wrought by their involvement with educational provision might ultimately impact more widely and profoundly on social order.

SOCIETY IN EARLY NINETEENTH-CENTURY IRELAND

A series of social and political upheavals had been experienced during the late eighteenth century in North America, continental Europe, Britain and Ireland. These upheavals engendered a consequent questioning of the *status quo*. Nevertheless, by the beginning of the nineteenth century, society in Ireland, as elsewhere in Europe, remained stratified in the main according to religion, gender and class. Ardently held, pervasive religious beliefs caused tensions, divisions and segregation. As with females throughout Europe at the time, social and civil rights were routinely and unquestioningly denied to women in

Ireland, regardless of class. Few people, female or male, were exercised by this lack of gender equity. Very few entertained 'the same notions of equality that characterise modern feminism'[10] and women themselves often spurned nascent stirrings regarding equality of the sexes.[11] With regard to class, there were the exalted and the lowly, with the 'middling sort'[12] in between. The upper and middle classes might display their munificence in alleviating the suffering of the poor, thereby ensuring eternal redemption for themselves and their families. It fell to the lowly to accommodate themselves to their ignoble station in life. To be deemed deserving, the poor must display 'humility; meekness; forgiveness; gratitude; self-denial; submission to the will and obedience to the law of God'.[13] It remained a widely held belief that the Lord had created the exalted and the lowly, that a stratified society was part of a divine plan.

At the top of the social scale in Ireland was the Ascendancy, the privileged group that controlled Irish politics and society at the time. The majority of Ascendancy members were Protestant.[14] Politically conservative, in general, the Ascendancy comprised aristocrats, ecclesiastics,[15] the landed gentry, and professional and business people. A comparatively small community, members of the Ascendancy met as frequently as early nineteenth-century travel allowed, at assemblies and balls. They spent long sojourns in each other's homes.[16] The Irish Ascendancy contracted apposite marriage alliances with members of the upper classes in Britain and further afield. There was also much intermarriage within the close-knit Ascendancy community in Ireland. This resulted in family ties that consolidated political allegiance and/or ownership of property and lands.[17] The size of these estates, and the income derived from them, differed. Nevertheless, ownership of land generally conferred wealth and power in a country that was at the time 'a predominantly rural and un-industrialised economy where a rapidly expanding population was almost exclusively dependent upon land for a livelihood'.[18] Ireland experienced little of an industrial revolution[19] and 'the vast majority of people…belonged to landed estate communities'.[20] 'By 1800 as many as one third of landlords owning Irish land were absentees'.[21] Some of these left the management of their estates in the hands of unscrupulous agents or middlemen[22] who 'gave never a thought to the welfare of the tenants or to the improvement of agriculture'.[23] Other landlords however took seriously their responsibilities towards the less advantaged in society. Once married, most Ascendancy women reared big families, managed large estates in the absence of husbands or sons, dealt with retinues of servants and supervised ambitious renovation plans. Many, like their husbands, were involved in philanthropic projects for the benefit of their poor neighbours and tenants.

At the other end of the social scale were Ireland's poor, comprising in the main the Roman Catholic majority, kept 'in a position of social, economic, and political inferiority' by the penal laws.[24] According to contemporary commentators, the condition of the impecunious Irish was remarkable among the poorer classes of Europe.[25] The majority eked out a living on the land, rarely leaving their native parishes.[26] They did not have security of tenure and, consequently, no permanent interest in the land. Irish peasants had little knowledge of agriculture and 'no capital to spend upon improvements'.[27] By 1800, the population of Ireland stood at almost five million, having doubled during the previous century.[28] This compounded the plight of the rural Irish by increasing subdivision of holdings.[29] The labours of entire families often went towards paying high rent for small tracts of land. From their meagre income poor Irish Roman Catholic householders paid tithes and dues to the clergy of the Anglican Church, who ministered to only one-sixth of the population. Dues were also payable to the Roman Catholic clergy. Not all tenants lived in deplorable conditions, of course. Some were afforded 'a decent way of life'.[30] However, this was generally not the case especially in the west and south-west of the country and, as Foster states, 'what cannot be rationalized away is the general unanimity of contemporary impressions: that where Ireland was poor and backward, it was astoundingly so'.[31]

Corkery contends that during the eighteenth century there was no middle class in Ireland, suggesting that there was 'a dearth of the virtues for which that class stands'.[32] Barnard, by comparison, discusses Protestants of the 'middle station'[33] and Kiberd illustrates how poems in Irish such as *Caoineadh Airt Uí Laoghaire* support not only the existence of affluent Roman Catholics but also their participation in the administrative affairs of the country.[34] Foster agrees that there was a middle class, Protestant and Roman Catholic, in Ireland, in the eighteenth and nineteenth centuries. These people concerned themselves with the establishment, with commerce, economics and the professions.[35]

WOMEN IN IRISH SOCIETY

In Ireland, as elsewhere, women were bartered in marriage arrangements; wife beating was legal and socially acceptable; abduction of marriageable heiresses was not unknown; mothers' rights regarding their children were secondary to those of fathers; women's inheritance entitlements were inferior to those of their male relatives; husbands controlled their wives' bodies, minds, money and property; women were rarely in a position to sue for divorce, regardless of circumstances, and it was not even acceptable for respectable females to venture out alone.[36] Unmarried women fared badly too, often reliant on fathers, brothers or brothers-in-law for their very existence. Sometimes viewed as a burden,[37] they regularly had to stifle their own opinions and comply with their benefactors' beliefs and decisions. Irish females also suffered from inequalities in the area of education. Like their sisters in other countries, Irish female intellects were frequently as 'restricted as their rib cages',[38] regardless of the international voices of Macaulay, Condorcet and Wollstonecraft, *inter alia*, calling for equality of opportunity and education.[39]

WOMEN AND EMPLOYMENT IN IRELAND

'All human beings are subject to some degree of social forces that limit freedom, but within those limits people are able to exercise greater or lesser degrees of control over their own lives'.[40] In nineteenth-century Ireland, females, especially poor females, were certainly oppressed. Nevertheless, some women possessed and displayed remarkable 'agency',[41] that 'ability and will to act purposefully, independently, and self-consciously'.[42]

'Biological and familial imperatives governed [women's] chief roles' in Ireland as elsewhere, regardless of wealth or status.[43] However, to dismiss nineteenth-century women as being solely involved in private, domestic concerns is not to paint the entire picture. Irish women were certainly concerned with the maintenance of homes, both humble and great. Contrary to modern conceptions though, many women of all social classes took part in work other than domestic. The novelist and educator Maria Edgeworth[44] and the estate agent Barbara Verschoyle[45] were among the women who worked outside the domestic milieu, supporting themselves and their families and thereby exercising a considerable measure of control over their own lives.

LAY WOMEN AND PHILANTHROPY

Women like Edgeworth and Verschoyle received financial recompense for their work. Others participated in unpaid, voluntary activity which was socially acceptable for women. Charitable work, especially in the area of education was particularly admissible, as it was deemed akin to women's natural role as mothers and nurturers. According to Foreman, education and schooling for poor children was an area that offered remarkable opportunity for female participation outside the domestic sphere.[46] In becoming involved with educational projects, women were not, therefore, stepping beyond society's arbitrary boundaries. The women observed the plight of the less fortunate around their homes. They put their ability, empathy and undeniable talents to good use, helping to ameliorate the 'conditions' of poor labourers and tenants.

An example of such a woman was Charlotte, Lady O'Brien, who opened several schools for poor children around her home in Co. Clare at the beginning of the nineteenth century. Charlotte had married Edward O'Brien of Dromoland Castle in 1799.[47] The couple had, in all, thirteen children – seven daughters and six sons.[48] The boys were sent away to school and the girls were educated at home, as was usual at the time. Charlotte took primary responsibility for this[49] but also employed dancing, music and drawing masters to impart the extra accomplishments which, at the time, were perceived necessary for young ladies. At the time of their marriage, Edward had been a member of the Irish Parliament in Dublin.[50] He was subsequently elected to Westminster and joined the ninety-nine other Irish MPs there, spending much time in London until his resignation in 1826.[51] Charlotte became an adept manager of their vast estates, demonstrating the business acumen she had inherited from her father.[52] She corresponded at length with Edward, detailing estate affairs. His letters to her outlined the economies he wanted practised, estate business to be carried out in his absence and instructions regarding ongoing renovations to their home.

Charlotte was said to have a 'benevolent heart'.[53] 'A renowned humanitarian',[54] she involved herself in the philanthropy that was sorely needed in nineteenth-century Clare, when localised potato famines caused much hardship throughout rural Ireland. 'Many poor persons bore testimony' to her 'benevolent disposition'.[55] Like other women of the time, she kept a book of medicinal recipes, some comprising lead and/or opium.[56] Most of these recipes had been given to her by doctors. Charlotte personally mixed many of the recipes and administered them to victims of cholera and other diseases apparently unafraid that she herself might become infected.[57] In 1827 Elizabeth Fry, prison reformer, visited the gaol in Ennis. Charlotte, who met Fry when the latter called to Dromoland, joined the Ladies Visiting Committee which was set up to encourage improvements for women prisoners in Ennis gaol.[58] During the Famine a daily ration of soup or meal was distributed by a member of the family near the 'famine' ash trees on the estate which stood on either side of the drive leading from Newmarket-on-Fergus, close to the coach road. Charlotte organised a local woman, Mary O'Grady, to sell food, thereby saving locals from an exhausting journey into town. Charlotte also taught Mary to make a rice porridge that was subsequently sold at a penny a quart.[59]

CHILDREN IN IRISH SOCIETY

During the eighteenth century, the writings of Jean-Jacques Rousseau, amongst others, had influenced the child-rearing of the upper classes. Henry Fox, a successful Whig politician, and his wife Caroline, followed Rousseau's advice on the education of children. In Ireland, Caroline's sister Emily, Duchess of Leinster was also a supporter of Rousseau. She was so moved by the death of her eldest son while he was in school in England that she decided against sending her other sons away, instead hiring a tutor to teach her children (boys and girls) along Rousseauvian lines at Frescati House, near the sea at Black Rock in Dublin.[60]

By the beginning of the nineteenth century, however, life remained bleak for many children, despite the influence of the eighteenth-century educators. Regardless of class, children were often viewed as inherently bad, insentient beings whose eternal souls might be saved by the intervention of religion, and, to a lesser degree, by education.[61] That perception was common amongst those who wrote about schooling for children of the lower classes. At the time, the concept of education as a process which enabled a person to achieve his or her potential was far from prevalent, except in the case of very rich and/or very bright males. In Ireland, as elsewhere, education for girls particularly was 'circumscribed by class, religion and gender'.[62]

Straitened family circumstances meant that very young children were forced to work to augment their parents' incomes. Society was undecided as to whether such children deserved or needed much schooling. Any education poor children did receive inevitably centred on religion and on the skills that might enable them to earn a living. Basic literacy and even less numeracy were deemed adequate for those destined to be 'hewers of wood and drawers of water'.[63] By emphasising their duties which were legion but not their rights which were few, it was envisaged that this restricted schooling would turn poor children into submissive servants and grateful, loyal subjects.[64]

Poor girls were doubly disadvantaged, being both female and poverty-stricken. As females they were perceived as inferior, their intellectual capacity reflecting their smaller craniums.[65] Some believed though that females who had been taught domestic skills would make thrifty wives and astute mothers. The education of poor girls could therefore improve the lot of the impecunious in general. The girls' families would be part of the 'deserving poor' while avoiding the slur of indigence and blameworthiness often associated with nineteenth-century poverty. Regardless of such possible benefits to society, girls' schooling remained constrained. They usually received a short rudimentary schooling fitting them for their station in life and for eternity. They were taught 'the principles of the christian [sic] religion'.[66] They learned to read primarily that they might have access to Holy Scripture. Girls were taught only the most basic arithmetic. Many learned only to write their names. Domestic crafts (sewing, knitting and spinning) formed a central part of their schooling. This was deemed all they would need for later life.

LAY WOMEN AND INSTITUTIONAL CARE FOR CHILDREN IN DUBLIN

At the beginning of the nineteenth century, kindly, philanthropic members of the public, male and female, concerned themselves with children in institutional care. Among these was the aforementioned Elizabeth La Touche who, in 1800, became one of four vice-presidents of the Female Orphan House on the city's North Circular Road. Of Huguenot origin, the La Touche family had come to Ireland in the late seventeenth century. They had prospered as manufacturers and bankers and were benevolent and altruistic. Elizabeth's involvement with an orphanage for girls and a day school[67] near her home in Delgany, Co. Wicklow may have led to her serendipitous appointment as one of the vice-presidents of the institution in Dublin. Elizabeth visited the Orphan House regularly and every Saturday had an account of each child's conduct sent to her. She appears to have been interested in the girls individually not only while they were in the orphanage but during their apprenticeships as servants and afterwards too. Her concern for the children seems to have been reciprocated.[68] While in the orphanage the girls were taught the principles of Christianity, to read, to write in a legible hand, do some arithmetic and to cast accounts. They were also taught needlework, knitting, spinning and housework to qualify them as servants. The orphanage took in sewing work for the girls to do. Some of the older girls worked as monitresses in the schoolroom while others served at table, kept rooms tidy, worked in the dairy and milked the orphanage's eight cows.[69] The Female Orphan House was fortunate too in the appointment of

Sarah Stephens as matron and principal schoolmistress. Teachers at the time were generally untrained. Sarah was unusual in that she had been trained by Dr. Bell in the Central School in Baldwin's Garden, London. Sarah resided with the girls and, according to the rules of the *Orphan House for Destitute Females*, she was enjoined, unusually for the time, to treat the children with 'tenderness and humanity'.[70]

VOLUNTARY EDUCATION SOCIETIES

In the absence of a State-run welfare system or many institutions comparable to the Female Orphan House, responsibility for abandoned or poor children usually devolved on parishes. Some of these were unwilling, ill-equipped and/ or unable to shoulder the burden. In the area of education, parishes' reluctance or inability was often offset by private charitable ventures which relied for help, financial and academic, on one of the many Protestant voluntary education societies in operation at the time. Societies such as the London Hibernian Society, the Baptist Society, and the KPS were all involved in education.[71] Because of its contemporaneous efficacy and its wide-reaching influence on the future education system in Ireland, the latter ranks as the most important of these. The KPS filled an advisory, fiscal and administrative role for the schools connected with it. It published books for the use of pupils and teachers. It pioneered the inspection of schools and formal teacher training for both men and women. The Society did not pay those teaching in the schools connected to it. Instead it awarded half-yearly or yearly gratuities (ranging generally from £1 to £10) to the teachers it deemed 'particularly worthy of Approbation'.[72]

The KPS was founded by wealthy Dublin philanthropists on 2 December 1811 with the purpose of 'diffusing the blessing of *well-ordered* Education amongst the labouring classes'.[73] Included among the philanthropic gentlemen were Samuel Bewley, William Guinness and Peter La Touche, Elizabeth's husband. The society depended initially on voluntary subscriptions but subsequently received parliamentary grants of varying amounts, beginning in 1815 with a grant of £6,980. There were applications from all parts of the country for assistance and by 1825 the society was supporting 1,490 schools catering for at least 100,000 children.[74] *Ab initio*, the society set out to be religiously neutral and to provide education for Ireland's poor without proselytising.[75] In schools that were 'in connexion' with the Society, the Bible, Authorised or Douay Version,[76] would be read 'without Note or Comment' by children who had attained a suitable proficiency in reading. No other religious instruction would be allowed. This tenet of the society caused much opposition. The Catholic Church 'prohibited the indiscriminate Use of Scripture…without Note or Comment' and 'the Interpretation of them by every One's private Judgement'.[77] The Church's hierarchy also disagreed with confining the teaching of Christian doctrine to Bible reading alone, feeling that a religious ethos should permeate all aspects of pupils' lives. Many Protestants also subscribed to this view. The predominance of Protestants on the society's committee was a further cause of unease to Roman Catholics. Furthermore, they suspected the society of proselytising activities. The Roman Catholic hierarchy also felt that if the society grew too successful then the government would be loath to fund denominational schools directly. The founding of the national school system in 1831 presaged the end of the KPS.

Another source of funding became available to school patrons in 1819 when parliament empowered the Lord Lieutenant to issue grants annually to schools that had already been established by voluntary subscriptions.[78] In practice, the Lord Lieutenant's School Fund aided the building or purchasing of schoolhouses. Applications for grants from this fund were generally rejected unless half the amount of estimated costs had already been raised locally.

PARLIAMENTARY COMMISSIONS AND EDUCATIONAL INQUIRY

The Commission of Irish Education Inquiry was established in 1825, largely at the behest of the Roman Catholic Church, which was beginning to assert its rights as the Church of the majority of Irish people.[79] The commissioners made 'a personal inspection of a great Variety of Schools for the Education of the lower Orders in every County of Ireland'.[80] Included were hedge schools and schools run by Roman Catholic orders, male and female.[81]

The country's clergymen, Roman Catholic and Protestant, were requested by the commission to make separate returns 'of the state of Education in their respective Parishes'.[82] The clergymen were requested to include the name and location of schools, the names, religious persuasion and salaries of masters and/or mistresses, the cost of building and the condition of the school houses, the numbers and religious persuasion of pupils and the names of societies and/or local patrons who supported the schools. They were also asked to state whether the Bible (Authorised or Douay Version) was read. The clergymen were required to swear that, to their knowledge, the returns were correct and that they had taken all possible care while compiling them in the autumn of 1824. The figures returned separately from the Roman Catholic and Protestant clergy certainly showed discrepancies. Nevertheless, the information contained in the commissioner's ultimate reports is remarkable for an age hampered by indifferent means of research and communication and by laborious travel. The resultant reports and appendices prepared by the commissioners paint in meticulous detail a picture of the education offered in Ireland at the time. According to the reports, more than 560,000[82] children attended 11,823 schools[84] throughout Ireland.[85] The provinces of Leinster, Ulster and Munster all boasted approximately 3,500 schools. Connaught had significantly fewer, with a little more than 1,500 schools.[86]

The commissioners published responses, county by county, as detailed in Appendix 22 of the *Second Report of the Commissioners of Irish Education Inquiry*. As mentioned above, the clerical correspondents had been asked to include the names of societies and/or local patrons who supported the schools as part of their returns. Many correspondents did not identify an association with which a school was connected and/or did not name a local patron. Instead they entered 'none' in the appropriate column. Perhaps such correspondents were simply stating facts. Perhaps there was no society or local patron involved. Alternatively the correspondents may have been unaware of such involvement. If, on the other hand, 'none' was an effort at evasion, perhaps it was due to 'the hostility of partisan school authorities' or even to 'ambiguous directions from the sponsors of the enquiry'.[87]

Some correspondents, however, were more expansive, identifying education societies and local patrons. The London Hibernian Society, the Baptist Society and the KPS were among the education associations named most often. Members of the middle and upper classes, including peers, were named as school patrons. Luminaries of the Protestant and Roman Catholic Churches were also identified as assisting schools.

LAY WOMEN AND EDUCATIONAL PROVISION

Commissioners' Reports indicate that women were certainly patrons of schools in the late eighteenth and early nineteenth centuries. It is, however, difficult to establish exactly the numbers of women involved with the provision of elementary education for poor children at the time. Female patrons were sometimes recorded anonymously as 'ladies of the neighbourhood', 'committee[s] of men and women' or 'parishioners'. Sometimes a family name was given but the individual female members of that family were not specified.[88] A further difficulty is that members of female religious orders (nuns) were often given the title 'Mrs', thereby appearing to be lay women. Regardless of these computational constraints, however, it is possible to identify lay women who were involved with almost 400 schools throughout the thirty-two counties of Ireland providing elementary education for poor children in the first quarter of the nineteenth century.

So, who were these women? What was the extent of their involvement? With which schools were they connected? It is possible to attempt these questions by scrutinising sources on female patrons and schools in Munster, where the percentage of the population attending school was higher than the national average.[89]

Like their male counterparts, women from the middle and upper classes of Irish society were named in the *Second Report* (1826–27) as patrons of schools. Some of these women were undoubtedly of relatively restricted means and consequently able to contribute only modest amounts to the upkeep of schools. Further up the social scale, others had greater funds at their disposal and could afford to be (and were) generous in their support of schools. 'Miss Lazenby, governess in the Bishop of Derry's family' belonged to the former group. As a governess, she was certainly of restricted personal means.[90] Nevertheless, she was patron of a school on the Inishowen Peninsula in Donegal where Margaret Gardiner taught eight or nine Protestant girls. Margaret earned £4 a year and was given a cabin and a potato garden.[91]

By comparison, Caroline, Countess of Dunraven, of Adare in Co. Limerick was socially and financially in a much stronger position than Miss Lazenby. In 1807 the church of the Augustinian Abbey had been given to the Protestant community of Adare, Co. Limerick as their parish church.[92] Some years after that, at the behest of Caroline, Countess of Dunraven, the abbey's refectory was converted into a schoolhouse.[93] The renovations, costing £350, were done with stone and lime.[94] The schoolroom was a 'spacious apartment lighted by fifteen windows, each of which [was] different from the rest'. Caroline was the school's patron. By 1824, almost 200 children, mainly Protestant, were attending the school which observed the rules of the KPS though it also received funds from the London Hibernian Society.[95] The Authorised Version of the Bible was read.[96] John Armstrong taught the boys in the school while his wife, Catherine, taught the girls. The couple, Protestants, were to remain in the school for more than ten years.[97] They received regular gratuities from the KPS, and some monies from their pupils. By 1824 their income amounted to £64 a year, over half of which was contributed by Caroline.[98] In addition, John earned £15 annually as clerk of the Church.[99] In 1825, Caroline built a 'good residence' for the Armstrongs in the same style as the original refectory that housed the school. There was a garden attached for the family's use. The Armstrongs were not the only teachers in the school: Ellen Lyons, also Protestant, began teaching there in 1838. Caroline recommended her for training in the KPS model school in Dublin, and Ellen began a short teacher-training course on 7 September, 1838. She finished her training in ten weeks, and was awarded a second-class certificate.[100]

A Sunday school was also conducted in the restored abbey. The surnames of the children in attendance suggest that members of the Palatine and Roman Catholic communities may have sent their children to the Sunday school along with pupils of the Anglican faith.[101] Pupils from the Sunday school were presented annually for examination in religious knowledge, and those who attained the required standard were given prizes of books.[102] Caroline's school maintained its links with the Kildare Place Society until 1838 before eventually joining the national school system.[103]

While the religious affiliation of school patrons is not generally given in the Appendix to the *Second Report* (1826–27), one exception to this is Mrs Meade, 'a Roman Catholic lady' who was patron of a free school in Denmark Street, in the city of Limerick. Some eighty-four Roman Catholic girls attended and, as might be expected, the Douay Version of the Bible was read. Bridget Burke, the school's mistress, was paid £28 8s. 9d. per year. An unnamed 'workwoman' was also employed. Her salary depended on the volume of sewing produced by the girls which when sold yielded £10 annually.[104]

The religious affiliations of the schoolmaster and/or mistress and of the children attending the school were invariably included in the Appendix. Female patrons, regardless of their own religious affiliations, were involved with schools that catered for all of the main Christian denominations in Ireland at the time. In the Dungannon area of Co. Tyrone, Elizabeth Beatie, Presbyterian, taught thirty-six girls, Protestant and Roman Catholic, for which she earned £4 per year. The schoolhouse was a thatched cottage, which contained two rooms that had been 'fitted up' by the Rev. Mr. Gore while Mrs Gore gave £4 to the school each year.[105] In Co. Tipperary, Cahir Chapel School was first aided by the Kildare Place Society in 1822.[106] Emily, Countess of Glengall was sometimes named as the school's sole patron[107] but Rev. John Power, P.P. and John Chaytor were also listed as patrons/correspondents. They were members of the Church of Ireland, the Roman Catholic Church, and the Society of Friends respectively. The school in Cahir cost £198 14s. 9d. to build; the Kildare Place Society contributed £49, the Lord Lieutenant's Fund provided £97 2s. 3d. and the rest was raised by subscription. The money from the Lord Lieutenant's Fund was officially awarded to the Earl of Glengall, Emily's son.[108] However, it was Emily who made the initial submission by which the funds were procured. The school, a slated house with a residence annexed for the teachers, originally catered for approximately 136 children, all Roman Catholic.[109] There were two schoolrooms, one each for girls and boys, which were well lit and ventilated. Mary and James Davin,[110] Roman Catholics, taught in the school, earning an annual salary of £15 each.[111] Pupils paid 1d. per week for tuition, which included reading, writing, arithmetic, and needlework for the girls. Despite the Roman Catholic profile, the Authorised Version of the Bible was read there and pupils could recite parts from memory.[112] On 12 October 1825, an inspector from the KPS visited the school. Of the 138 children on the school rolls, 111 were present. On this occasion the inspector recorded, however, that 'Scriptures [were] not regularly read in School'. This was hardly surprising. Rev. Power, P.P. was one of the school's patrons/correspondents and the Roman Catholic Church frowned on its flock reading the Bible 'without Note or Comment'. Despite this breach of the society's rules, a £5 gratuity was paid to both Mary and James Davin in December that year. Cahir Chapel School subsequently became known as Cahir National School having joined the national school system founded in 1831. It thereby terminated its association with the Kildare Place Society.[113]

The level of female patrons' contribution to schools varied greatly. There were those, like Caroline, Countess of Dunraven and Emily, Countess of Glengall, who were intimately involved with the running of the schools. Then there were those whose involvement was more peripheral. The Countess of Desart appears to have been closely connected with the school built by the late Earl of Desart in Knocktopher, Co. Kilkenny. James Shearman was master in the 'commodious house' that had cost £25 to build. The Bible was not read in the school possibly because the majority of the school's eighty pupils (sixty boys and twenty girls) were Roman Catholic. The Countess visited the school every Monday to give premiums or prizes to the pupils.[114] By comparison, Mrs Burke's involvement with the school in Ower, Co. Galway appears to have been limited to giving 'the use of the school-house', 'a miserable thatched barn' which had cost approximately £9 to build.[115] Other female patrons were involved with the schools they supported to the extent that they were also the only teachers in those schools. In Cork city, Ann Shehan taught up to 130 Roman Catholic girls, *gratis* in an 'apartment in Mr. Shehan's dwelling-house' on Friars-walk. The children were 'clothed by the exertions of Miss Shehan's family, assisted by a collection made in the neighbourhood, which [came] to about £5 and a donation from Jeremiah Murphy, esq.' The Bible was not read in the school.[116] Neither was it read in a school in Co. Tipperary, supported by Mrs Baron Pennefather and her daughters. The school educated twelve Roman Catholic girls *gratis* in a school housed in the demesne lodge.[117]

Members of banking and merchant families were also involved with the provision of education for poor children during the early nineteenth century. As noted earlier, the Guinness, Bewley and La Touche families were among the founders of the KPS. Evidence suggests that the prominent Cork brewing families of Beamish and Crawford were involved in education, through the efforts of the ladies of each family. Mrs Beamish supported a pay school for approximately twenty girls and a small number of Roman Catholic boys in the Ballintemple area of the city, giving the teacher five shillings per week, and coals and meat at Christmas. Mrs Beamish was also involved with another school in the Blackrock area of the city, together with Mrs and Miss Crawford. Just as philanthropic members of the Guinness brewing family were involved with education in Dublin, so members of Cork's brewing elite appear to have supported schools in that city.

Women of social prominence were also involved with educational provision for the poor. A school at Slane, Co. Meath, was supported by Lady Elizabeth of Slane Castle, a leading light in Irish society and the putative mistress of King George IV.[118] Susanna, Marchioness of Waterford was the sole patron of a school on Curraghmore estate near the village of Portlaw. Born into the notorious Delaval family of Seaton Delaval in Northumberland, Susanna had married Henry le Poer Beresford, 2nd Marquis of Waterford in 1805. At her behest a 'handsome', 'excellent schoolhouse' was built in the cottage style just inside the demesne gates, at a cost of £500.[119] Lewis and Ryland contend that this school was built for the purpose of educating the children of the 'neighbouring peasantry'.[120] However, as alternative schools were available in the area for such children, Susanna's may have been founded solely for the daughters of people working on the Curraghmore estate.[121]

Just as the patrons and their involvement varied, so the schools they supported ranged from large to small, and were attended by children of one denomination or many. Generally teachers were untrained, but occasionally they were sent to Dublin at the patrons' expense to undergo a short course there, usually at the KPS teacher training institution. In Clogheen, in Co. Tipperary, Eliza Thornhill taught only six Protestant girls in a pay school that was 'in connexion' with the KPS and under the patronage of the Misses Grub.[122] They collected 1d. per week from the pupils, paying Eliza £10 per year.[123] By comparison, Lady Caroline Damer supported a large school for more than 120 children in the Roscrea area of Co. Tipperary. John and Jane Atkinson taught the almost equal number of boys and girls, both Protestant and Roman Catholic. Lady Caroline subscribed £300 towards the construction of this 'very good' schoolhouse, which had cost £900 in total to build. The Board of Erasmus Smith, a charitable educational trust, had contributed the remaining £600. Lady Caroline gave two acres of land to the master and mistress, John and Jane, who also enjoyed rent-free accommodation and a joint salary of £60 per annum.[124]

Eleanor, Lady Godfrey, was committed to securing a school for the 'worthy' poor of Milltown in Co. Kerry.[125] A school supported by her in the early years of her marriage had fallen into disuse by 1810. Determined to re-establish it,[126] Eleanor opened a school in the local session's house for girls and boys, Roman Catholic and Protestant, on 1 July 1821. This proved unsatisfactory so, regardless of opposition from local Roman Catholic clergy, Eleanor had a new school built. It is debatable whether this school was 'violently opposed'[127] by the priests, as claimed by some because, in essence, it was intended for the substantial Protestant population of Kilcoleman Parish. At the time this consisted of approximately fifty families.[128] Some years later, some fifty Protestant but only three Roman Catholic children were listed on the school's rolls.[129] The new school, known as Kilcoleman School, cost £196 17s. 11d. to build, and was a slated stone and mortar building. Finished in 1824, it was 'in the cottage style', with a garden.[130] It had accommodation for seventy males and for fifty females, and all 'except 1 child' were educated *gratis*.[131] Local subscriptions amounted to £15, while the Lord Lieutenant's Fund provided £100 and the Kildare Place Society gave £30. John Godfrey donated £50 and turf to heat the school.[132] The Godfreys also paid the teachers' salaries.[133] Eleanor was identified as patron of the school, and Rev. R. Hewson as correspondent. Nevertheless, Eleanor herself did much of the early secretarial work on the school's behalf. In March 1824, Eleanor applied for, and was granted, training for a teacher for the school. In 1845, Eleanor's school joined the Anglican Church Education Society, which had been founded in 1839. However, from 1876 until *circa* 1914 it functioned as a national school.[134]

PRACTICAL VERSUS ACADEMIC

Some of the women who were involved with the provision of schooling for poor children were aware of enlightened educational theories. Eleanor, Lady Godfrey, for example, was *au fait* with Rousseau's educational theories.[135] However, when it came to the education of the poor, she and most of the women named above identified more closely with the less progressive teachings of Trimmer and More, Lancaster and Bell, subscribing to voluntary societies that promulgated the ideas and theories of these prominent educators. Women who provided schooling for the poor emphasised the practical over the academic, particularly with regard to the education of poor females. The emphasis on practical subjects for the girls in Eleanor, Lady Godfrey's school is a case in point. Caroline, Countess of Kingston, Mitchelstown, Co. Cork believed that by teaching poor girls in her school to be industrious, to weave, spin and sew, she was promoting 'their comfort and happiness' and consequently that of the wider community.[136] Girls in the Co. Clare schools of Charlotte, Lady O'Brien, followed the curtailed academic curriculum offered to many females at the time, but they also learned to embroider, following her ladyship's patterns and designs.[137] Embroidery was a skill which could help support them and their families.

In a thatched house at Springfield in Co. Tipperary, Mary Shins taught eight girls and one boy. Mary received about £6 6s. per year from Lady Barker. Illustrating the importance attached to the practical over the academic, Lady Barker paid the mistress 5s. per quarter for such children 'as were learning needle work' but just '2/2 for those learning only to read & spell'.[138] Emily, Countess of Glengall supported Cahir Chapel School where girls admittedly learned to read and write. Nevertheless, similar to many female educators of the time, she rated the inculcation of habits of cleanliness and industry in girls above intellectual activity. Like Caroline, Countess of Kingston, her neighbour and rival, Emily believed that 'nothing [would] so much tend to meliorate the condition of the poor, as attention to the habits of the females'. Corresponding with the General Board of Health in 1821, Emily wrote that '… to teach [women] industry, and how to wash, work, spin and knit, [was] of more use than to teach them to read and write'. She suggested that the Linen Board might be induced to grant small annual salaries to spinning mistresses. Were spinning schools to be established for three or four years, so many women could be taught that 'the art would then be disseminated through the country'. 'With respect to industry', she wrote, 'it is more the means than the will of the poor that are deficient'.[139] Given this practical viewpoint, it is not surprising that Emily promoted the manufacture of straw hats in Cahir.[140] In 1823, the 'Leghorn, Tuscan, British, and fancy straw plat manufactory', also known as the Cahir Straw Platting School, was established in the Co. Tipperary town. An inspector from Kildare Place Society visited the school in the spring of 1827. He found it shut because the master was ill. This situation was to prevail and the Cahir Straw Platting School subsequently closed permanently.[141] Emily and the Cahir Local Association had succeeded in introducing flax growing to Cahir in 1823,[142] and 'for the purpose of giving employment to the female population' Emily established a spinning school, once again in the Market House.[143] Before the Linen Board became involved with the project, Emily organised and financed the project herself. Local women were anxious to be part of the venture and attended 'with great obedience to the rules of the establishment'. Each day they grew 'more cleanly'. Emily had 'no fault to find with their want of industry'. Indeed she had to turn away hopeful employees. The yarn produced in Emily's spinning school was woven by weavers in the town, who were consequently in full-time employment instead of being 'idle and penniless'.[144] Unfortunately, however, 'for want of an advantageous market', this project also was doomed to failure.[145]

MOTIVATION

Why did women of the upper ranks become involved with educational provision for the poor? Many women were doubtless moved by sympathy and a sense of charitable duty, or *noblesse oblige*. They were also doing what other women, of similar social status, were doing in Britain and continental Europe. For some of the women, philanthropy may have given purpose to their lives. Citing Leadbeater, O'Connell suggests that practical involvement by women was 'a resource against ennui'[146] which allowed them to lead lives 'of purpose and duty far removed from anyone deserving the description of idle rich'.[147]

Most of the women mentioned above began founding schools during the first quarter of the nineteenth century. The relatively short time-span in which their schools were established merits comment. Following the Repeal of the Penal Laws, specifically Gardiner's Relief Act of 1782,[148] it became legal for lay Roman Catholics along with teaching orders to provide for the education of co-religionists, rich and/or poor. At the time there were comparatively small numbers of female religious orders involved in the provision of education in Ireland. This *lacuna* allowed some lay women to pursue their interest in educational philanthropy. After 1782, Ireland witnessed change as the Roman Catholic Church changed from one under siege to one of vigour. This metamorphosis doubtlessly encouraged charitable Roman Catholic women to become involved with the education of poor co-religionists. Similarly, the increasingly vigorous opposition of many Roman Catholic clerics to any education for Roman Catholic children with which they were not directly involved may also have galvanised evangelical Protestant women into action, as suggested by Robins.[149] Just as the Roman Catholic Church in Ireland was experiencing growth, some sections of the Church of Ireland underwent a 'period of vehement evangelicalism' during the Second Reformation of the 1820s.[150] Some deeply evangelical women, such as Charlotte, Lady O'Brien, of Dromoland Castle, became involved with elementary education. She and others like her were therefore prepared to go to great lengths and brook little opposition in their efforts to provide for the schooling and, importantly, the religious instruction of the poor children of their neighbourhoods.

The efforts of these women provided an antidote to the illegal hedge schools, discussed in Chapter One, that were suspected of spreading sedition.[151] Some of these women believed that their schools would encourage work and productivity, and eradicate backwardness.[152] In the wake of the 1798 Rebellion, some women may have believed that educating poor children in a carefully controlled environment could prevent further upheavals.

Women may also have enjoyed developing their business acumen, by fund-raising and managing money. For example, some looked to the Lord Lieutenant's School Fund for financial backing for their schools. This fund, which rose from £3,250 in 1819 to almost £11,000 in 1824,[153] attracted the attention of women like Emily, Countess of Glengall. They were also attracted to the KPS as a source of support. From 1820, parliamentary grants to the KPS amounted annually to tens of thousands, peaking at £30,000 in 1831.[154] Some women who had established schools were quick to apply to connect their schools with the KPS, not only for monetary backing but to ensure that the schools remained Protestant, particularly after the establishment of a non-denominational state system of National Schools in 1831. Eleanor, Lady Godfrey, and Caroline, Countess of Dunraven, both placed their schools 'in connexion' with the KPS. Having observed the changes wrought by the Act of Union, and the vigour of the renewed Roman Catholic Church after Catholic Emancipation, perhaps

Eleanor and Caroline wished to guarantee the *status quo* at their schools. In this they would not have been unusual or alone.

The women included in this chapter were often staunch Protestants and were actively involved in their respective parishes. Some doubtlessly tended towards proselytism. However, in a school where the majority of children were Protestant to begin with, proselytism was hardly a primary motivation. By comparison, there were no Protestant children on the rolls of Emily, Countess of Glengall's school in Cahir, Co. Tipperary. No suggestion of proselytism attaches to her involvement with the school, though she and her husband were actively involved in the parish affairs of the Anglican community there. Concerned as she was with encouraging cleanliness and providing employment, Emily may have realised that if the poor children of Cahir were to be educated, it would be sensible to acquiesce with the wishes of their spiritual leaders and with those of their parents in matters of faith. This suggests pragmatism in the face of an increasingly confident Roman Catholic clergy and people.

CONCLUSION

William Herschel, court astronomer to George III, opined that *quicquid nitet notandum* (whatever shines should be observed).[155] The contribution of the women who became involved with educational provision at the beginning of the nineteenth century shines. These women overcame obstacles to pursue their interest in founding and overseeing schools. They were committed to providing basic elementary education for poor children, concerning themselves with social needs rather than confining their lives to the social calendar. Their enterprise in education was often significant, and they deployed a range of skills – managerial, financial, and social – to ensure the success of their schools. The enterprise displayed by these women in an inequitable era has been a missing chapter in Irish women's history and in the history of education.

NOTES

1.   Caroline, Dowager Countess of Kingston (statement to the 'Catholic Clergy and their flock', Mitchelstown, Co. Cork, November 13, 1809) in Right Rev. Dr. Coppinger, *Letter to the Right Honorable (sic) and Honorable (sic) The Dublin Society from the Right Rev. Doctor Coppinger Titular Bishop of Cloyne & Ross, occasioned by Certain Observations and Misstatements of the Rev. Horatio Townsend, in his Statistical Survey of the County Cork* (Cork: executed and published by the direction and under the patronage of this Society, 1811), 19–20.

2. Mary Leadbeater, *The Landlord's Friend: Intended as a Sequel to Cottage Dialogues* (Dublin: Hibernia Press Office, 1813), 112.

3. Jim Brennan and Aileen Short, 'La Touche History', The La Touche Legacy, http://latouchelegacy.com/history-of-the-la-touche-family.php (accessed 17 February 2011); *Sixth Report of the Commissioners on Education in Ireland, (Hibernian Society for Soldiers' and Sailors' Children)* 1826-27 (442) XIII. 385, 12–4.

4. Brendan Behan, 'The Confirmation Suit', in Augustine Martin (ed.), *Exploring English 1* (Dublin: Gill and Macmillan, 1967), 245.

5. Second Report of the Commissioners of Inquiry (Abstract of Returns in 1824, from the Protestant and Roman Catholic Clergy in Ireland, of the State of Education in their respective Parishes) 1826-27 (12.) XII. 1, Appendix 22, 328-9, 868-9, 1006-7, 1066–7.

6. Rev. Martin Brenan, *Schools of Kildare and Leighlin A.D. 1775-1835* (Dublin: M.H. Gill and Son Ltd., 1935); Patrick John Dowling, *The Hedge Schools of Ireland* (Cork: Mercier Press, 1968); Norman Atkinson, *Irish Education: A History of Educational Institutions* (Dublin: Allen Figgis, 1969); Donald Harman Akenson, *The Irish Education Experiment – The National System of Education in the Nineteenth Century* (London: Routledge & Kegan Paul; Toronto: University of Toronto Press, 1970); Thomas Joseph Durcan, *History of Irish Education from 1800 with special reference to manual instruction* (Bala, North Wales: Dragon Books, 1972); John Coolahan, *Irish Education: its history and structure* (Dublin: Institute of Public Administration, 1981); Áine Hyland and Kenneth Milne, *Irish Educational Documents*, vol. I (Dublin: CICE, 1987); Séamus Ó Buachalla, *Education Policy in Twentieth-Century Ireland* (Dublin: Wolfhound, 1988); Kenneth Milne, *The Irish Charter Schools 1730–1830* (Dublin: Four Courts Press, 1997).

7. Caitríona Clear, *Nuns in Nineteenth-Century Ireland* (Dublin: Gill and Macmillan; Washington, DC: The Catholic University of America Press, 1987); Mary Cullen (ed.), *Girls Don't Do Honours* (Dublin: Women's Education Bureau, 1987); Myrtle Hill and Vivienne Pollock, *Image and Experience: Photographs of Irishwomen c.1880–1920* (Belfast: The Blackstaff Press, 1993); Mary Cullen and Maria Luddy (eds), *Women, Power and Consciousness in Nineteenth-Century Ireland* (Dublin: Attic Press, 1995); Maria Luddy, *Women and Philanthropy in Nineteenth-Century Ireland* (London: Cambridge University Press, 1995); Deirdre Raftery and Susan M. Parkes, *Female Education in Ireland 1700–1900: Minerva or Madonna?* (Dublin: Irish Academic Press, 2007).

8. Leadbeater, *The Landlord's Friend*, 112. Leadbeater's fictional work contains one of the few references to lay women, in this instance 'Mrs Peter La Touche', and their efforts regarding educational provision for the poor. Constantia Maxwell, *Country and Town in Ireland under the Georges* (London: Harrap and Co. Ltd., 1940), 203, 204. The involvement of Caroline, Countess of Kingston is mentioned by Maxwell in another such rare reference. Another reference occurs in Maria Luddy, *Women in Ireland, 1800–1918 – A Documentary History* (Cork: Cork University Press, 1995), 93 citing Doc. 31.1: MS Lady Shaw's Day School, Murray Papers, File 33/5 (Education, undated) Dublin Diocesan Archives.

9. Eilís O'Sullivan, 'The Training of Women Teachers in Ireland, 1824–1919, with special reference to Mary Immaculate College and Limerick' (unpublished MA thesis, Mary Immaculate College, University of Limerick, 1998), 57-8. The Kildare Place Society was a voluntary education association founded in 1811.

10. Amanda Foreman, introduction to *Georgina Duchess of Devonshire* (London: Harper Collins, 1998), xvi.

11. Hannah More, *Strictures on the Modern System of Female Education*, 5th edition (Dublin: Wogan and Porter, 1800), 222.

12. Stella Tillyard, *Aristocrats: Caroline, Emily, Louisa and Sarah Lennox 1740–1832* (London: Vintage, 1995), 352; Daniel Corkery, *The Hidden Ireland: A Study of Gaelic Munster in the Eighteenth Century* (Dublin: M.H. Gill and Son, Ltd., 1925), 10; Robert Fitzroy Foster, *Modern Ireland 1600–1972* (London: Penguin Books Ltd., 1989), 210; Declan Kiberd, *Irish Classics* (London: Granta Books, 2000), 161–82; Seán Ó Tuama, *Caoineadh Airt Uí Laoghaire* (Baile Átha Cliath: An Clóchomhar Tta., 1961), 33–4.

13. Victor Edward Neuburg, *Popular Education in Eighteenth-Century England* (London: Woburn Books Ltd., 1971), 10.

14. Though the term 'Protestant' is an umbrella term for members of several Churches, in Ireland, historically, it has been taken to mean Anglican adherents of the Established Church, formally the Church of Ireland.

15. Alan Acheson, *A History of the Church of Ireland 1691–2001*, 2nd revised edition (Dublin: Columba Press and APCK, 2002), 73. Anglican bishops enjoyed 'wealth, prestige and power of patronage'. By 1789 they controlled 5 per cent of the land in Ireland which equalled the amount controlled by Roman Catholics.

16. Dorothea Herbert, *Retrospections of Dorothea Herbert 1770–1806* (Dublin: Town House, 1988), 66–74, 164–6.

17. Robert Douglas King-Harmon, *The Kings, Earls of Kingston – An Account of the Family and their Estates in Ireland between the Reigns of the two Queens Elizabeth* (printed for private circulation by W. Heffer and Sons Ltd., Cambridge, copyright R.D. King-Harman, 1959), 59; Tillyard, *Aristocrats*, 104–119; Hugh Montgomery-Massingberd (ed.), *Burke's Irish family records*, 5th edition (London: Burke's Peerage, 1976), 431; Bernard Burke, *Peerage and Baronetage*, 105th edition (London: Burke's Peerage Ltd., 1975), 612–4.

18. Terence Dooley, *The Big House and Landed Estates of Ireland: A Research Guide* (Dublin: Four Courts Press, 2007), 10.

19. Foster, *Modern Ireland*, 203; Thomas Hunt, 'Portlaw, County Waterford 1825–1876: Portrait of an Industrial Village and its Cotton Industry' in *Maynooth Studies in Local History*, No. 33, (ed.), Raymond Gillespie (Dublin: Irish Academic Press, 2000), 11–4. Hunt cites D. MacNeice, 'Factory workers' housing in counties Down and Armagh' (PhD thesis, Queen's University, Belfast, 1981), 8.

20. Dooley, *Big House*, 9.

21. Ibid., 18.

22. Corkery, *Hidden Ireland*, 23–4; Maxwell, *Country and Town*, 114–5.

23. Foster, *Modern Ireland*, 221; Maxwell, *Country and Town*, 114–5.

24. James Camlin Beckett, *The Making of Modern Ireland* (London: Faber and Faber, 1966), 158–9.

25. Constantia Maxwell, *The Stranger in Ireland from the reign of Elizabeth to the Great Famine* (London: Jonathan Cape, 1954), 290, citing Johann Georg Kohl, a German, who visited Ireland during the nineteenth century.

26. Corkery, *Hidden Ireland*, 8.

27. Maxwell, *Country and Town*, 114.
28. Foster, *Modern Ireland*, 217–9; Maxwell, *Country and Town*, 119.
29. Maxwell, *Country and Town*, 114, 119.
30. Foster, *Modern Ireland*, 221.
31. Ibid., 197, 221–2.
32. Corkery, *Hidden Ireland*, 10.
33. Toby Barnard, *A New Anatomy of Ireland: The Irish Protestants, 1649–1770* (New Haven and London: Yale University Press, 2003), 239–278.
34. Kiberd, Irish Classics, 161–82; Ó Tuama, Caoineadh Airt Uí Laoghaire, 33–4.
35. Foster, *Modern Ireland*, 195–225, 296.
36. Herbert, *Retrospections*, 112, 129, 337; William LeFanu (ed.), *Betsy Sheridan's Journal: Letters from Sheridan's sister 1784–1786 and 1788–1790* (Oxford: Oxford University Press, 1986), 52, 137, 141; Lawrence Stone, *Road to Divorce: England 1530–1987* (Oxford: Oxford University Press, 1992), 139–367; Toby Barnard, 'The Abduction of a Limerick Heiress: Social and Political Relations in Mid-Eighteenth-Century Ireland' in *Maynooth Studies in Local History*, No. 20, Raymond Gillespie (ed.), (Dublin: Irish Academic Press, 1998).
37. Lucy Moore, Liberty: The Lives and Times of Six Women in Revolutionary France (London: Harper Perennial, 2006), 310, 347.
38. Sarah Bayliss, introduction to *Munster Village*, by Mary Hamilton, (London and New York: Pandora, 1987), x.
39. Catharine Macaulay, 'Letter on Education' in *Female Education in the Age of Enlightenment*, vol. 3, Janet Todd (ed.), (London: Pickering & Chatto, 1996); Bernard Jolibert, 'Condorcet (1743–94)', in *Prospects: the quarterly review of comparative education*, vol. XXIII, no. 1/2 (Paris: UNESCO: International Bureau of Education, 1993), 197-209; Mary Wollstonecraft, 'A Vindication of the Rights of Women' (Boston: Peter Edes, 1792), Project Gutenberg, http://www.gutenberg.org/cache/epub/3420/pg3420.html (accessed 18 April 2009).
40. Paul Halsall, 'Women's History Sourcebook', Fordham University, the Jesuit University of New York, http://www.fordham.edu/halsall/women/womensbook.asp (accessed 25 June 2012).
41. Ibid.
42. Paula R. Backscheider, *Eighteenth-Century Women Poets and Their Poetry: Inventing Agency, Inventing Genre* (Baltimore: The John Hopkins University Press, 2005), 22–7.
43. Amanda Vickery, *The Gentleman's Daughter: Women's Lives in Georgian England* (USA: Yale Nota Bene, 2003), 7.
44. Marian Broderick, *Wild Irish Women: Extraordinary Lives from History* (Dublin: The O'Brien Press, 2001), 12-6. Edgeworth spent much of her life in Edgeworthstown, Co. Longford in Ireland but she won international acclaim for her remarkable literary ability. Her works included numerous elegant novels, *Letters for Literary Ladies*, *The Parent's Assistant* and *Practical Education*, co-written with her father, Richard Lovell Edgeworth. She was also possessed of significant business acumen.
45. Nicola Matthews, 'Merrion Square' in *The Georgian Squares of Dublin: An Architectural History* (Dublin: Dublin City Council, 2006), 57–87. Verschoyle had financial expertise and organisational strengths. She had followed in her mother's footsteps in 1776 by becoming estate agent to the 7th Viscount Fitzwilliam, proving a devoted and

indefatigable employee. She had been in charge 'during the vital and difficult years of the building of Merrion Square, Fitzwilliam Square and surrounding streets' in Dublin.

46. Foreman, *Duchess*, 428, footnote 27.
47. Burke, *Peerage*,1414.
48. Grania Weir, *These My Friends and Forebears: the O'Briens at Dromoland* (Whitegate: Ballinakella Press, 1991), 80, 99.
49. Ibid., 113.
50. Stephen Gwynn, *Charlotte Grace O'Brien Selections from her Writings and Correspondence with a Memoir* (Dublin: Maunsel and Co., Ltd., 1909), 5.
51. Weir, *Friends and Forebears*, 102; 105–6; 113.
52. Acheson, *History of the Church of Ireland*, 126.
53. Aubrey de Vere, *Recollections of Aubrey de Vere* (New York: London : Edward Arnold, 1897), 78.
54. Acheson, *History of the Church of Ireland*, 126.
55. CLASP, *Poverty Before the Famine – County Clare 1835, First Report From His Majesty's Commissioners for Inquiring into the Condition of the Poorer Classes in Ireland* (Ennis: CLASP PRESS, 1996), 143–4.
56. Elizabeth Burton, *The Georgians at Home 1714–1830*, (London: Longmans, 1967), 251; Elizabeth Gaskell, *The Cranford Chronicles* (London: Vintage, 2007), 298, 299.
57. Weir, Friends and Forebears, 103, 120.
58. Patricia Downes, 'The Downes Brothers: Wren Boys from County Clare: Newspaper Reports of the Clare Assizes', PC Users Group (ACT) Incorporated, http://members.pcug.org.au/~pdownes/dps/newspapers.htm (accessed 31 July 2010). Downes cites *The Ennis Chronicle and Clare Advertiser*, 4 April 1827 and 7 April 1827.
59. Weir, *Friends and Forebears*, 103, 120, 132.
60. Tillyard, *Aristocrats*, 34–42, 86–8, 235–251.
61. Antonia McManus, *The Irish Hedge School and Its Books, 1695–1831* (Dublin: Four Courts Press, 2002), 145; Sarah Trimmer, *The Oeconomy of Charity; or, an Address to ladies concerning Sunday-schools; the establishment of schools of industry under female inspection; and the distribution of voluntary benefactions to which is added an appendix, containing an account of the Sunday-schools in Old Brentford* (Dublin: Messrs. White, H., Whitestone, Moore and Jones, 1787), 32, 37, 126; Hannah More, 'The History of Hester Wilmot: Part One', 101-5 and 'The History of Hester Wilmot: Part Two', 111-5 in *Tales for the Common People and Other Cheap Repository Tracts* (Nottingham: Trent Editions, 2002).
62. Ruth Watts (address at the launch of Raftery and Parkes, *Minerva or Madonna*, Trinity College, Dublin, 29 March 2007).
63. Joshua, 9:27 (New Revised Standard Version).
64. *First Report of the Commissioners of Irish Education Inquiry* 1825 (400.) XII. 1, 5 citing petition to George II, signed by Archbishops, Bishops, dignitaries of the Church, and members of the laity requesting a charter 'for the Support and Maintenance of Schools wherein the Children of the Poor might be taught gratis'.
65. David Bodanis, *Passionate Minds: The Great Enlightenment Love Affair* (London: Little, Brown, 2006), 7 citing Molière, *Les Femmes Savantes* and Schiebinger, *The Mind has no sex*, 197.
66. Horatio Townsend, *Statistical Survey of the County of Cork with Observations on the Means of Improvement. Drawn up for the Consideration, and by Direction of the Dublin*

Society (Dublin: Graisberry and Campbell, 10 Backlane, printers to the Dublin Society, 1810), 528.

67. *Second Report*, 1826–27, Appendix 22, 848–9.

68. Ibid.

69. O'Sullivan, 'The Training of Women Teachers in Ireland, 1824–1919', 59. The monitorial system was pioneered separately by Joseph Lancaster and by the Rev. Andrew Bell, their methods differing only in detail. Able pupils were selected to work as teachers' helpers, effectively. They served apprenticeships as monitors or monitresses under teachers' supervision and subsequently became teachers themselves. Thus the majority of teachers received training in the nineteenth century before courses in colleges became the norm. The monitorial system was not just a method of teaching but also a method of school management and it proved a very effective way of recruiting young people into the teaching force.

70. Sixth Report of the Commissioners on Education in Ireland, 1826-27, Appendix 42.

71. *First Report*, 1825, 65 citing the regulations of the London Hibernian Society printed in 1808 and 1882, and Appendix 249, 'Examination of the Rev. J. West, on Oath; 4th January, 1825', 736. The London Hibernian Society was founded in 1806 for the 'Purpose of diffusing religious Knowledge in Ireland'; The Baptist Society was founded in London in the year 1814 'for the Purpose of employing itinerant Preachers in Ireland, of establishing Schools, and of distributing Bibles and Tracts, either gratuitously or at reduced Prices'.

72. Ibid., 40.

73. *Eighth Report of the Society for Promoting the Education of the Poor of Ireland*, 1820, Appendix No. VI, 60. Italics as in original.

74. *First Report*, 1825, 39–40.

75. Susan M. Parkes, *Kildare Place: The History of the Church of Ireland Training College and College of Education 1811–2010* (Dublin: C.I.C.E., 2005), 17 citing Regulations of the Society for Promoting the Education of the Poor in Ireland, *4th Annual Report*, 1816 and Kingsmill Moore, *An Unwritten Chapter in the History of Education* (London, 1904).

76. The Vulgate, an official text of the Roman Catholic Church, is the Latin version of the Bible prepared in the main by St. Jerome, *circa* 382–404. The Douay-Rheims Bible is the English translation of the Vulgate. The Authorised Version of the Bible, used by Protestant churches, is an English translation prepared in 1611 during the reign of James I of England and who was also known as James VI of of Scotland.

77. *First Report*, 1825, 46.

78. Ibid., 58–9.

79. Ibid.,1; McManus, *The Irish Hedge School*, 56–7; Akenson, *Irish Educational Experiment*, 94–5.

80. *First Report*, 1825, 3.

81. *Second Report*, 1826–27, 17, 23.

82. Ibid., 3. Presbyterian congregations, though not set up as parishes, were also involved.

83. Ibid., 4.

84. *Second Report*, 1826–27, Appendix 3, 48.

85. *Second Report*, 1826–27, 5. Just over 200,000 (approximately 37 per cent) of the pupils were girls.

86. Ibid., Appendix 3, 48–9. There were 3492 schools in Leinster, 3,449 in Ulster and 3,359 in Munster.

87. John Logan, 'How many pupils went to school in the nineteenth century?' in *Irish Educational Studies*, 8, ed. Jim McKernan (Dublin: Educational Studies Association of Ireland, 1989), 24, 25.

88. Ibid., 592–3, 608–9, 966–7, 1060–1, 1218–9, 1220–1, 1308–9. On occasion, references to families of females were made e.g. 'the Ladies Bernard' or 'the ladies of C. Ferguson's family'. For the purposes of this chapter, such references were counted as two women but could, of course, have been more. Similarly, references such as 'Mrs Strangman and her daughters', for example, were counted as three women, but again could have been more.

89. *First Report*, 1825, Appendix 239, 670; *Second Report*, 1826–27, 4. According to the census of 1821, the population of Ireland was almost seven million. With over two million inhabitants, Munster was the most populous province. In 1824, 0.08 per cent, approximately, of the country's population was attending school. In Munster, slightly less than 200,000 children (0.90 per cent of the province's overall population) were attending school.

90. For a study of governesses in Ireland see Deirdre Raftery, 'The nineteenth-century governess: image and reality', in B. Whelan (ed.), *Women and Paid Work in Ireland, 1500–1930* (Dublin: Four Courts Press, 2000).

91. *Second Report*, 1826-27, Appendix 22, 328–9.

92. Caroline, Countess of Dunraven, *Memorials of Adare Manor by Caroline, Countess of Dunraven with historical notices of Adare by her son, the Earl of Dunraven* (Oxford: printed for private circulation by Messrs. Parker, 1865), 3; The Diocese of Limerick, 'Adare Churches: Augustinian Friary', http://www.limerickdioceseheritage.org/Adare. htm (accessed 18 April 2010).

93. Countess of Dunraven, *Memorials*, 3. Caroline herself gives the date for this conversion as 1814 as does The Diocese of Limerick, 'Adare Churches: Augustinian Friary', http:// www.limerickdioceseheritage.org/Adare.htm (accessed 18 April 2010); Samuel Lewis, *A topographical dictionary of Ireland with historical and statistical descriptions* (Port Washington, London: Kennikat Press, 1970), vol. 1, 10 gives 1815 as does *Second Report*, 1826–27, Appendix 12, 'Schools in connection with the Society for Promoting the Education of the Poor in Ireland', 163 while MS, 354, folio 120 in Kildare Place Society (KPS) Archives, Church of Ireland College of Education, Dublin (CICE), suggests the later date of 1816.

94. Lewis, *Topographical Dictionary*, vol. 1,10. Lewis records (incorrectly) that it was the refectory of the Franciscan Abbey that was restored by Caroline; The Diocese of Limerick, 'Adare Churches: Augustinian Friary', http://www.limerickdioceseheritage. org/Adare.htm (accessed April 18, 2010).

95. Lewis, *Topographical Dictionary*, vol. 1,10; *Second Report*, 1826-27, Appendix 22, 1090-1. Lewis gives the total attendance figure as 300; according to the *Second Report*, 1826-27, 180 children (168 of the Established Church and 12 Roman Catholic; 76 girls and 104 boys) attended the school.

96. *Second Report*, 1826-27, Appendix 12, 163; Appendix 22, 1090–1.

97. MS 416, KPS Archives, CICE.

98. *Second Report*, 1826-27, Appendix 22, 1090–1.

99. MS 416, KPS Archives, CICE.

100. MS 685, 'List of mistresses instructed in the Education Society's model school, December 1824–March 1855', KPS Archives, CICE.
101. Tom Upshaw, 'Irish Palatine History', Teskey Family Genealogy Page, http://www.teskey.org/ (accessed 26 March 2010).
102. Glucksman Library, University of Limerick, The Earl of Dunraven Papers, D/3196 /C/18/1 Sunday Schools.
103. MS, 354, folio 120, KPS Archives, CICE; MS 685, 'List of mistresses instructed in the Education Society's model school, December 1824–March 1855', KPS Archives, CICE.
104. *Second Report*, 1826–27, Appendix 22, 1066–7. It is possible that 'Mrs Meade' may have been a member of a female religious order. However, members of female religious orders usually taught in the schools with which they were connected. Given that Bridget Burke was named as the school's mistress and that a 'workwoman' was also employed, it is more likely therefore that 'Mrs Meade' was a lay woman, involved only as patron of the school.
105. Ibid., 488–9.
106. *Cahir Heritage Newsletter*, 7, 1 gives the date as *circa* 1818. MS Ledger 353, folio 131 KPS Archives, CICE records correspondence regarding the school's establishment in 1822 as does MS Ledger 360, folio 49, 'A Return of the Schools in connection with The Society for Promoting the Education of the Poor of Ireland in the Province of Munster on the 5th day of January, 1825', KPS Archives, CICE. MS Ledger 354, folio 21, KPS Archives, CICE states that the school was established in July 1824.
107. MS Ledger 360, folio 49, KPS Archives, CICE.
108. Ibid., Appendix 238, 661.
109. *Second Report*, 1826–27, Appendix 22, 1124–5; *Cahir Heritage Newsletter*, 7, 1.
110. In *Second Report*, 1826–27, Appendix 22, 1124–5 the couple is named 'Dixon' but in MS Ledger 354, folio 21, KPS Archives, CICE the school's teachers are listed as 'Davin'.
111. MS Ledger 354, folio 21, KPS Archives, CICE.
112. *Second Report*, 1826–27, Appendix 22, 1124–5; MS Ledger 354, folio 21, KPS Archives, CICE; *Cahir Heritage Newsletter*, 7, 1.
113. MS Ledger 354, folio 21, KPS Archives, CICE.
114. *Second Report*, 1826–27, Appendix 22, 660–1.
115. Ibid., 1198–9
116. Ibid., 1006-7.
117. Ibid., 1122–3.
118. John Boynton Priestley, *The Prince of Pleasures and his Regency* (London: Heinemann, 1969), 279–281.
119. Rev. Richard Hopkins Ryland, *The History, Topography and Antiquities of the County and City of Waterford with an account of the present state of the peasantry of that part of the south of Ireland* (London: John Murray, 1824), 281; *Second Report*, 1826–27, Appendix 22, 1186–7.
120. Lewis, Topographical Dictionary, vol. 1, 357–8; Ryland, County and City of Waterford, 281.
121. William Power, Portlaw, Co. Waterford, interview with this author, 7 July 2007.
122. *Tipperary Historical Journal*, 1990, Michael Ahern, 'The Quaker Schools in Clonmel', 128–132. Grub was a Quaker family name in the Clonmel area of South Tipperary.
123. *Second Report*, 1826–27, Appendix 22, 1126–7.

124. *Second Report*, 1826–27, Appendix 22, 1130–1, 1132–3. Lady Caroline also supported two other schools in Co. Tipperary.
125. Dr. John G. Knightly, Milltown, Co. Kerry, private papers.
126. John G. Knightly, interview with this author, 7 September 2007.
127. John G. Knightly, 'Eleanor Godfrey: A Tradition of Landlord Philanthropy', in *Journal of Kerry Archaeological and Historical Society*, Series 2, vol. 2 (Tralee: Kerry Archaeological and Historical Society, 2002), 95.
128. Ibid.
129. *Second Report*, 1826–27, Appendix 22, 1050–1.
130. Lewis, *Topographical Dictionary*, vol. II, 371; MS Ledger 354, folio 56, KPS Archives, CICE; John G. Knightly email to this author, 26 November 2001.
131. *Second Report*, 1826–27, Appendix 22, 1050–1.
132. Knightly, 'Eleanor Godfrey: A Tradition of Landlord Philanthropy', in *Journal of Kerry Archaeological and Historical Society*, Series 2, vol. 2, 95.
133. *Second Report*, 1826–27, Appendix 22, 1050–1.
134. Knightly, private papers and email message to author, 26 November 2001. In 1914 the school was transferred to nearby Castlemaine where it continues to serve local members of the Church of Ireland. The building erected by Eleanor in 1824, although modified and reduced in size, continues in use as an annex to the local secondary school.
135. Knightly, 'Eleanor Godfrey: A Tradition of Landlord Philanthropy', in *Journal of Kerry Archaeological and Historical Society*, Series 2, vol. 2 (Tralee: Kerry Archaeological and Historical Society, 2002), 87.
136. Caroline, Dowager Countess of Kingston (statement to the 'Catholic Clergy and their flock', Mitchelstown, Co. Cork, 13 November 1809) in Coppinger, *Letter to the Dublin Society*, 19, 20.
137. CLASP, *Poverty Before the Famine County Clare*, 156; Weir, *Friends and Forebears*, 111, 200.
138. *Second Report*, 1826–27, Appendix 22, 1154–5.
139. Maria Luddy, 'The Lives of the Poor in Cahir in 1821', *Tipperary Historical Journal*, 1991: 79.
140. Joe Walsh (ed.), *Cahir Heritage Newsletter*, private papers, citing Cahir Archive, Butler-Charteris Hall, *Cahir Heritage Newsletter* ISSN 0790-7265 and Quaker Regional Archive, c/o Cahir Heritage Society.
141. MS Ledger 354, folio 22, KPS Archives, CICE.
142. Walsh, private papers; Lewis, *Topographical Dictionary*, vol. I, 238.
143. *Cahir Heritage Newsletter*, 37, 3; Luddy, 'Poor in Cahir', 78–9.
144. Luddy, 'Poor in Cahir', 78–9.
145. Ibid., 78–9; Thomas P. Power, *Land, Politics, and Society in Eighteenth-Century Tipperary* (Oxford: Clarendon Press, 1993), 45, citing Public Record Office, Northern Ireland, D207/28/365, 367, 369.
146. Helen O'Connell, *Ireland and the Fiction of Improvement* (Oxford: Oxford University Press, 2006), 74–5. O'Connell notes that 'Leadbeater's use of the word 'ennui'...is an explicit reference to Edgeworth's novel *Ennui* (1809)'.
147. Rosemary Baird, *Mistress of the House: Great Ladies and Grand Houses* (London: Phoenix, 2004), 45–46.
148. Hyland and Milne, *Irish Educational Documents*, Vol. I, 59–60, citing 21 and 22 Geo. III c. 62 (1782).

149. Joseph Robins, *The Lost Children: A Study of Charity Children in Ireland 1700–1900* (Dublin: Institute of Public Administration, 1980), 38, 122–3.
150. O'Connell, *Fiction of Improvement*, 68.
151. *First Report*, 1825, 102.
152. O'Connell, *Fiction of Improvement*, 6; 8; 73.
153. *First Report*, 1825, 58–9.
154. Akenson, *Irish Education Experiment*, 86–7 citing *Report from the select committee on foundation schools and education in Ireland*, 11.
155. Susan M.P. McKenna-Lawlor, introduction to *Whatever Shines Should Be Observed [quicquid nited notandum]* (Dublin: Samton Ltd., 1998), 12.

5 THE MUSEUM OF IRISH INDUSTRY AND SCIENTIFIC EDUCATION IN MID-VICTORIAN IRELAND

CLARA CULLEN

At his inaugural address as director of the new Government School of Science applied to Mining and the Arts at the Museum of Irish Industry (MII) in Dublin, on the afternoon of 9 November 1854, Sir Robert Kane declared that the purpose of this School of Science was to provide a

> system of scientific education … a project which he trusted … would eventuate in the happiest results, as regarding the improvement, the well being and the prosperity of the country – a prosperity arising from practical improvement in manufacturing skill, in the science of agriculture, and in the affairs of commercial enterprise.[1]

The occasion, attended by a 'densely crowded assemblage of the very *elite* [*sic*] of the learned and scientific men of the Irish metropolis' celebrated a new role for the Museum of Irish Industry (MII). In this new educational role, the MII was intended to be as a central College for the Arts and Sciences in Dublin and a place where the popular public lectures and courses of 'systematic' lectures were open to all, regardless of class, creed or gender, in mid-nineteenth-century Ireland.

THE MUSEUM OF IRISH INDUSTRY (MII)

The MII had been established by the British government in 1845 as the Museum of Economic Geology – in the same year as its counterpart, the Museum of Practical Geology, was established in London – and it was originally intended to provide a showcase for the geological findings of the Irish branch of the Geological Survey. A building on St. Stephen's Green was purchased to house the new museum,[2] funding was provided to convert it for its new purpose and a director, Sir Robert John Kane, appointed. Within two years the name of the museum was changed to the Museum of Irish Industry and its remit expanded to be a museum 'embracing the general range of the industrial arts'.[3]

Although established in 1845, it was 1853 before the museum opened its doors to the public. There were several reasons for this, some of them local. Efforts to identify the causes and to find remedies for the potato blight occupied the attention of Irish scientists, including Robert Kane, in the years of the Great Famine (1845–50). Kane also had other responsibilities as president of the newly-established Queen's College in Cork and chairman of the board establishing the structures of the Queen's University. A more prosaic reason for the delay was that the funding for the renovation and extension of the old Georgian building on St. Stephen's Green that was to house the museum was allocated in a piecemeal and intermittent fashion by Her Majesty's Treasury. However, by August 1853 (just in time for Dublin's Great Industrial Exhibition) the renovated museum, with exhibition galleries extending over the former gardens of the Georgian house, opened its doors to the public. Immediately, it became a very popular venue for Dubliners. The number of visitors to the museum in 1854 was 47,544 and by 1857, 'instead of merely opening the Museum on the nights of Lectures which can be but imperfectly known to a general public', the museum also opened 'on certain fixed nights of the week'.[4] Until 1867, when the public galleries closed, an average of 35,000 people visited the Museum of Irish Industry every year.

In the intervening years, under Kane's direction, the collections at the museum were developed to provide public exhibitions illustrating Ireland's natural resources and the practical application of science to industry.[5] The findings of the Geological Survey of Ireland were analysed, catalogued and exhibited,[6] a library created for the students and laboratories equipped for both teaching and research. The officers at the museum worked hard to create an educational environment 'where education in applied science, such as chemistry applied to the arts, or metallurgy or geology applied to mining, or any other department of science applied to the arts, can be obtained'.[7] The museum's laboratories also provided a practical service to local and educational authorities.

But Kane had another role in mind for the museum – that of a teaching institution. The completed museum buildings in St. Stephen's Green contained not only offices, galleries and laboratories and a library, but also a 650-seat lecture theatre which formed the fourth side of the quadrangle of buildings housing the museum's activities. In his 1853 report to his new masters, the Department of Science and Art (DSA) in London, Kane reported:

> The organization of the Museum as to its internal exhibitional arrangements being now so far advanced towards completion, it becomes advisable to provide for the systematic instruction in industrial science by means of lectures, etc., which shall enable its collections, geological and industrial to be made properly available for practical educational purposes.[8]

The following year the newly-established DSA in London confirmed that the teaching of popular science in Ireland should be put on a formal basis. The Royal Dublin Society (RDS), which had been providing public science lectures for almost half a century, were informed by the department that their science professors, together with the proportion of the society's annual grant which paid their salaries, were to be transferred to the MII's new School of Science, confirming that institution's role as the provider of scientific education in Ireland, outside the universities. Understandably, the society objected and a compromise was later agreed whereby the resources and expertise of both the MII and the RDS would be shared to provide popular public courses on physics, chemistry, botany, zoology and geology. As with all compromises, this was not a very satisfactory one and was subsequently acknowledged to be a half-measure which led to future difficulties between Kane, the society and the government.

HISTORICAL CONTEXT

Ireland at mid-century was a predominantly agricultural country with whatever industries that existed based in the urban areas, especially Dublin and the rapidly developing town of Belfast. In 1854 the country was still recovering from the effects of the Great Famine and experiencing significant demographic and social change. Ireland had been joined to Britain in a political Union since 1800 and all administrative and legislative decisions were taken in London. The vast majority of the population were Catholics but at mid-century most political power and influence was still in the hands of the Ascendancy – members of the Church of Ireland.

A system of government-funded national schools had been established in 1831 and the level of illiteracy in Ireland declined from 53 per cent in 1841 to 39 per cent by 1861.[9] As noted in earlier chapters, those secondary schools which existed in the middle of the nineteenth century were mostly denominational.[10] Apart from these, there were numbers of small private academies and 'seminaries' which provided an education beyond that provided by the national school system, albeit of very varying standards. Until 1845 Ireland had only one university, the University of Dublin, with one constituent college, Trinity College, Dublin (hereafter TCD). A series of religious tests had excluded Catholics and dissenters from openly attending the college until 1793, when a Relief Act removed these requirements for primary degrees, whilst continuing to reserve scholarships and senior academic posts for members of the Church of Ireland.[11] This effective exclusion from higher education of all but members of the Established Church was addressed by the British government in 1845 when three non-denominational colleges were established in Cork, Galway and Belfast, offering degrees in a range of practical subjects (arts, engineering and medicine). However, reaction to the new colleges was mixed. The Catholic hierarchy's initial reaction hardened into a determined opposition to the Queen's Colleges[12] and in response in 1854 a Catholic University was established in Dublin.

Science, and the support of science, in Ireland was predominantly rooted within the Protestant Ascendancy group and the major scientific institutions, the RDS and the Royal Irish Academy (RIA), together with TCD, in their origins and membership, reflected this constituency. Locally, the establishment of the new Government School of Science in Dublin as the provider of popular scientific education in Ireland was opposed by the long established and politically powerful RDS which considered itself 'the great central association for the diffusion throughout Ireland of a knowledge of Practical Science'.[13]

For women educational opportunities were even more limited. In 1850s and 1860s Ireland, there were few opportunities available for Irish women who wished, from personal interest, to extend their education or who sought qualifications which might enable them to support themselves independently.

Before the establishment of Alexandra College in Dublin in 1866, women without independent means but anxious to acquire some qualification attended classes in institutions such as the Government School of Art at the RDS, classes at the Queen's Institute and at the MII. Education for women beyond the elementary level was rarely seen as a gateway to employment but rather as a means to acquire useful accomplishments and prepare for marriage.[14] This approach to education was condemned by Anne Jellicoe when she established the Queen's Institute in 1861 and discovered:

> the light, the inaccurate, vague, and fragmentary nature of the education generally given to girls, the neglect of the rules of spelling, of the principles of grammar, the downright ignorance of arithmetic, the absence of any training of the mind, the meagreness of the so-called accomplishments on which so much time and energy had been wasted.[15]

It was against this background that the Government School of Science at the MII was established.

THE DIRECTOR OF THE MUSEUM OF IRISH INDUSTRY, ROBERT KANE, AND HIS PROFESSORS

Robert Kane was born in Dublin in 1809, the son of a successful chemical manufacturer.[16] He was a Catholic and one of the first generation of a professional middle class, many of them Catholic, that emerged in post-Union Ireland. Educated privately, Robert, the second son, began his scientific education by attending lectures on chemistry in the Royal Dublin Society, possibly with the intention of following a medical career. At the age of eighteen, he published his first scientific paper and by 1829 he was a Licentiate of the Apothecaries Hall and entitled to practise medicine. In the same year he entered TCD and by the time he graduated, five years later, he had published his first book, *Elements of Practical Pharmacy*[17], become Professor of Chemistry at Apothecaries Hall, been elected to the Royal Irish Academy (RIA) and founded the *Dublin Journal of Medical and Chemical Science*. Between 1835 and 1845 Kane held two professorships simultaneously, wrote and lectured on a range of scientific subjects and had became an internationally recognised scientist with a lucrative private practice.[18]

However, Kane's interests were changing. The subject of his writings moved away from pure science to exploring the application of science to industry, most notably in his *Industrial Resources of Ireland*.[19] Linked to this was his increasing interest and commitment to scientific education. In 1845, the year he became director of the new museum in Dublin, he was also appointed as President of the recently-established Queen's College in Cork. The following year Kane, now Sir Robert, declared that in future he would be devoting his life to scientific education for the future material and social prosperity of Ireland. All of Kane's innovative thinking on education is exemplified in the MII, the institution with which he was most directly involved – a place he was determined, where 'the rivalries of creeds and parties [would] find no admission'[20] and where the facilities of the museum would be open to all.[21]

Supporting Kane's educational endeavours was a small staff of professors. In the words of one Irish newspaper:

> The museum has been singularly fortunate in securing a first-rate staff of professors ... Jukes whose scientific and literary reputation requires no comment ...[and] Professor Sullivan, the talented pupil of Liebig.[22]

The professor of chemistry, William Kirby Sullivan had a lot in common with Robert Kane and, in many respects, their careers could be described as complementary. Both men were Catholic, and were the sons of middle-class businessmen.[23] Both had studied in scientific institutions in Europe, had worked in the laboratories at the University of Giessen with Liebig and had taught in various schools. They shared a common view on the need for a proper system of industrial education on the continental model in Ireland. They served together on the governing authorities of the Queen's University, the Royal University of Ireland and as officers of the RIA and in 1873 Sullivan succeeded Kane as president of Queen's College Cork.[24] They were both nationalists but differed in their political affiliations, Sullivan having been a member of Young Ireland in 1848 while Kane followed a more constitutional path.

The Local Director of the Geological Survey in Ireland, Joseph Beete Jukes, who has been described as 'one of the finest field-geologists of his generation'[25], became the professor of geology. He also subscribed to Kane and Sullivan's principles of scientific education. He had experience in Australia,

Newfoundland, New Guinea, Java and Wales before coming to Ireland. The professor of botany was William Henry Harvey, a distinguished botanist who had been colonial treasurer in Cape Town before returning to Ireland in 1844. John Robert Kinahan, who became professor of zoology, was a graduate of TCD in arts and medicine. He had visited Australia, Peru and other countries in order to extend his knowledge of natural history but ill-health brought him back to Dublin in 1856. He was described as 'a truthful, genial, and instructive companion by those with whom he was familiar, and by scientists in his department as a highly-cultured naturalist, who had enlarged the boundaries of the domain of science'.[26]

The professors and scientists who worked and researched at the MII were career scientists. They were 'men of science',[27] rather than 'gentlemen of science'. With the exception of Robert Kane, they derived their main income from their scientific research, teaching and writings – not an easy thing to do in nineteenth-century Britain or Ireland. They differed in their opinions on some of the new scientific theories of the day. Jukes, for example, supported Charles Darwin's evolutionary theories, including them in his geology curriculum.[28] His colleague Harvey disagreed with the theory of natural selection and published a pamphlet (which he later regretted) attacking Darwin's theories.[29] The professors also held varied political views, differed in their religious affiliations and came from a range of backgrounds. Kane and Sullivan were Catholic, Harvey, was 'a frugal bachelor of Quaker upbringing' who had converted to the Church of Ireland in 1846.[30] Jukes was a member of the Church of Ireland and a later colleague, John Morgan came from a Baptist family.[31] The majority were graduates of TCD – the exceptions being Sullivan whose doctorate came from a German university and another chemist, Robert Galloway, who had 'studied under Hoffman at the Royal College of Chemistry in London'.[32] Several had medical qualifications, although Harvey's was an honorary award.[33] Many were members of the RDS and, almost without exception, they were members of the RIA.[34]

Almost all of the professors were experienced teachers, were active in professional associations and in the societies in Dublin relating to their particular disciplines, wrote for the scientific journals and published both learned monographs and text books. Galloway and Jukes had come to Ireland from England but the majority of the professors were Irish. Many of them had travelled widely in pursuit of scientific knowledge. They represented a wide spectrum of the sciences of their day and brought their professional experience and commitment to their teaching. The professors earned their salaries – their workload was enormous. One later described his working day at the museum to a government committee:

> for many years I taught a class from ten till four; then I got some dinner; came back again between six and seven and started to work, and worked till ten, and then I went home and prepared my lessons for the next day till two or three o'clock the next morning.[35]

THE COURSES

From 1854 until 1867, the museum offered courses of lectures on botany, chemistry, zoology, geology and the natural sciences during the day, with corresponding courses delivered in the evening, to 'those who are occupied in the day time with the means of employing their leisure hours in the evening in learning more thoroughly the more practically useful branches of science'.[36] The more popular and introductory lectures were free and were intended to raise general interest in and to provide popular elementary instruction in science, reflecting Kane's own interest in popular education. Official government reports and reports in contemporary newspapers confirm that these courses were extremely popular and were attended by audiences of hundreds, both men and women. In 1855, for example, the average number attending the lectures in geology was 365. Beyond these popular courses, the professors were responsible for more advanced 'systematic' courses, held in the museum's lecture theatre and laboratories.

The MII published programmes of their educational arrangements every year and included in these programmes a very detailed syllabus for each subject, to:

> Provide the student with such an index to each branch of science, that however differently the text-book which he employs may be arranged, he may still be able to follow in his reading the order of subjects adopted by the professor.[37]

The detailed syllabus expanded, from a thirty-two page programme in 1856 to one of eighty-six pages in 1865. By then, the courses had expanded from the original subjects of physics, chemistry, natural history, geology and analytical chemistry to include zoology, organic and inorganic chemistry, chrystallography and practical zoological instruction. Within many of the subjects, the range of topics covered had also increased. The courses offered were detailed and very current. In 1860, for example, the theory of evolution was included in the palaeontology course at the museum, although Charles Darwin's *The Origin of Species* had been published only a year earlier.[38] These advanced courses could be considered as the first initiative in Ireland, outside the universities, to give ordinary people access to scientific education.

The lectures given by the professors went beyond simple classroom teaching. Robert Kane believed in 'industrial instruction given in the Museum by courses of lectures and other appropriate means',[39] making use of the museum's collections and laboratories in support of the lecture programmes. The students had access to the industrial and geological collections in the museum's exhibition galleries, the professors used the specimens and models in the museum's collections to illustrate their lectures and, in some subjects, established small 'working' collections of samples for the students' use.[40]

The third strand of the education programme was laboratory work. As might be expected in an institution whose director and professors of chemistry had been trained in the teaching of practical chemistry by, or through, the laboratory-based education methods of Justus von Liebig, the laboratories played a significant role in the education programmes at the Museum of Irish Industry. The museum's professor of chemistry, Sullivan, believed that his practical chemistry class 'was the feature of the whole system which had afforded the most gratifying proof of the value of industrial education. The persons attending belonged chiefly to the working classes'.[41]

A fee was charged for these lectures which were held in the museum's lecture theatre and laboratories. This fee was small, about two shillings and six pence for a course of lectures, and was intended to encourage serious students and 'to test the reality of the wish to learn on the part of those attending'.[42]

Those who attended these lectures were expected to have at least an elementary knowledge of the subject, although the professor of chemistry, W.K. Sullivan, on occasion complained about the poor arithmetic of the students in his chemistry classes. Again, the numbers who registered for, and attended, these advanced courses were high.

Examinations were held at the close of each course and ambitious students had the opportunity to recoup their fees by entering these end of session examinations and winning one of the prizes offered to the best students. All the successful candidates received certificates, and prizes of £5, £2 and £1 were awarded to those who gained top marks in the examinations. The intention behind these monetary prizes was that they would provide financial assistance to enable the students to continue their studies.

THE STUDENTS

The Under-Secretary for Ireland, Thomas Larcom, wrote in 1858 that 'The students are of the class very much of assistants in mercantile houses and downwards to artisans. There are however very many of a higher station.'[43] However, it is impossible to form a complete picture of the student community at the museum. The primary sources for the student community at the MII, such as the student registers or attendance lists, no longer exist. Nevertheless, despite the missing records, it is possible to put together a profile of the students from the lists of prizewinners, using contemporary newspapers and commercial directories.[44] These sources confirm that students were a mix of the artisan and middle classes, and many were 'adults already engaged in business.'[45] Their backgrounds reflected the upwardly mobile as well as the established professional classes.

The annual prize-givings were very social occasions, attended by the Lord Lieutenant of Ireland, and there were detailed reports of the events in the contemporary newspapers. It is from these reports that we know the names of those students who attended the courses of lectures in the Museum of Irish Industry and were successful in the school's annual examinations.

Names of university students (especially medical students, students at TCD and at the Catholic University of Ireland) dominate the lists of known students. However, it would be an error to assume that they constituted a major part of the student body. There were clerks and artisans intent on acquiring qualifications which would enable them to gain appointments in the civil service.[46] Others were engineers, entrepreneurs, manufacturers, commercial photographers, the children of clergymen, bank managers, soldiers, builders and a very significant number were teachers. Subsequently, these students joined their fathers' firms, or became analytical chemists in the hospitals and the Excise service; others became civil servants or officers in the Geological Survey, and some joined the Indian civil service and the army. One student's description of his class illustrates their possible future careers:

> The tall young man at the centre table, is employed during the day by the Gas Company; he does well to spend his evenings here,

the knowledge acquired will form no unimportant qualification in enabling him to fill a higher position. Directly opposite him observe that student ... An engineer by profession, he intends India or China to be the scene of his future labours.[47]

Ten years later, in 1868, the students 'attending the institution which has been transformed into the College of Science' were described as 'the sons of the working managers of several very large manufacturers' establishments'.[48] Later again, the background of the students was described as being 'smelting, gasworks, pharmaceuticals, chemical works [owners as well as workers], photographic establishments, teachers, practicing physicians, TCD students'.[49] For the most part the students who attended courses at the museum were Irish. Regarding religious affiliation, the Museum of Irish Industry was open to all regardless of creed but, despite the lack of any official register, the surviving records indicate a range of religious backgrounds – Catholic, Quaker, Presbyterian and Church of Ireland.

WOMEN AND THE MUSEUM OF IRISH HISTORY

Giving evidence to a government committee in 1863, Robert Kane said that women attended the classes at the museum on an equal basis to men and in the competition for prizes: '... [t]hey compete with the best of the male pupils and carry off a great number of the prizes – not only in Zoology and Botany ... [but also] ... in Natural Philosophy, Chemistry and Geology'.[50] Robert Kane was very proud of the achievements of the women students who attended the courses at the MII. He took every opportunity of referring to them and to their achievements in official reports, in evidence given to various government committees, and at the annual distribution of prizes at the museum. At the first annual prize-giving in 1856, Kane reported that 'in the formation of the classes of the present institution ... several ladies had been students, and in the competition for prizes distinguished themselves in a high degree'.[51] In the examination in natural history that year, for example, there were fifteen candidates and four women among the ten successful students. This first prize-giving set the pattern for the future, and year after year, in the words of the *Daily Express*, 'A very interesting feature of the [prize-giving] proceedings was that ladies entered the list as competitors, and vindicated the genius of their sex by carrying off the highest prizes'.[52] Again, in 1868 he described the science lectures:

[They are] attended by large numbers of girls and ladies of the middle class, and thus they supplemented in a most valuable manner the ordinary elements of female education. I think that the system of public instruction of an elementary and popular character in Dublin has exercised, for the last couple of generations, a most valuable influence upon the training of female society in the middle classes.[53]

Kane was justified in emphasising the examination successes of the women students. It is not known what percentage of the student body were women, but given that women made up at least 13 per cent of the prizewinners we can assume they attended courses at the MII in very significant numbers. The women students appear to have enjoyed and appreciated the opportunities available to them at the MII. One woman, probably Matilda Coneys, described her experience as a student there:

The most perfect harmony, courtesy and good feeling has always existed there. We sit on the same benches in the lecture theatre and read in the same library [as the men]... I was the first lady who worked in the laboratory, and I found my fellow students as ready to tender me any little civility I needed, as if I were in a drawing room.[54]

From 1854 to 1867, every year, without exception, saw the names of some of the women students appearing in the lists of prizewinners at the museum and almost every year, they also figured in the lists of students awarded medals by the DSA. A number of these women students took examinations in several subjects at the museum, notably Frances Armstrong, Matilda and Zoe Leigh Coneys and the Hare and Harman sisters. These women did not confine their studies to the 'softer' sciences and were very successful in the more technical subjects. Robert Kane seemed to have been particularly proud of this. Considering the limited access to education for girls beyond the elementary level, and the even more limited access to mathematics and science teaching, the achievement of these women is remarkable.[55]

Tracing the story of the women who attended the courses at the MII is frustrating. The absence of student records, the paucity of female entries in contemporary commercial and residential directories, and the probability that many women subsequently married and changed their names, combine to ensure that most of the women who attended the MII have vanished from the printed record. For example, the author of a letter in files of the Natural History Museum, discussed two women students thus:

> Do you know anybody who wants a visiting governess - I have two in view who are invaluable. They took all the premiums at Sir R. Kane's in Botany, Chemistry, &c, &c. They are well up in French & that sort of thing. They can teach the young ... how to shoot, or ... to contend for honours in T. C. D. In fact if they were boys, instead of girls, they might stand for fellowships or cadetships or any other sort of ships ... you will benefit three parties by doing what I ask.[56]

For those for whom there are records it is clear that, like the men, the majority of them were middle class. Because of the museum's determined 'interdenominational' stand, we can only guess about these women's religious background but there were Catholics, daughters of Presbyterian and Methodist ministers, of Church of Ireland clergymen and some of the students were Quakers. The addresses given by female students suggest that they were the daughters or sisters of solicitors, merchants, farmers, builders, Church of Ireland clerics, bank managers, and widows. There were several sets of sisters, such as Hester, Henrietta and Harriet Harman, Halgena and Frances Anne Hare, and the two Miss Coneys (Matilda and Zoe Leigh), both of whom continued as students at the Royal College of Science for Ireland. Many of them were teachers, either in the model and national schools or in private seminaries. Certainly some of these women students were 'young women of the middle classes, living in reduced circumstances',[57] who were forced to earn their living. Others are typified by Jeannie Leeper who, like her mother before her, greatly resented that as a woman she was barred from higher education and attended these courses as her only option in furthering her own knowledge.[58]

Robert Kane and his colleagues continually emphasised the educational role of many of the women students and certainly the majority of these women were intent on a career in the field of education. In 1862, for example, Kane gave evidence:

> Practically all the ladies who attend the day systematic courses are either governesses or persons preparing to be governesses. They

receive here an instruction which they would get nowhere else, and similar to that which is given in the Ladies' College in London [Queen's College London, founded in 1848].[59]

Certainly the educational efforts and scholastic attainments of the Hare sisters, Halgena and Frances (both prizewinners at the MII), must have been intended to contribute to the family enterprise, the Dublin High School, of which their father Mathias was proprietor. Adelina Rorke, who took a first prize in botany in 1865, was another woman student who derived her income from education. In the 1860s, in partnership with her brother John, she ran a 'ladies academy' in Dublin.[60]

Other women sought careers in different fields. Harriett and Hester Harman were employed by the MII to draw diagrams to illustrate lectures, and they made quite a good living. By 1901, they were living in London and supporting themselves by their drawing and art work. The Hare sisters had returned from the US with their father in the late 1850s and, following the closure of Mathias Hare's school in 1862, probably left Ireland. By 1869, Frances Anne Hare (now Mrs Appleton), 'has since been a successful student at the Female Medical College, London'.[61] Jane Leeper spent the rest of her days in Dublin, trying to maintain herself by her writings and some teaching. By 1876 she had taken over as housekeeper for her family and had become involved in the movement for women's rights, although she always maintained her interest in science and education. She typified the *corpus* of women students who, in the 1870s and 1880s, benefited from the establishment of Alexandra College and similar educational institutions for girls and women. She never married and her brother in Melbourne supported her, guaranteeing her £60 a year for life. She died in 1921.

CONCLUSION

For several years the MII prospered. Courses expanded, student numbers increased, and through their participation in the courses of provincial lectures held around Ireland during the summer months, the professors and the institution gained a wider national profile. However, in 1862 a government commission, originally intended to inquire into the financial dealings of the RDS, had its remit changed and instead it investigated the role of the MII and the RDS in science education in Ireland. It concluded that the MII should be closed and that the RDS (a private society) should become the provider of popular science education. This was met with public outrage in Ireland, and the recommendation was overturned. However, the incident focused government attention on the future role of the MII. It was suggested that the museum become a fourth Queen's College (a suggestion opposed by the Catholic University and TCD), but in 1867 the Museum of Irish Industry ceased to exist as a teaching institution and it became the Royal College of Science for Ireland (RCScI).[62]

However, the more formal and academic College of Science meant the end of the popular courses of lectures intended for interested audiences in Dublin. The museum's collections were dispersed, and the galleries converted to lecture rooms. This new college was described as 'more complete as a pure school of science than anything of the kind existing in Scotland or England'[63] but, despite the eminence of its professors and the comprehensive courses on science, the RCScI never captured the popular imagination in Ireland.[64] Nevertheless, the principles of science education, linking classroom and laboratory teaching, established at the MII continued in the new college.

The Museum of Irish Industry, with its exhibition collections, its laboratories, and the range of educational courses organised by its staff was one of the British Government's innovative experiments in education in Victorian Ireland. Beyond this, Kane's determination that the courses offered by the museum would be available to all, with no distinctions of creed or sex, distinguishes this institution as a pioneer in providing equal access to scientific education to all in the mid-nineteenth century.

NOTES

AUTHOR'S NOTE:
I would like to acknowledge the Humanities Institute, UCD, for supporting this research.

1. *Freeman's Journal*, 10 November 1854.
2. The building which housed the Museum of Irish industry at 51-52 St Stephen's Green is still in existence. Until recently, it was the Office of Public Works.
3. [Museum of Irish Industry] *General Descriptive Guide to the Museum of Irish Industry* (Dublin: Thom, 1857), 3
4. *Fifth Report of the Science and Art Department ... [1857]*, H.C. 1857-58 [2385] xxiv, 219,10.
5. Kane's pride, and the only part of these exhibits to survive today, is the arrangement of Irish marbles in the entrance hall, which inspired the use of Irish marbles rather than imported materials in public buildings for the next seventy years.

6. The Geological Survey of Ireland had its offices in the Museum of Irish Industry building until 1873.

7. *Report from the Select Committee on Scientific Institutions, Dublin); together with the Proceedings of the Committee, Minutes of evidence, Appendix, and Index*, H.C. 1864 (495), xiii,1, 70 (hereafter *Select Committee ... 1864).*

8. *First Report of the Department of Science and Art ... [1853]*, H.C. 1854 (1783), xxviii, 269, 461.

9. *Census of Ireland, 1901, pt II: general report with illustrative maps, diagrams, tables and appendix* H.C. 1902 [C. 1190], cxxix, 527; quoted by Donald H. Akenson, *The Irish education experiment: the national system of education in Ireland* (London, Routledge and Kegan Paul, 1970), 376.

10. For Catholics, the Christian Brothers, founded in 1802, provided both elementary and, in some schools, a more advanced education. By the 1850s the Jesuits, Vincentians and Carmelites, among others, had founded schools which catered for the education of the new Catholic middle classes of Ireland. For girls, the Loreto Order had founded schools, as had the Presentation Sisters, the Ursulines, the Sisters of Mercy, the Dominicans and the Society of the Sacred Heart.

11. Robert Kane, a Catholic, was a graduate of TCD but was one of those excluded from higher academic degrees.

12. T.W. Moody and J.C. Beckett, *Queen's, Belfast 1845–1949: the History of a University.* (2 vols, London: Faber and Faber for Q.U.B., 1959), 1, 78.

13. *Report from the Select Committee on the Royal Dublin Society; Together with the Minutes of Evidence, and Appendix*, H.C. 1836 (445), xii, 355, xx (hereafter *Report ... RDS 1836).*

14. An example of the curriculum offered by these private seminaries for ladies is one offered by the Misses Williams, where the course of education offered at their Ladies School comprised 'the English, French and Italian languages, history, geography, writing, arithmetic, music, singing, drawing, dancing, the size of the globe, plain and fancy needlework.' *Freeman's Journal*, 7 April, 1862.

15. Royal Commission on ... Primary Education (Ireland), *Report ... V. 8, Miscellaneous Papers,* H.C. 1870 [C-VII], Pt.5, 917, 241-3.

16. According to family legend, his father, John Kean (d. 1832), who came from Westmeath, settled in Dublin, married Eleanor Troy, the niece of the Catholic archbishop of Dublin and was a United Irishman who had been forced in 1798 to flee to France. John Kean changed his name to John Kane when he returned to Ireland in 1803.

17. Robert Kane, *Elements of Practical Pharmacy* (Dublin: Hodges and Smith,1831).

18. Charles Alexander Cameron , *History of the Royal College of Surgeons in Ireland: and of the Irish Schools of Medicine, Including Numberous Biographical Sketches, also a Medical Bibliography* (Dublin: Fannin, 1866), 607–8.

19. Robert Kane, *The Industrial Resources of Ireland* (Dublin: Hodges and Smith, 1844).

20. The *Irish Times*, 21 October 1859.

21. *Report upon the Royal Dublin Society, the Museum of Irish Industry, and on the System of Scientific Instruction in Ireland*, H.C., 1863, (3180), XVII, Pt. I.1, 89-90 [hereafter *Report on the RDS ... 1863*].

22. *Freeman's Journal*, 7 October 1856.

23. Sullivan's father was a paper manufacturer in Cork; *Report from the Select Committee on Industries (Ireland) together with the Proceedings of the Committee, Minutes of Evidence, and Appendix …[1885],* H.C. 1884–5 (288), ix, 1, 5.

24. Sullivan was elected a member of the RIA in 1857, vice-President 1866, Secretary 1867-74; Kane was elected a member 1832, President 1877-82 of the RIA.

25. Gordon L. Herries Davies, 'Joseph Beete Jukes' in Charles Mollan, Charles, William Davis and Brendan Finucane (eds) *Irish Innovators in Science and Technology* (Dublin: RIA, 2002), 109.

26. Cameron, *History of the College of Surgeons,* 612.

27. 'Men of science' was a widely embraced term, but in 1874 Galton estimated there were only three hundred 'truly scientific' men in Britain. See Francis Galton, *English Men of Science; their Nature and Nurture* (London, 1874), 6.

28. [Museum of Irish Industry] *Programme of educational arrangements for the Session of the Government School of Science applied to Mining and the Arts for the Session of 1860-1861* (Dublin, 1860), 91.

29. William Henry Harvey, *An Inquiry into the Probable Origin of the Human Animal* ([Dublin: printed privately], 1860); Jukes to Darwin, 27 February, 1860 (Darwin correspondence project, correspondence 8: 112-113), Harvey to Darwin, 24 August, 1860; Darwin to Harvey [September] 1860, (http://darwinproiect.ac.uk/darwins-letters (accessed 14 February 2014)).

30. He converted to the Church of Ireland in 1846 and married in 1861; R.B. McDowell and D.A. Webb, *Trinity College Dublin, 1592-1952: an Academic History* (Cambridge: Cambridge University Press, 1982), 196.

31. Cameron, *History of the College of Surgeons in Ireland,* 493.

32. Brian Kelham, 'The Royal College of Science for Ireland (1867–1926)' in *Studies,* 56, (Autumn 1967), 309.

33. William Henry Harvey's was an honorary degree, awarded to him by TCD in 1844; *Alumni Dublinenses,* George Dames Burtchaell and Thomas Ulick Sadlier (eds), (Bristol: Thoemmes, 2001), 1771.

34. Robert Kane had been given an honorary life membership of the RDS in 1846, Sullivan was elected to the society in 1850 but let his membership lapse after 1854 while Jukes, who regarded the society as elitist, refused to apply for membership. W.H. Harvey, who demonstrated that his loyalty was to the RDS, was a member, as was William Barker.

35. *Report from the Select Committee on Industries (Ireland) together with the Proceedings of the Committee, Minutes of Evidence, and Appendix … [1885],* H.C. 1884–5 (288), ix, 1, 397 (hereafter *Committee on Industries 1885*).

36. [Museum of Irish Industry] *Programme of Educational Arrangements for the Session of 1859-1860,* (Dublin: Thom, 1859), vii.

37. [Museum of Irish Industry] *Programme of Educational Arrangements for the Session of the Government School of Science applied to Mining and the Arts for the session of 1856-1857* (Dublin: Thom, 1856), 15.

38. [Museum of Irish Industry] *Programme of Educational Arrangements for the Session of the Government School of Science applied to Mining and the Arts for the session of 1860-1861* (Dublin: Thom, 1860), 91.

39. *Statement of Amount Voted by Parliament for the Museum of Industry, Stephen's Green, during each year since the Formation of that Institution,* H.C. 1854 (331) lviii, 387, 6.

40. *Select Committee ... 1864*, 69.

41. *Freeman's Journal*, 29 May 1856.

42. *Third Report of the department of Science and Art ...* H.C. 1856 [2123] xxiv. 191, 101.

43. Memo from Larcom to Lord Eglinton, 12 June 1858, briefing him on the Museum of Irish Industry (Larcom papers 7601 NLI MS 7601).

44. UCDA MII/1-7; UCDA RCSI.; Department of Science and Art, First Report, 1852-53 – Fifteenth report, 1867–68; contemporary *Thom's directories*; contemporary newspapers; membership lists of the Royal Dublin Society, etc.

45. *Freeman's Journal*, 26 November 1855.

46. *Report from the Select Committee on Scientific Instruction; together with the Proceedings of the Committee, Minutes of Evidence and Appendix ... 1868*, H.C.1867–8, H.C. (432), xv, 1, 153 (hereafter *Committee on Scientific Instruction 1868*).

47. Letter to the editor, *Freeman's Journal*, 5 June 1857.

48. *Committee on Scientific Instruction 1868*, 8.

49. *Committee on Industries 1885*, 465.

50. *Report on the RDS... 1863*, 97.

51. *Freeman's Journal*, 29 May 1856.

52. *Daily Express*, 15 June 1858.

53. *Report from the Commission on the Science and Art Department in Ireland;* Vol. 2, Minutes of evidence, appendix and index, H.C. 1868-69 [4103-1], xxiv, 43, 374 (hereafter *Commission on DSA, 2*).

54. Lydia Ernestine Becker, 'On the study of science by women' in *Contemporary Review*, x (1869), 396.

55. Clara Cullen, '"Laurels for fair as well as manly brows": women at Dublin's Museum of Irish Industry, 1854–1867', in Mary Mulvihill (ed.), *Lab Coats and Lace* (Dublin: WITS, 2009), 1–13.

56. E. Clibborn to Alexander Carte, 2 October 1865. Natural History Museum Dublin, Correspondence Files, C file.

57. Anne V. O'Connor and Susan M. Parkes, *Gladly Learn and Gladly Teach: Alexandra College and School, 1866–1966* (Dublin: Blackwater Press, 1984), 4.

58. The biographer of her brother, Alexander Leeper, described Jane Anne [Jeannie] Leeper, as 'one of Leeper's gritty sisters' who 'greatly resented that as a woman she was barred from higher education, and made her views well known to him [Leeper] (as she later made them known generally, in assiduous correspondence in *The Irish Times*)'. See John Poynter, *Doubts and Uncertainties: a Life of Alexander Leeper* (Melbourne: Melbourne University Press, 1997), 14.

59. *Report on RDS and MII, 1863*, 97.

60. *Thom's Directory... 1860* (Dublin: Thom, 1860), 1633.

61. Lydia Ernestine Becker, 'On the study of science by women' in *Contemporary Review*, x (1869), 395.

62. *Fifteenth Report of the Department of Science and Art*, H.C. 1867-68 [4049] xxvii, 419, 289–92.

63. *Report from the Commission on the Science and Art Department in Ireland; Report, vol.1* H.C. 1868-9 [4103], xxiv, 1, xxxiii.

64. Clara Cullen, "'A pure school of science": the Royal College of Science for Ireland and scientific education in Victorian Ireland', in Juliana Adelman and Éadaoin Agnew (eds), *Science and Technology in Nineteenth-Century Ireland* (Dublin: Four Courts Press, 2011), 136–49; *The College of Science for Ireland: its Origin and Development, with Notes on Similar Institutions in Other Countries, and a Bibliography of the Work Published by the Staff and Students (1900–1923)* (Dublin: College of Science Association, 1923); W.F. Barrett, *An Historical Sketch of the Royal College of Science from its Foundation to the Year 1900* (Dublin: John Falconer, 1907); Brian Kelham, 'The Royal College of Science for Ireland (1867–1926)', in *Studies*, 56, (Autumn 1967), 297–309.

6 THE NINETEENTH-CENTURY GOVERNESS AND EDUCATION IN IRELAND

DEIRDRE RAFTERY

As noted by Maria Luddy 'an aspect of [Irish] education which has received little attention is that of governessing'.[1] This is in contrast to the other form of unofficial nineteenth-century education, the 'hedge school', discussed in Chapter One. Governesses formed a significant proportion of all those employed in teaching: the *Census of Ireland, 1841* indicates that almost 10 per cent of the total (male and female) teaching force were governesses. However, they left few records of their work and any evaluation of their contribution to education relies, perforce, upon a close examination of a small range of sources. Papers of a few institutions for governesses are extant, and they are included in certain census returns. They are also mentioned in some nineteenth-century newspapers and journals, and feature in autobiographies of some Anglo-Irish writers. In addition, there were links between the Governesses Association of Ireland (GAI), Alexandra College, Dublin, and the movement for higher education for women. This chapter examines the profile of the profession, and the work of governesses, through a detailed analysis of available sources.[2]

THE GOVERNESS: IMAGES AND ARCHETYPES

In 1847, Charlotte Brontë created one of fiction's best-known heroines: a governess who was 'plain, poor and disconnected'.[3] In doing so, she created the defining image of the nineteenth-century governess. But it is arguably a romantic image that has obscured reality. The influences of the Romantic period are evident in *Jane Eyre*, which takes an ordinary woman as its central character, and allows her to venture beyond her limits. Jane's challenging of tradition is central to the novel. Upon taking up her first teaching position at Thornfield, she reflects:

> Women are supposed to be very calm generally: but women feel just as men feel; they need exercise for their faculties ... just as their brothers do; they suffer from too rigid a restraint, too absolute a stagnation, precisely as men would suffer; and it is narrow-minded in their more privileged creatures to say that they ought to confine themselves to making puddings and knitting stockings, to playing on the piano and embroidering bags.[4]

Virginia Woolf, commenting on this passage in 1929, argued that it was the voice of Charlotte Brontë, herself a governess, who had been starved of experience. Brontë's biographer, Mrs Gaskell, equally recognised the autobiographical nature of *Jane Eyre*, remarking that Brontë's occupation as a governess 'was not sufficient for her great forces of intellect'.[5] It is particularly significant that a woman who recognised all the frustrations of the profession should have penned the defining portrait of a Victorian governess. Brontë articulated her frustrations through Jane, whose passionate longing for change is in the tradition of Romantic writing: 'It is in vain to say that human beings ought to be satisfied with tranquility: they must have action and they will make it if they cannot find it. Millions are condemned to a stiller doom than mine, and millions are in silent revolt against it.'[6] The 'silent revolt' of nineteenth-century governesses is the concern of this study, which attempts to rescue the lives of real governesses from the shadow cast by images, and to examine the realities of their work, pay and prospects in nineteenth-century England and Ireland.

Nineteenth-century fiction is rich with representations of governesses. This owes much to the fact that the nineteenth century was also the century of the woman writer, and it was through the work of George Eliot, Anne and Charlotte Brontë, Harriet Martineau, Charlotte Yonge and Maria Edgeworth that the governess found a voice. Their works invariably focused on the plain and persecuted members of the profession, eclipsing the images of more powerful antecedents, who are met, infrequently, in the pages of history.

It is not surprising to find that Victorian iconography recorded the low status of the governess throughout the nineteenth century. Book and magazine illustrations, including cartoons in *Punch* magazine,[7] frequently portrayed the governess as a spirit-broken woman, persecuted by her young charges, and possessing neither fortune nor beauty. Richard Dadd painted 'The Music Lesson, or The Governess' in 1855, depicting the governess as a drab creature, while Thomas Ballard's subject in 'The New Governess' in 1877 was equally dejected.[8] But the image was captured most famously by Richard Redgrave in his 1884 painting 'The Governess'. One of the best known of Victorian *genre* paintings, it was imitated by a number of painters and was one of a highly regarded series intended to elicit sympathy for gentlewomen who had fallen on hard times and were forced to work. It suggested clearly that, whilst the subject was surrounded by evidence of her accomplishments (music, reading and sewing), she was isolated from her employer's family, and it hinted at what M Jeanne Peterson has termed the 'status incongruence' of Victorian governesses. Peterson examined the peculiar status of the governess, noting that 'she was a lady, and therefore not a servant, but she was an employee and therefore not of equal status with the wife or daughters of the house'.[9] It was this uneasy position of the governess within the structure of upper middle-class life which became a recurrent theme in fiction and iconography directed at an upper middle-class audience. But it is necessary to question the degree, if any, to which images of nineteenth-century governesses accord with reality, and to construct a picture of their working lives based on a variety of sources of evidence.

THE GOVERNESS IN ENGLAND

In 1801 Maria Edgeworth described governessing as 'an honourable profession, which a gentle-woman might follow without losing any degree of the estimation in which she is held.'[10] Indeed, from Tudor times to the late eighteenth century, the governess was held in some esteem in the homes of the upper middle ranks, though she was, it would seem, always stereotyped as a plain and serious character. Possibly the earliest mention of a governess comes from the letters of St Jerome to the Roman Lady Laeta, advising her to find a female tutor for her clever daughter, and suggesting that such a woman should be '*gravis, pallens, sordidata, subtristis*'.[11] Medieval sources suggest that governesses had attained a position of some influence because of their proximity to the nobility. Chaucer's sister, Catherine Swynford, was one of the more renowned women whom 'lords' daughters had 'in governaunce'.[12] As the duties of the governess included teaching court customs, many governesses were themselves the wives of earls or barons.

Throughout the seventeenth, eighteenth and nineteenth centuries, some of the most significant steps towards the education of women were made either by governesses or by royal women of spirit and conviction.[13] In 1673, Bathsua Makin, governess at the court of Charles I, founded Tottenham High Cross school for girls, and developed a curriculum for women. Kathryn Ashley, governess to Princess Elizabeth, had a profound and lasting influence on her pupil, and had the singular fame of being the first and last royal governess to be lodged in the Tower of London on a charge of high treason.[14] Equally devoted to her governess, Lehzen, was Queen Victoria. In adulthood she continued to refer to Lehzen for advice, and was to eventually support the Governesses' Benevolent Institution (GBI).

By the time the Edgeworths were writing *Practical Education*, the governess was no longer the exclusive property of the upper classes. Census returns from the last decades of the eighteenth century show that governesses could be found teaching in the homes of wine merchants, army officers, grocers and coach-builders, suggesting that the governess had lost some of her earlier significance as a symbol of status and wealth. By the mid-nineteenth century, newspapers and journals advertised the services of a variety of types of governesses. The 'daily governess' travelled each day to her employer's home to give lessons, while the 'resident governess' lived in her employer's home and was both teacher and companion to the children. The 'finishing governess' was employed merely to provide older daughters with lessons in polite accomplishments and social graces.[15]

Many governesses were women of the upper middle classes who were obliged to earn a living due to a change in family circumstances, whilst others were women of the rising lower-middle ranks. Indeed, Bessie Rayner Parkes observed that governessing was 'a platform on which middle and upper classes meet, the one struggling up, the other drifting down'.[16] But because the majority of governesses were 'ladies', the work of a governess was perceived as genteel and, therefore, enjoyed a higher status than elementary school teaching. Dina Copleman's study of women teachers in nineteenth-century England indicates clearly that the vast majority of women who taught, worked in elementary schools. These were not, however, described as 'lady teachers': they were women drawn almost exclusively from comfortable working-class (or labour aristocratic) and lower middle-class families. Indeed, attempts to encourage 'ladies' to become elementary school teachers failed signally.[17] It was thought that ladies would have a civilising influence on elementary pupils. At village schools, it was argued, children would be improved by 'a lady's gently refining influence'.[18] But, while gentlewomen involved themselves in school management and school boards, few were attracted into a profession that would call their status into question, even though a salary of between £80 and £90 per annum was often greater than a governess could hope to earn.

Upon securing a position, most governesses lived with the family. Salaries averaged between £30 and £50 per year, with laundry expenses deducted from this. Maria Edgeworth argued that a governess needed 'three hundred a year for twelve or fourteen years' in order to secure her retirement, for it was at retirement that a governess found herself most vulnerable. In 1849, the *Quarterly Review* described the typical treatment of the governess:

> When she has lived with the family for perhaps fifteen years and finished the sixth daughter, [they dismiss] her with every recommendation as a "treasure", but without a fragment of help in the shape of a pension or provision to ease her approaching incapacity. In nine cases out of ten, the old servant is more cared for than the governess.[19]

By the middle of the century, the conditions of employment for governesses had become a pressing issue for English philanthropists. Census returns for 1851 indicated that there was a 'surplus' of a quarter of a million women of marriageable age in the population. This was largely due to the economic uncertainties of the time that had led many middle-class men to postpone marriage or to emigrate to Britain's colonies.[20] Many middle-class women could expect to support themselves throughout their lives, and indeed the same census returns reported that 21,373 women were identified as governesses. But clearly these women were not able to provide adequately for themselves. The census indicates that 1.5 per cent of female inmates in insane asylums were governesses, and Florence Nightingale had, by 1853, all but filled her Institution for the Care of Sick Gentlewomen with homeless governesses.

Perhaps as a consequence of the changing expectations of middle-class women, philanthropists concerned themselves with the fate of unqualified and ill-prepared governesses. An option for unemployed governesses was emigration, though as Swaisland indicated, many women did not survive the sea passage to their new life.[21] Between 1861 and 1872, the Society for Promoting the Employment of Women (SPEW) placed 160 women in governessing positions in Australia and New Zealand. The Female Middle Class Emigration Society (FMCES), which placed 300 governesses in Australia and New Zealand between 1862 and 1882, also sent a small number of women to southern Africa, though this was a less popular destination. Between 1862 and 1880, the FMCES sent eighteen governesses to Natal and sixteen to the Cape. One of these women, Sophie Beddoe, kept a diary of her life as a governess for over twenty-two years, providing an important source of information on the daily hardships suffered by emigrant women. Most of the governesses placed by FMCES were either orphaned or destitute, and had no preparation for their profession or for the huge change that emigration would bring. Many feminists, including Frances Power Cobbe, were critical of the societies that offered emigration as a solution to the problem of 'surplus women'. They argued that it simply removed the problem, rather than dealing with the fact that women were unsuitably educated to work in a variety of other professions at home. The first sustained attempts to deal with the poverty of English women who worked as governesses were made in 1843, when the Governesses' Benevolent Institution was established at Harley Street, London, by a group of Anglican clergymen. While it was later to establish Queen's College, London, it originally aimed at establishing a retirement home for indigent governesses, and compiling an employment register. From its inception, the GBI attracted the attention of many influential people. Bessie Rayner Parkes noted that the duchess of Gloucester, the duchess of Cambridge and the queen dowager all gave their names in support,[22] while support was also given by writers including William Makepeace Thackeray and Charles Dickens. But, while the GBI was a popular 'genteel' charity with which to be associated, it did not attract much funding and financial aid was spread thinly over the hundreds of governesses who applied to Harley Street each year. The women who applied for assistance were invariably from middle and upper middle-class families. Lady Eastlake noted that a significant number of applications were from women 'with aristocratic names'.[23] The first report of the GBI indicated that a number of women turned to governessing to support their fathers' failing efforts in business, while some were supporting orphaned nieces and nephews, younger siblings, and aged parents.[24] A mother, recruiting a governess from the pages of *The Times* could have as many as one hundred advertisements from which to choose. But the standard of teaching provided by governesses depended largely on the education they had themselves received. At a time when formal schooling for girls was still inadequate, it became clear to the GBI that the training and certification of governesses could only serve to raise generally the standard of female education.

Efforts to provide training for governesses began when the GBI started a lecture series for governesses and other young women. Lectures were provided by some of the staff of King's College, London, and Professor Dennison Maurice arranged a teaching diploma. The GBI acquired additional neighbouring premises, and in 1848 Queen's College, London, was opened. Amongst the earliest students to attend Queen's were Sophia Jex-Blake who won the battle for the entry of women into the medical profession; Dorothy Beale who became principal of Cheltenham Ladies College; and Frances Mary Buss, who became principal of the North London Collegiate School. Buss later wrote that the establishment of Queen's College began the women's education movement. By the end of the century, women teachers could hold certificates from the Colleges of Preceptors, from Queen's, and some had been to the women's colleges at Cambridge and Oxford. Indeed, a significant percentage of all first-generation graduates from Cambridge and Oxford chose secondary school teaching as their profession, and many of them pioneered the new high school education movement for girls.[25] But by this time the role of the governess had become redundant. In calling attention to the state of female education and training for women teachers, governesses had precipitated the demise of their profession.

THE GOVERNESS IN IRELAND

While some scholars have examined the history of the governess in England in the last decade, there are few, if any, studies of Irish governesses, either at home or abroad, and there are few records of governessing in Ireland. However, a picture of the life and work of Irish governesses can be pieced together from a variety of sources. Governesses are included in certain census returns; some archives of a few institutions for governesses are extant; governesses feature in autobiographies of some Anglo-Irish writers, and governesses are mentioned in some nineteenth-century newspapers and journals published in Ireland. In addition, there were links between the Governess Association of Ireland (GAI) and Alexandra College, Dublin, not unlike the links that existed between the GBI and Queen's College, London. A place in history for these governesses' institutions has been assured, if only because they were affiliated to two pioneering women's colleges.

Governesses at work in Ireland in the first half of the nineteenth century were most likely to be employed in the homes of the upper and upper-middle classes and, therefore, were dependent on a small, and largely Protestant, section of the population for employment. From the 1840s until the early 1860s, governesses formed almost 10 per cent of the total teaching force. The majority of governesses were, at this time, Protestant. Census returns for 1861, for example, show that some 74 per cent of Irish governesses were Protestant.[26] Catholic unmarried women who wanted, or needed, to devote their lives to teaching could consider entering a religious order. Once fully professed, religious women were guaranteed shelter, companionship and useful occupation for the rest of their lives. While many women entered religious life primarily in response to what they referred to as a 'calling' from God, others were drawn towards semi-cloistered life as the only alternative to marriage and motherhood.[27] As Fahey has commented, through its female religious orders, 'the Catholic Church provided an option in life to its female members that had no counterpart in the Protestant churches and denominations.'[28] It is, then, perhaps not surprising that governessing was mainly a Protestant profession in nineteenth-century Ireland, though there is evidence that by the last decades of the century, increasing numbers of Catholic women were earning a living in this way. By 1881, of a total female teaching force of 12,846, some 5,316 women were governesses and, as the denominational profile of the profession changed, so too did the economic profile.[29] It is likely that the profession expanded with daughters of the rising middle classes: Catholic girls who had benefited from the national and intermediate programmes of education which gave to them opportunities not afforded to their foremothers. The Association of Irish Schoolmistresses and Other Ladies Interested in Education (AISE) observed in its annual report in 1887:

> Girls who some years ago only thought of going into service, to some trade, or at most becoming teachers in the primary schools are now, encouraged by the good education they get at the expense of the country either in the national schools or through the help of the Intermediate Board, either going in for Civil Service appointments, looking for private tuitions or for teaching in superior schools.[30]

However, by the end of the century, employment in formal education (such as national schools and second-level schools) was becoming more commonplace than employment in private teaching. In the last decades of the century there was a marked decline in the number of women who became governesses, and an increase in the number of schoolmistresses and assistant mistresses.

The few surviving records of institutions for governesses tell us something of the status of the profession and the nature of the education which governesses provided in Irish homes. These records, together with autobiographical sources, make it possible to reconstruct some picture of Maria Edgeworth's 'honourable profession'. In 1801, Edgeworth had noted with concern the content of the education given at home by private teachers. She was particularly scathing of the education provided for girls, concluding that 'a girl who runs through a course of natural history, hears something about chemistry, has been taught something of botany … is in a miserable situation, in danger of becoming ridiculous, and insupportably tiresome to men of sense and science'.[31]

Other prominent writers such as Edith Somerville and Frances Power Cobbe also noted the haphazard content of the education provided by governesses. Somerville's biographical writings suggest that governesses in Ireland, like their counterparts in England, obliged their pupils to learn by rote meaningless facts, dates and rules. This was probably to avoid revealing the inadequacy of their own education and their complete lack of teacher training. Somerville recalled that she 'had to learn by heart the Church Catechism, Rules of Grammar … [and] dates of the Kings of England'.[32] Textbooks used in Irish homes were similar to those used by governesses in England, and those used by Somerville included *A child's guide to general knowledge*, Mrs Markham's *History of England* and Richmal Mangall's *Historical and miscellaneous questions for the use of young people*. These were quite outdated by the middle of the century, and even as Somerville was using them, children within the Irish national school system were using texts that were more varied and solid in content. Both Somerville and Frances Power Cobbe were taught by a variety of governesses including foreign women. In her autobiography, Cobbe recalled a particularly competent French governess, while Somerville remembered 'going from system to system' with a series of English, French and German governesses.[33]

The uneven nature of the education provided by governesses reflected their own poor training. Some women, as Clara Cullen has shown in Chapter Five, took lectures at the Museum of Irish Industry, studying botany and chemistry, in addition to having a good knowledge of French, and the ability to shoot.[34] But there were a few organisations that prepared girls properly for the profession, and their records indicate that they were less concerned with teacher training than with preparing women, some as young as fifteen years of age, to find some kind of respectable employment. One such institution was the Seminary for Young Persons Designed to be Governesses in Cork city which attempted to train young Protestant girls whose parents could not support them. The trainee governesses lived within the seminary and parents had to pay 5s per quarter towards their keep.

Another organisation which promoted the training of governesses was the Governesses Association of Ireland (hereafter GAI), established in 1869. It was formed as a consequence of the endeavours of a number of prominent middle-class Dublin Protestants, and owed its inception in particular to Anne Jellicoe, who had founded the Irish Society for Promoting the Training and Employment of Educated Women (later the Queen's Institute) in 1861. The Queen's Institute quickly found that many of the 'distressed gentlewomen' who came to it could not afford to pay the required fees, and many could not avail of training because they lacked basic education. Whilst Jellicoe had hoped that the Queen's Institute would become involved in the training of governesses, this idea was unpopular with its board. It remained for Jellicoe, together with Archbishop Trench, to found a college for women that would provide them with a sound education. Alexandra College opened in 1866. Eventually in 1869, Jellicoe formed the GAI to 'promote the education of ladies as teachers'.[35] It opened at 3 Lower Leeson Street, Dublin, and played an important role in furthering the higher education of women by persuading Trinity College, Dublin, to establish special examinations for women. The GAI concerned itself specifically with raising scholarships to Alexandra College for 'persons intending to become governesses'. Its committee wrote in 1884:

> It seems to be generally supposed that, without any preparation, every woman is fit to teach, if she is fit for nothing else. Hence, the large number of persons, wholly unqualified, labouring as governesses on miserable wages ... and the low tone of the education which is the rule in private houses.[36]

The aim of the GAI was to provide a library and an agency for governesses, and two years of training 'in the best methods of imparting instruction'.[37] This form of teacher training was examined, somewhat unusually, with an academic test: the 'Examinations for women' held by Trinity College. A certificate of proficiency was also presented to successful students and trainees gained teaching experience by assisting at Alexandra School. The GAI estimated that a successful student could expect to take up a governessing position at £80 per annum. This was a significantly higher salary than an untrained governess could expect. The average salary for a resident governess in Ireland in the middle of the century was between £40 and £60. AISE reported in 1887 that nursery governesses were often paid as little as £20 per annum, while daily governesses earned as little as £1 per month.[38] Daily governesses were the most vulnerable members of the profession, as they had to provide their own accommodation and food. All governesses were vulnerable once old age approached, as few of them were provided with a pension, and residential governesses could suddenly find themselves homeless.

Research has indicated that in England at this time, indigent governesses made up a small but not insignificant number of inmates of poor houses and asylums. Records examined suggest that governesses in Ireland were inmates of asylums and other charitable institutions. One such asylum which has left valuable records was the Home for Aged Governesses (later the Governesses' Home, and now Harcourt Home), established in 1838 at Marlborough Street, and later permanently relocated to Harcourt Terrace, Dublin. Originally titled the Asylum for Aged Single Females, it was founded by a small independent voluntary committee of Protestant men and women. By 1851 it had recognised and committed itself to the needs of 'a class of persons, justly claiming much sympathy…aged governesses', and it had admitted a number of destitute governesses who otherwise 'would have had to shelter in the poor house … as the widows houses, servants asylums, and all other institutions were … closed to them'.[39]

By the end of the century, the Governesses' Home had admitted 175 women. Their ages ranged from 31 to 80 years, though the majority of inmates were between 50 and 60 years of age. They were, doubtless, at an age when the likelihood of resuming employment was small, and only six inmates had left to take up a situation.[40] Nineteen women were expelled for 'improper conduct' such as being quarrelsome or uncooperative. The remaining women lived there until they died, and many were buried in 'The Governesses' Grave' at Mount Saint Jerome cemetery in Dublin. The poverty into which these women sank in middle age is indicated not only by the fact that they relied on a charitable asylum to provide them with a home and a burial place, but also by the fact that the few who were removed were subsequently cared for in such institutions as the Whitefriars' Alms House and the Hospital for Destitute Incurables, Donnybrook.

During the nineteenth century, Ireland had witnessed the growth of the national school system and the intermediate examination system. In line with developments in England at the same time, it was perceived that girls should be educated outside the home and that their education should approximate more closely to the education of boys. The governess, at one time a symbol of social superiority, became a victim of much needed educational change. However, in both Ireland and England the profession of governessing had played a significant role in bringing attention to the working conditions of this branch of women teachers, and to the importance of providing an academic education for women who would, in turn, educate young girls. The GBI, closely connected to Queen's College, and the GAI, connected to Alexandra College, were positioned at the centre of the debate about higher education for women. Women who studied at Queen's, such as Dorothy Beale, Sophia Jex-Blake and Frances Mary Buss, were at the forefront of the battle for female education in England. Similarly, women attached to Alexandra, including Anne Jellicoe and Isabella Mulvaney (the latter was a recipient of a GAI scholarship, and later principal of Alexandra College), gave leadership to the growing movement for female education in Ireland.

CONCLUSION

While English literature and iconography offers a greater range of images of the nineteenth-century governess than Irish sources provide, it can be seen that the stereotype of the Victorian governess was the same in England and Ireland. This is not surprising, since governesses in Ireland for much of the century were both drawn from and employed by Anglo-Irish families. As the profession widened in England and Ireland to include women of the rising lower middle classes, it did not accommodate social difference and demanded that women who entered the profession acquired a veneer of gentility and some accomplishments. But although the profession grew to embrace women of different social ranks, it did not develop in status. In both England and Ireland, governesses were poorly paid and had no security, and many relied on charitable institutions in their old age. The popular image of the 'plain, poor and disconnected' governess, romanticised in fiction and iconography, had some basis in reality. It is arguable, however, that such an image has served to obscure the significance of the profession both as a form of respectable female employment and an agency for social mobility, and it is important to position the work of governesses within the history of female education in nineteenth-century Ireland.

NOTES

1. Maria Luddy, 'An agenda for Irish women's history, 1800–1900', *Irish Historical Studies*: 28, 109 (1992), 34.

2. This is a revised and updated version of a chapter in Bernadette Whelan (ed.), *Women and Paid Work in Ireland, 1500–1930* (Dublin: Four Courts Press, 2000). Reproduced with permission of Four Courts Press.

3. Charlotte Brontë, *Jane Eyre* (1847; this edn. London: 1982), 4.

4. Brontë, *Jane Eyre*, 64.

5. Cited in Julia Swindells, *Victorian Writing and Working Women* (Oxford, 1985), x.

6. Brontë, *Jane Eyre*, 141.

7. See, for example, John Leech, 'Class of humility', *Punch*, 2 October 1847; Charles Keene, 'Considerate – Very!', *Punch*, 22 October 1864, 174; Charles Keene, 'Simple addition', *Punch*, May 1871, 202.

8. For a sample of illustrations of governesses, see Trev Broughton and Ruth Symes, *The Governess* (Gloucester, 1997).

9. M Jeanne Peterson, 'The Victorian governess: status incongruence in family and society' in Martha Vicinus, *Suffer and be Still: Women in the Victorian Age* (London, 1980), 5.

10. Maria Edgeworth, *Practical Education* (2 vols, London, 1801), vol. 2, 101.

11. 'Serious, pale, shabby, sad'.

12. Geoffrey Chaucer, quoted by Bea Howe, *A Galaxy of Governesses* (London, 1954), 18.

13. For a study of the opening of formal education to women, see Deirdre Raftery, *Women and Learning in English Writing, 1600–1900* (Dublin, 1997).

14. See Howe, *A Galaxy of Governesses*.

15. For descriptions of the lives and work of governesses see Pamela Horn, 'The Victorian governess', *History of Education*, 18, 4 (December 1989); Howe, *A Galaxy of Governesses*; Alicia C Percival, *The English Miss Today and Yesterday* (London, 1939); Kathryn Hughes, *The Victorian Governess* (London, 1993) and Broughton and Symes, *The Governess*.

16. Bessie Rayner Parkes, 'The profession of the teacher', *English Woman's Journal*, 1,1 (March 1858), 1.

17. See Dina Copleman, *London's Women Teachers: Gender, Class and Feminism, 1870–1930* (London, 1996).

18. Cited in Copleman, *London's Women Teachers*, 3.

19. Elizabeth Eastlake, '*Vanity Fair, Jane Eyre* and the Governesses Benevolent Institution', *Quarterly Review*, lxxxiv (1848), 180.

20. See Margaret Bryant, *The Unexpected Revolution* (London, 1979), 35.

21. Cecilie Swaisland, *Servants and Gentlewomen to the Golden Land: the Emigration of Single Women from Britain to Southern Africa, 1820–1939* (Oxford, 1993).

22. Bessie Rayner Parkes, *Essays on Women's Work* (London, 1865), 338.

23. Eastlake, '*Vanity Fair, Jane Eyre*', 184.

24. Ibid., 181.

25. Governesses are treated in John Logan, 'Governesses, tutors and parents: domestic education in Ireland, 1700-1800', *Irish Educational Studies*, 7 (1988), 1–20. See Deirdre Raftery, 'Teaching as a profession for first-generation women graduates: a comparison of sources from Ireland, England and North America', *Irish Educational Studies*, 16 (1997), 99–109.

26. *Census of Ireland*, 1861.

27. See Deirdre Raftery, '"*Je suis d'aucune Nation*": the recruitment and identity of Irish women religious in the international mission field, c. 1840–1940', *Paedagogica Historica: International Journal of the History of Education*, 49, 4:(2013), 513–530.

28. Anthony Fahey, "Female Asceticism in the Catholic Church: A Case Study of Nuns in Ireland in the Nineteenth Century" (unpublished PhD thesis, University of Illinois, 1982), 5.

29. *Census of Ireland*, 1881.

30. *Annual Report of the Association of Irish Schoolmistresses and Other Ladies Interested in Education*, 1887 cited in Maria Luddy (ed.), *Women in Ireland, 1800-1918: a documentary history* (Cork, 1995), 150.

31. Edgeworth, *Practical Education*, 144.

32. Edith Somerville, *Wheel Tracks* (London, 1929), 43.

33. For lively portraits of governesses at work in Anglo-Irish homes, see Frances Power Cobbe, *Life* (London, 1904) and Somerville, *Wheel Tracks*.

34. See Clara Cullen, Chapter Five of this volume, citing E. Clibborn to Alexander Carte, 2 October 1865. Natural History Museum Dublin, Correspondence Files, C File.

35. Anne V. O'Connor, 'Anne Jellicoe' in Mary Cullen and Maria Luddy (eds), *Women, Power and Consciousness in Nineteenth-Century Ireland* (Dublin, 1995), 143.

36. Alexandra College Archives (hereafter ACA), MS Bell. The cooperation of the Principal and Board of Alexandra College, Dublin is gratefully acknowledged.

37. ACA, Governesses Association of Ireland to Executor of Mr JB Ball, 22 January 1884.

38. *Annual Report* cited in Luddy, *Women in Ireland*, 148–9.

39. Harcourt Home Archives (hereafter HHA), *Thirteenth Annual Report of the Governesses Home* (1851), 1. The cooperation of the Board of Harcourt Home is gratefully acknowledged. At the time of researching this piece, these archives were at Harcourt House. They are now at the Representative Church Body Library, Dublin.

40. HHA, MS Register of the Governesses Home 1839–1900, Harcourt Home, Dublin.

7 THE PRESENTATION ORDER AND NATIONAL EDUCATION IN NINETEENTH-CENTURY IRELAND

CATHERINE NOWLAN-ROEBUCK

During the nineteenth century the emergence and growth of female religious congregations was a distinguishing feature of life in the Roman Catholic Church. From the middle of the seventeenth century, the movement to let women religious out of the cloister and into the world of practical pastoral service gained momentum, and countries across Europe saw an increase in their numbers of convents and nuns.[1] This growth was represented in a pronounced move from enclosure to more open and active congregations. For its part, the Catholic Church looked on these female congregations as a new missionary force. In focusing on the areas of education and healthcare nuns became new agents of the Church, emphasising its commitment to the welfare of the hitherto neglected masses. By the end of the nineteenth century, in the cause of Catholic propagation, nuns visited the sick and poor in their homes, worked in hospitals and other types of welfare service and taught in public schools.[2] In Ireland, this expansion had the dual effect of answering the obligations of the Church to respond to the vast amount of poverty and distress that existed in the country at the time, whilst at the same time providing relatively wealthy single women with the opportunity to engage in socially active work.

The native Irish congregations were founded by independently wealthy women, who had engaged in charitable work before establishing religious communities. Nano Nagle (Presentation Order), Mary Aikenhead (Sisters of Charity), Frances Ball (Loreto), Catherine McAuley (Sisters of Mercy) and Margaret Aylward (Sisters of the Holy Faith) had all been involved in philanthropic work.[3] These institutes were established between the 1770s and 1850, and were complemented by Irish houses of congregations with continental origins and adapted versions of female orders with a more traditional heritage. In this way the organisational basis was laid for the growth that took place after 1850.[4]

Although this movement was gaining momentum in Europe from the middle of the seventeenth century onwards, its start was delayed until the end of the eighteenth century in both England and Ireland. Barbara Walsh (2002) examines the nature and extent of institutions of women religious in England and Wales from 1800 onwards, and assesses their response to the changing needs of a growing Catholic community.[5] In Ireland the effects of the Penal Laws also contributed to the later start. The work of both Fahey and Clear (1987; 1989)[6] focuses on the establishment, growth and development of the orders and congregations that opened in Ireland from the end of the eighteenth century and into the nineteenth century. Mary Peckham Magray's (1998) work examines the way in which religious women became central to the religious and cultural change that occurred in Ireland during the nineteenth century, and how nuns used the powerful position they gained through the course of their work.[7] Maria Luddy (1995; 2004) and Rosemary Raughter (1997; 2005) place the establishment and growth of the new congregations and orders within the context of the philanthropic movement that had come to prominence during the eighteenth century, and continued into the nineteenth century.[8] The first substantial history of the Presentation Order was written by William Hutch (1875) to mark the centenary of the Order and it became the standard history of the foundress Nano Nagle.[9] Hutch's work contains a considerable amount of detail relating to many of the early Irish foundations and information on various convents established overseas. T.J. Walsh's (1959) work provides a comprehensive account of the Institute, detailing the establishment and development of the Order both in Ireland and abroad, and an overview of the Institute within the arena of national education in the nineteenth and into the twentieth centuries.[10] Both Raphael Consedine PBVM (1983) and Mary Pius O'Farrell PBVM (1996; 2001) have made significant contributions as historians of their congregation.[11] While the existing body of research into the Presentation Sisters examines the development of Presentation convents as a group (Luddy 1992; Coonerty 1996; Scully 1973), little research into the way in which Presentation Sisters in Ireland established and conducted their schools during the nineteenth century has been presented until now.[12]

Religious congregations are distinguished from religious orders on the basis of their religious vows. Members of congregations take simple vows, whilst members of orders take solemn vows. In both cases the vows are generally of poverty, chastity and obedience. Theologians have disputed the exact meaning of the distinction between simple and solemn vows but, traditionally, solemn vows of religious orders gave them a higher religious standing than congregations. Although not widely applied in everyday language, the term 'nun' refers to a member of a religious order and the term 'sister' to a member of a congregation. Observing the rule of enclosure required that the members of a community remain within the area enclosed by the convent buildings and grounds. All duties and activities were carried out by the community within this 'enclosure'. Work that brought them outside the convent enclosure, such as visiting the aged and sick in their homes or the infirmaries, and teaching in schools that were located at a distance from the convent, was incompatible with the rule.[13]

THE FOUNDATION OF THE PRESENTATION ORDER

The emergence and subsequent growth of the modern Irish congregations of women that occurred in the nineteenth century began in the second half of the eighteenth century with the aspirations of Nano Nagle to teach poor children. Her work is located within the context of the philanthropic activity that emerged during the eighteenth century in Ireland, and mirrored similar drives that occurred across Europe and the United Kingdom.[14] Born in County Cork in 1718, Nano was the eldest of seven children born to Garret and Ann Nagle. They were a wealthy Roman Catholic family, whose ancestry has been traced back to the Norman invasion of Ireland in 1169.[15] Having completed her education abroad, Nano lived in Paris for a number of years before returning to Ireland. Following the deaths of her parents and one of her sisters, she moved back to the family home in Ballygriffin some time after 1749. During the eighteenth century, conditions for the majority of the population in Ireland, the Catholic peasantry, were characterised by poverty, deprivation and wretchedness. Having witnessed the impact of these conditions on the people around her and, overwhelmed by the helplessness of the situation, Nagle decided to enter the religious life on the continent. However, her stay there was brief and she did not reach the stage of religious profession. Following the advice of her spiritual director, she returned home and resolved to dedicate herself and her resources to the poor of Cork city.[16]

Sometime between 1754–55, Nano Nagle opened her first school in a little cabin in Cove Lane (now Douglas Street) near her brother's residence. The schoolhouse was a rented mud cabin that had two earthen-floored rooms, a garret and a thatched roof.[17] Within nine months a second cabin was secured to cater for the 200 children who were attending the school. This success resulted in a request to establish schools in the northern part of the city. Nano agreed to this on the understanding that these schools would receive local financial support. Within a similar timeframe, 200 more children were accommodated in a two-storey disused warehouse in Philpot Lane (Clarence Street), which meant that over a period of two years Nano's schools were catering for more children than the other known schools in the city combined.[18] Initially, Nano's intention was to cater for girls only, but at the insistence of her family she obtained another cabin in Cove Lane in which forty boys were taught by a master whose salary she paid. As the promised local finance for the schools in the north of the city did not materialise, Nano supported all the schools from her own resources until the death of her uncle in April 1757. Under the administration of Joseph Nagle's estate, Nano received considerable assistance and by 1769 she had opened seven schools, five for girls and two for boys.[19]

Although she may have drawn on a variety of influences in devising a daily programme for the schools, the one on which she settled owed much to the French *petites écoles*.[20] She outlined the programme as follows:

> … At present I have two schools for boys and five for girls. The former learn to read, and when they have the Douai catechism by heart they learn to write and cypher. There are three schools where the girls learn to read, and when they have the catechism by heart they learn to work. They all hear Mass every day, say their morning and night prayers, say the Catechism in each school by question and answer all together. Every Saturday they all say beads, the grown girls every evening. They go to Confession every month and to Communion when their Confessors think proper. The schools are opened at eight, at twelve the children go to dinner, at five o'clock they leave school. The workers do not begin their night prayers until six, after the beads…[21]

The teaching of secular subjects was left to lay mistresses and masters, whilst Nano explained the catechism in one school or another every day. She prepared the children for the sacraments of Confession and Communion, instructing and preparing a group in each of the seven schools twice a year, an arduous task that extracted a significant toll on her health.[22] After the hours at the schools were finished, she visited and tended the sick, the aged and the poor in their homes and in the infirmaries of Cork before she returned to her brother's house.[23]

By her work up to this point, Nano Nagle had taken a major step in the cause of Roman Catholic education for the poor. However, it was evident to her that, under the circumstances that pertained, her schools could have no permanence beyond her lifetime. In the hope of ensuring this permanence and continuity, Nano resolved to introduce a religious congregation to Cork.[24] Her first attempt at establishing a religious institute led to the successful foundation of the Ursuline Order in Ireland in 1771. Formed by Angela Merici in Italy in the early sixteenth century, the Company of St. Ursula was the first modern teaching order of women to be established. Although Merici's intention was to set up a society of women devoted to teaching the young and caring for the sick and the poor, the evolution of the institute into a religious congregation whose members professed solemn vows and observed strict enclosure altered the original character of the institute. The focus of their education mission also changed from the lower to the wealthier classes.[25] For Nano the Cork Ursulines' observance of their rule of enclosure, and the fact that they worked with the daughters of the wealthy classes meant that her hopes for them could not be realised. In 1774 she decided to establish a society that would devote itself exclusively to the poor, but she was unable to find someone who was willing to undertake the project. Although she considered herself to be unsuited to the task, in 1775 Nano Nagle embarked upon the establishment of a new religious congregation.[26] Initially this initiative drew opposition from the Ursuline community and Fr Francis Moylan, her adviser and collaborator. Nano persisted however and, along with three other women, began her novitiate on 24 December 1775. Taking simple vows, all four sisters were professed in the presence of the Bishop of Cork, Dr. John Butler, on 24 June 1777, and were the first members of the new congregation called the Sisters of the Charitable Instruction of the Sacred Heart of Jesus.[27] Finding fault with those who lived far away from her, and unable to supervise the schools they took care of every day, Nano discharged all but one of the mistresses she had employed. In their place the Sisters took charge of the schools and, according to Nano, tended them better than they had been before in every respect.[28] Between 1777 and her death in 1784 Nano built a new convent for the congregation, and began work on the selection of a French congregation whose rules and constitutions would meet Irish religious and social conditions. She already had some clear views on this, specifically, that foreign religious discipline was not suited to Ireland; that rules needed to be balanced between prayer and action; and that priority must be given to the work of the schools over every other activity.[29] Although she hoped to extend the society with foundations in Killarney and Dublin, this proved beyond her resources both in terms of finances and personnel. With the sisters of her community assembled around her, Nano Nagle died on 26 April 1784 aged sixty-five years.

CONSOLIDATION AND EXPANSION

For twenty years after the death of the foundress until her own sudden death in 1804, Mother Angela Collins directed the sisterhood and the poor schools. In the days after Nano Nagle's death the existence of the society was in serious doubt – a situation that lasted for nearly a decade. Illness and death, the embezzlement of funds and the scarcity and insecurity of postulants, reduced the small congregation almost to vanishing point. The combination of the unhygienic conditions that prevailed, and the demands of teaching and visitation, had devastating effects on the health of the first sisters. By August 1785, almost eight years after the foundation of the congregation, it still only had four sisters in its community.[30] While under the terms of her will Nano made considerable bequests to Mother Angela Collins and Sr Joseph Fouhy for the support of the sisters and the schools, her will was not proved until 1793. In the intervening years the agent appointed to act as administrator to Nano's estate had removed all of her papers from the convent, and appropriated and dissipated the funds intended for the support of the community. The women were left penniless.[31] The survival of the community was placed on a more permanent footing through the intervention of Joseph Nagle who became interested in the affairs of the community. From 1799 until his death in 1813 he undertook liability for payments to the sisters, and made further provision for the congregation in his will.[32]

Once it was established, the nature and form of Nano Nagle's new congregation was clear. In 1776 she called the foundation the Sisters of the Charitable Instruction of the Sacred Heart of Jesus, and in 1779 she added that the religious rule observed by the community had been drawn up by the Curé of St Sulpice. The constitutions followed by the sisters were considered a temporary measure until more permanent decisions could be made. Although she had been actively engaged in the search for permanent rules and constitutions, this task was still undecided at the time of Nano's death.[33] Compared with the flourishing Ursuline foundation, the society was ambiguous and ill defined. On his translation to the position of Bishop of Cork in 1787, Francis Moylan realised that approval by the Holy See would enhance the prestige and membership of the sisterhood.[34] He first approached the Vatican for pontifical approval in May 1788 and submitted a set of *Constitutions* for the consideration of the Congregation of Faith in March 1790. It was Moylan's belief that the observance of enclosure was incompatible with the charitable work of the sisters in Cork, and whilst he based these new statutes on the already approved Constitutions of the Ursulines, he incorporated modifications that followed the spirit more than the letter of the Ursuline code.[35] An apostolic brief (*Decretum Laudis*) of Pope Pius VI in September 1791 gave a qualified approval to the foundation. This was accompanied by a letter from the Sacred Congregation which stated that the *Constitutions* as set out by Moylan were deemed to be too austere, and instructed him to draw up new rules that resembled, as closely as possible, the Constitutions of the Ursulines.[36] Fr. Laurence Callanan, Nano Nagle's confessor, was appointed to this task and in 1791, at the request of the sisters, gave the society the new title of the Presentation of the Blessed Virgin Mary.[37] The completed draft of the new *Constitutions* was submitted by Bishop Moylan to the four Metropolitan Archbishops of Ireland in 1793. The formal observance began on 15 August of the same year when Moylan received the simple vows of the four professed sisters of the community. A copy of the *Constitutions* written and attested by the bishop, and bearing the names of the four archbishops and three other bishops, was deposited in the convent archives.[38]

The Presentation Sisters considered that recognition as a traditional religious order with solemn vows and enclosure was necessary to establish the society on a more solid foundation. The strain of teaching in the schools and visiting the sick proved to be a great burden on the small community. Their arduous life discouraged girls who were willing to devote their lives in religion to the education of the young. They were advised by Laurence Callanan and Fr. Michael J. Collins, brother of Mother Angela, that to achieve recognition as a religious order they would have to confine themselves to the education of the poor within their own enclosure. By 1800 a form of voluntary enclosure was observed by the sisters, a move with which the five other convents that had been established by then fully co-operated. Clearly this was contrary to the original intention of Nano Nagle.[39] Having initially opposed their decision Dr. Moylan relented and presented the new *Constitutions* of the Presentation Sisters to the Holy See for final approval in 1802. This was granted by Pope Pius VII on 9 April 1805, just over a year after the death of Mother Angela Collins. On 15 August 1806, and after a twelve-month probationary period, the entire community of the motherhouse in Cove Lane made profession of solemn vows in the presence of Bishop Moylan, with similar ceremonies held in the other Presentation convents.[40] By adopting the rule of enclosure, the Presentation Sisters ensured that the education of girls attending the schools attached to their convents became the primary focus of their mission.

In her first extant letter to Teresa Mulally, Nano Nagle stated her intention to send two of her small community to Dr Moylan for a foundation in Kerry and expressed a wish that Teresa would join her in the new society. However, she died before realising the extension of her institute to Killarney and Dublin.[41] The precarious state of the community in Cove Lane in its early years, and the problems it encountered after Nano's death meant that there were not enough sisters to establish the foundations in either place. To overcome this difficulty, both Moylan and Mulally decided to send postulants for training and profession to the house in Cork.[42] When Lucy Curtayne arrived in Cove Lane in January 1786 to begin her novitiate for a foundation in Killarney, it marked the beginning of the expansion of the new institute. In the fourteen years between 1786 and 1800 women from Dublin, Waterford, Cork and Kilkenny followed Curtayne's lead, serving their novitiate and professing their final vows in the convent in Cove Lane. They returned to their home towns to establish what became known as the Primary Foundations of the Presentation Order at Killarney (1793), George's Hill in Dublin (1794), Waterford (1798), North Presentation in Cork (1799) and Kilkenny (1800).

Between 1807 and 1830 the Presentation Order experienced its most active period of expansion in Ireland, a period during which the Primary Foundations came into their own. Twenty-two new houses of the order were opened in fourteen counties.[43] The first of these convents opened in James's Street in Dublin on 17 August 1807 and was a filiation of the house in George's Hill, which, by this time, had twelve sisters in its community. The sisters moved from here to Richmond Road, Fairview, on the north side of Dublin in September 1820 and again to Terenure in south Co. Dublin in 1866.[44] George's Hill established two more convents before 1830, Drogheda (1813) and Rahan (1817). The Richmond/Terenure convent went on to open its own filiations within this time-frame also, in Maynooth (1823) and Mullingar (1825).[45] Three of the other Primary Foundations opened convents within this period. Two sisters from the house in Killarney opened a new foundation in Tralee (1809). Twenty years later the Tralee convent opened a house in Dingle in October 1829. The Presentation Convent in Waterford opened three filiations before 1820. They established Dungarvan in September 1809, Carrick-on-Suir on 3 May 1813 and Clonmel on 3 October 1813.[46]

The difficulties experienced by North Presentation in the early years of its existence meant that the community was unable to open a filiation until 1834. Their first and only Irish foundation during the nineteenth century opened in Midleton on 29 April.[47] Between 1803 and 1838 sixty-six postulants entered the Presentation Convent Kilkenny, which established its first filiation in Carlow (1811). This was the first of seven houses to be established from Kilkenny during the nineteenth century, six of which were open by 1830. South Presentation established two more filiations before 1830 – Doneraile in September 1818, and Bandon in May 1829. The first Presentation convent to be established outside of Ireland was opened in St John's Newfoundland in October 1833 by five sisters from the community in Galway. It became mother-house to the network of Presentation convents that were established in Newfoundland throughout the nineteenth and twentieth centuries. Other foreign-based foundations opened in Manchester (1836), Madras (1842), San Francisco (1854) and Tasmania (1866), marking the beginnings of the international Presentation community that has subsequently developed into the International Presentation Association.[48] The period between 1834 and 1875 was a time of sustained growth for the institute in which the number of Presentation convents in Ireland nearly doubled. The twenty-four houses that opened during these years, combined with the existing convents, meant that fifty-two Presentation communities in Ireland and twenty-two overseas celebrated the centenary of the order in 1875.[49] The convents appear to have opened in phases, so that eleven houses opened during the six years 1834–40, six between 1844 and 1854; three between 1856 and 1866, and four between 1867 and 1874. In the last quarter of the nineteenth century eight new convents were established in Ireland with a further thirty-two opened overseas.[50] In his history to mark the centenary, Hutch recorded that the international community of Presentation nuns numbered at least 1139, whilst the Irish community had reached 974.[51]

PRESENTATION CONVENT SCHOOLS AND NATIONAL EDUCATION

In the early decades of the nineteenth century nuns had little impact on public education. In 1824 there were forty-six schools attached to 'nunneries' as compared to 9,352 hedge schools and 1,727 schools connected with the various Protestant education societies.[52] For her part, Nano Nagle's vision of education centred on the quality of life, the quality of society and the relationship of people with God. Her schools acted as a vehicle to service this vision. The supernatural basis of Roman Catholic education formed an integral part of the ethos in the schools of the Presentation Sisters. A system of education that did not include the hope of eternal happiness and reduced education to the mundane transactions of this world, proved problematic for her successors.[53] As prescribed by the *Constitutions*, teaching was a co-ordinated act of love of God. The first chapter outlines the spiritual and catechetical values in education. The sisters:

> … must …have in view what is peculiarly characteristic of this Institute, that is, a most serious application to the instruction of poor female children in the principles of Religion and Christian Piety…[54]

The daily routine in the Presentation schools prior to 1831 was as follows: morning prayers were said at 9.00 am, followed by half an hour of instruction in the catechism. For younger children the lesson was oral and accompanied by simple hymns, whilst in older classes the text was the catechism of Christian Doctrine compiled by Dr. Butler, Archbishop of Cashel. Appointed passages were explained and committed to memory, question and answer. The class reading was taken from Reeve's *Bible History* or Gahan's *Summary of Christian Doctrine*. A large part of the morning session was occupied with reading, writing and simple arithmetic. From 11.45 am until midday complete silence was observed in all classes, during which the children tried to place themselves in the presence of God, discover their faults and make acts of perseverance. At noon, the Angelus was recited followed by recitations of Acts of Faith, Hope and Charity. At 1.00pm the girls were occupied with knitting, needlework and spinning with secular work resuming at 2.30 pm. Half an hour later the sister in charge of the class gave an instruction on an appropriate subject or read aloud from a spiritual work. At the close of the day the children said "…five Paters and five Aves for the Benefactors of the Institute…" and before dispersal, at 3.30 pm, the rosary or litany of Loreto was recited.[55] By the time that the National System of Education was established (1831), the twenty-eight Presentation convents in existence already had their schools operating efficiently.

In October 1831 Lord Stanley, the Chief Secretary to Ireland, wrote to the Lord Lieutenant outlining the government plan regarding a system of national education for Ireland. This became known as the Stanley Letter.[56] The main aims of the proposed system were to afford 'a combined literary and separate religious education … for the poorer classes of the community' and 'to unite in one system children of different creeds'.[57] To achieve this, the Letter proposed that a government-appointed board of commissioners be created, which should have representations from the Established Church, the Catholic Church and the Presbyterian Church. The board would have control over schools built by or placed under its auspices. It would also have control over all the books to be used in the schools and the funds voted annually by parliament. Stanley proposed that the schools be kept open for four or five days a week for literary instruction, while separate religious instruction could take place on the remaining one or two days and either before or after school hours on the school days. A system of inspection was also proposed to ensure that regulations were enforced. The commissioners drew up a set of rules to operate the proposed system, which, in subsequent years, were altered and adapted under pressure from the different religious bodies. This manipulation by the Churches was compounded by the failure of the board to implement the scheme as it was intended from the outset. The result was a system of national education that was denominational in practice, over which the local patrons, and by extension the Churches, had a significant degree of control.[58] Some of the earliest applications for aid from the newly-established National Board came from convent schools, with twenty-six of them connected to the system by April 1837.[59]

By 1853, the first year in which figures were compiled on convent and monastic schools as a specific group, ninety-nine convent schools had joined the system. This rose to 111 in 1857, 132 in 1864, and 145 in 1870.[60] The first Presentation convent to join the National system of Education was the house in Killarney. The capitation grant of £10 per annum for every 100 children, paid to convent schools connected to the System, was a boon to struggling communities. Yet, not all of the early foundations within the order embraced the system. The schools at South Presentation and George's Hill did not join until twenty years after its introduction, and the sisters of the North Convent in Cork waited until

1881 to connect to it.[61] However, almost all the houses founded between 1834 and 1871 were placed in connection with the board eventually.[62]

Although clearly not in keeping with the non-denominational nature of Stanley's plan, the Presentation schools that joined the National System managed to retain the acts of piety that were prescribed by the *Constitutions*. The 1837 alteration to the regulation concerning times of religious instruction, made to accommodate the Presbyterian Synod of Ulster, worked to their advantage. Morning and evening prayers were offered, the Angelus was recited at noon and the Hail Mary was said inaudibly at the hourly striking of the clock.[63] The early to mid-1850s were a difficult time for the convent schools. The basis on which the capitation fee was paid changed, from the number of children on the rolls to the daily average attendance. The chaos of these post-Famine years resulted in a low average, which reduced the payments to convents. Difficulties between some inspectors and the convent schools in their districts resulted in the withdrawal from the system of the Presentation Convents at Castlecomer and Mooncoin and the Sienna Convent in Drogheda. The re-statement of the Rules and Regulations of the Board in 1855 reinforced an amendment to the 1837 alteration that prevented the saying of prayers at intermediate times during the day.[64] However, the denominational nature of the system in practice indicates that religious schools worked out a solution to these apparent difficulties that allowed them to operate within its structures.

ORGANISING OF SCHOOLING

When drawing up the *Rules and Constitutions* in 1793 Laurence Callanan devoted its second chapter to the schools of the proposed new order.[65] Consedine points out that whilst the sisters were influenced by the Lancastrian model, the *Constitutions* drew on the Ursuline experience. She also suggests that by the time the *Presentation Directory* was published in 1850, the sisters had assimilated more of the educational theory and practice of the Ursulines than is indicated by the *Constitutions*.[66] For Presentation schools the Ursuline principle of shared responsibility was maintained, but the large numbers of children in attendance combined with the small numbers of sisters available, particularly in the early stages, meant that adjustments were necessary.[67] The *Directory* recommended that, "The number of schools in each Monastery, shall be regulated according to the number of children who attend. ...".[68] The schools were to be situated as conveniently to the convents as could be allowed within the rules of the institute, yet separated as much as possible from the convent house itself. Schools were to keep a record of the names of the children, their age on entrance, the names and occupations of their parents, their address and the exact date of reception into the school. Visitors were to be admitted to the schools only with the express permission of the Superioress, and only the members of the community who were engaged in instruction were allowed to be in the schools with the children.[69]

According to the *Constitutions*, schools were to open each day from 9.00am until 12.00pm, and 2.00pm until 5.00pm, however the *Directory* altered these hours to 9.00am until 3.15pm. In addition to the periods of vacation that were set out in the *Constitutions*, the *Directory* suggested that holidays '... may also be granted on the feasts of the Conception, Nativity and Purification of our Blessed Lady.' It further recommended that the school should not be open when particular ceremonies took place in the convent, such as the reception, profession or burial of a member of the community.[70] A final suggestion was that a clock should be hung in each school to regulate the different exercises of the day. On the approval of the Superioress the children were to discontinue their activities, bless themselves and '... devoutly recommend themselves to the protection of the Holy Mother of God, saying a Hail Mary' whenever the clock struck.[71]

Regardless of when the convents connected their schools with the National Board, they agreed to be bound by the conditions of the Commissioners regarding the general running of a school within the system.[72] These entailed keeping a register of the daily attendance of the children and the average attendance in each week and quarter; the conspicuous positioning of the inscription 'National School' on the school-house; the exhibition of the General Lesson in the schoolroom and the inculcation of its principles.[73] They also required that the school be open to receive children of all religious denominations; that the commissioners be allowed to visit and examine the school, and that the public, of all religious persuasions, have access to visit the school, inspect the register, witness the mode of teaching and see that the regulations were observed.[74] The changes to the rules of the National System in 1855 meant that convents were entitled to receive assistance in relation to only one of the schools they were operating. However, Presentation convent schools were located close to the convent houses and as such were centralised in one part of a city, town or village. This meant that in practice the change in rules had no impact on their operation as they had been in receipt of assistance from the commissioners for only one school up to that point.

CURRICULUM

The secular subjects at the heart of the curriculum in Presentation schools were reflective of contemporary attitudes regarding the appropriate subjects for the education of girls. The *Directory* outlined the purpose of these subjects and the particular importance of needlework thus:

> As the poor cannot receive a more precious inheritance than a spirit of economy and industry, particular attention shall be paid to instil it into the minds of the children. That pernicious propensity to talk and idleness, should as much as possible, be banished from amongst them. Besides, therefore, the more serious and to them, less interesting studies of Reading, Writing, Arithmetic, Geography, and Grammar, they should be carefully instructed in all sorts of needle-work, as being the means by which they may in after life, obtain more securely a decent livelihood. To the poor, this is certainly, the most essential acquirement which they can obtain; and it should therefore be to every Presentation Religious, one of the chief objects of her care and attention. To the young and less advanced children, knitting, will during the vacant moments of the day, prove a fruitful source of both amusement and industry.[75]

In reading, the children were only allowed to read books that would inculcate the practice of virtue and devotion, whilst the reading of books for amusement was forbidden. Bringing into school books that could lead to the destruction of pious and prudent sentiments in the minds of others was viewed as a most punishable offence.[76] In writing, the children were taught to hold the pen properly to begin with and having learned this were instructed in the exact formation of the letters. Writing on slates took place first and the progression to paper occurred when they had mastered the combinations of letters. They were not taught to write in small hand until they could form a good bold large hand. Finally, to write freely from dictation, children were taught to write in a running hand with speed and precision. All through the instruction in writing children were taught to leave equal distances between each two strokes in the formation of a letter and to allow the space of one letter between each two words.[77] Arithmetic was described as '...one of the most important branches of profane knowledge...' and, when properly taught, was viewed as an excellent way of strengthening the mind and preparing it for the acquisition of any other kind of knowledge to which it may be applied. Knowledge of tables and notations was deemed absolutely necessary for acquiring any facility in arithmetic. After knitting, children were taught to hem, sew and how to mark out on canvas or coarse linen. When they had advanced from this level they were taught to cut out and arrange the work for themselves, with particular attention paid to finishing. Instruction in needlework was done for the hour between twelve and one o'clock every day.[78]

In the National System the syllabus for the literary or secular education was laid down in the Programmes of Instruction for Pupils in National Schools.[79] There were separate programmes for girls and boys each describing the minimum level of proficiency required for pupils enrolled for at least one quarter in each class. The subject areas covered by these programmes were reading, writing, spelling, grammar, arithmetic and geography. Along with this basic curriculum, subjects such as sewing, knitting, netting, embroidery, straw plaiting and cutting out were taught to females. Beyond that, extra subjects including mensuration, geometry, bookkeeping, agriculture, music and drawing could also be offered by schools.[80] Up until the introduction of payment-by-results, classes in national schools were determined by the Lesson Books with progress dictated by the pupil's competence in the books. Thus the First, Second, Sequel and Third Classes corresponded to the First, Second, Sequel and Third Books with Fourth and Fifth Classes equating to the Fourth Book and higher.[81] In 1855 the Programmes of Instruction for girls and boys in the First, Second and Sequel Classes were the same. However, differences arose between the programmes in Third, Fourth and Fifth Classes. In Third Class the difference between the programmes related to arithmetic. Boys were expected 'To work readily questions in the Simple and Compound Rules of Arithmetic,' whilst girls were to work questions '... in all the simple rules of Arithmetic, and in Addition, Subtraction, Multiplication, and Division of Money.'[82] Differences also existed between the programmes for Fourth Class. The boys were expected 'To know all the Arithmetical Tables, and to be able to write out from memory, and in a neat and correct form, any one of them,' and to be able to '...work sums in Proportion, Fractions, and Practice.' Girls were 'To be able to write out from memory, and in a neat and correct form, any of the more useful Arithmetical Tables,' and to be able '…to work sums in the Compound Rules, Simple Proportion, and Practice.' There were also slight differences in grammar between the programmes.[83] In Fifth Class the differences in the arithmetic content increased. Boys were expected to know the commercial rules of arithmetic and the mensuration of superficies; how to keep cash, personal, real and farm accounts; how to write out bills and shop accounts and to be able to draw on slate any of the simple plane geometrical forms. For girls the requirements were to know fractions, practices and interest, how to keep a cash account and write out a short shop bill. In grammar boys were 'To analyse and parse correctly complex sentences' and "To analyse the words of their ordinary lessons, pointing out their roots, prefixes, and affixes, and to explain their meaning with clearness and precision.' Girls had to parse compound sentences and explain the composition and meaning of the words of their ordinary reading lesson. Although both boys and girls were expected to know the geography of the British Empire, boys were required to know the simpler portions of the *Geography Generalized* whilst girls were to explain the ordinary proofs of the Earth's sphericity.[84] As with all schools joining the National System, the Presentation Convent Schools undertook to follow the secular curriculum as defined by the commissioners. In addition to the core subjects, the sisters offered vocal music, drawing and embroidery as extra subjects in their schools. However, they met with varying degrees of success in these subject areas.

METHODS OF INSTRUCTION

The Programme of Instruction devised by the Commissioners of National Education promoted explanation, interrogation and repetition as the three great means of instruction to be employed in their schools.[85] These methods were also reflected in the approach of the sisters within their convent schools. According to the recommendation of the *Directory*, instruction in the various subject areas was based on a process of instruction, questioning and repetition. The Catechism was to be taught by reciting, repetition and questioning.[86] Whilst the instruction of reading receives little attention in the *Directory*, it recommended that very little advice was necessary in relation to instruction in writing. It was most important to pay close attention to the pupils when they first learnt to write, as this was the phase during which habits were formed. To teach writing effectively the teacher needed to move between the children constantly. She was to model the writing of any words or sentences given to the child to transcribe, wait for the child to complete the exercise and correct the work then so that any mistakes in formation or spacing could be addressed. Those pupils who were weak at writing would require more particular attention, most effective of which was to hold their hand to help them to control the pen.[87] Children were forbidden to scribble and were only ever to be allowed to write in their papers. They were to be accustomed to great neatness, never allowed to spatter their clothes or blot their paper, and to be supplied with pieces of old material for wiping their pens. The children were not allowed to talk amongst themselves during the writing hour and those children who were constantly noisy and negligent were to be admonished. The sister was advised to have appropriate copper-plate pieces or some pious verses prepared so that the pupils could practice their skills. The *Directory* also suggested that in the absence of printed billets on the saints for each month, the Writing Mistress should get the best writers to print them.[88]

The importance of a good knowledge of arithmetic to daily life meant that it was necessary to adopt a good method of teaching it. Accuracy and speed were the two essential characteristics of a good 'arithmetician', neither of which could be obtained without a knowledge of the principles and rules, and continuous practice in their application. The teaching of arithmetic began with instruction in the nine figures along with zero or nought. Having mastered these, the pupils were arranged into groups of ten or twenty and were instructed in addition, as numeration could be combined with it.[89] The monitress then began by telling them that:

> ... there are nine significant figures; and that all operations of modern arithmetic are performed by means of these, [and] the zero or nought, which by itself signifies nothing; that a figure in the first place expresses units; in the second, tens; in the third, hundreds; in the fourth, thousands; and may then ask, What does a figure in the first place express? What in the second? What in the third?...[90]

She then continued with a lesson in place value using the slates, with each child in the group entering the figures on their individual slate and holding it up for inspection after each entry. The *Directory* stressed that in teaching arithmetic, nothing was to be considered as done that was not thoroughly understood – a meaning and a reason was to be attached to every step of the process.[91]

Needlework was to be taught by imitation and constant practice. The sister was to practise great patience and forbearance in the annoyances the pupils might cause her, and encourage them to be attentive and to learn well by every means at her disposal. The girls were to be taught how to hem and sew at first, then to mark out on canvas or coarse linen. Once these skills were mastered, they were to advance to more difficult areas.[92] Work was to be examined often and, when necessary, was to be ripped and done again – more than once if required. Those children who were having difficulty were to be instructed on an individual basis, which was considered to be the most successful method of helping them. She was also expected to foster an environment of silence and recollection, and never to engage in useless discourse with them.[93]

CONCLUSION

In establishing the first modern Irish religious institute that was dedicated to working with the poor, Nano Nagle pioneered a new type of congregational life for women religious, and ensured the permanence and continuity of the success she had already achieved in this area. The Presentation Sisters who followed her consolidated the position of the new congregation by adopting the rule of enclosure, professing solemn vows and adding the fourth vow of instruction that became the essence of the order. The expansion and development of the Presentation network that took place during the nineteenth century provided the institute with a strong profile amongst the Catholic population both at home and overseas. This network had already established a structured method of conducting its schools before the establishment of the National System.

The denominational nature of the system in practice facilitated the work of the sisters in particular as their mission focussed on the poor. Whilst the sponsors of the system and the Presentation Order shared the common goal of providing secular education to the children of the poorer classes, the content of the programme of religious instruction in Presentation schools was centred on the catechism and sacraments of the Roman Catholic Church. The sisters' adherence to the inculcation of religious practices, rituals and ceremonies throughout the school day and across the year, meant that they could maintain their identity and ethos within the structures of the system. Both the secular and religious programmes were taught by means of the monitorial system and the sisters' efforts were met with a favourable response from the district inspectors who reported on the schools. The successful operation of the Presentation schools within the National System came as a result of their accommodating its structures within the greater Presentation approach, rather than being absorbed by the system. This meant that the Sisters began the twentieth century in the vanguard of Catholic education in Ireland, a position they consolidated and expanded upon during the following decades.

NOTES

1. Tony Fahey, 'Nuns in the Catholic Church in Ireland in the Nineteenth Century', in Mary Cullen (ed.), *Girls Don't Do Honours: Irish Women in Education in the Nineteenth and Twentieth Centuries* (Dublin: WEB Press, 1987), 7-9. In Ireland, the number of nuns rose from 120 in 1800 to 1,500 in 1850 and to over 8,000 in 1901.
2. Ibid., 9–12.
3. Maria Luddy, *Women and Philanthropy in Nineteenth-Century Ireland* (Cambridge: Cambridge University Press, 1995), 24.
4. Fahey, 'Nuns in the Catholic Church' in Cullen (ed.), *Girls Don't Do Honours*, 10 & 11.
5. Barbara Walsh, *Roman Catholic Nuns in England and Wales 1800–1937 A Social History* (Dublin: Irish Academic Press, 2002).
6. Caitríona Clear, *Nuns in Nineteenth-Century Ireland*, (Dublin: Gill and Macmillan, 1987); and 'The Limits of Female Autonomy: Nuns in Nineteenth-Century Ireland', in Maria Luddy and Cliona Murphy (eds), *Women Surviving: Studies in Irish Women's History in the Nineteenth and Twentieth Centuries* (Dublin: Poolbeg Press, 1989).
7. Mary Peckham Magray, *The Transforming Power of the Nuns. Women, Religion, and Cultural Change in Ireland 1750-1900* (Oxford: Oxford University Press, 1985).
8. Maria Luddy, Foreword, in Margaret H. Preston, *Charitable Words Women, Philanthropy, and the Language of Charity in Nineteenth-Century Dublin* (Connecticut: London: Praeger, 2004); Rosemary Raughter, 'A Natural Tenderness: The Ideal & Reality of Eighteenth-Century Female Philanthropy', in Maryann Gialanella Valiulis and Mary O'Dowd (eds), *Women & Irish History Essays in Honour of Margaret MacCurtain* (Dublin: Wolfhound Press Ltd., 1997); and 'Pious Occupations: Female Activism and the Catholic Revival in Eighteenth-Century Ireland', in Rosemary Raughter (ed.), *Religious Women and Their History: Breaking the Silence* (Dublin: Irish Academic Press, 2005).
9. William Hutch, *Nano Nagle: Her Life, Her Labours and Their Fruits* (Dublin: McGlashan and Gill, 1875).
10. T.J. Walsh, *Nano Nagle and the Presentation Sisters* (Dublin: M.H. Gill & Son, 1959).
11. M. Raphael Consedine, PBVM, *Listening Journey: A Study of the Spirit and Ideals of Nano Nagle and the Presentation Sisters* (Victoria: The Congregation of the Presentation of the Blessed Virgin Mary, 1983); Mary Pius O'Farrell, PBVM, *Nano Nagle: Woman of the Gospel* (Cork: Cork Publishing Limited, 1996); idem, *Breaking of Morn: Nano Nagle (1718-1784) & Francis Moylan (1735–1815) A Book of Documents* (Cork: Cork Publishing Limited, 2001).
12. Maria Luddy, 'Presentation Convents in County Tipperary 1806–1900', in *Tipperary Historical Journal*, (1992); Paula Coonerty, 'The Presentation Sisters and the Education of "Poor Female Children" in Limerick, 1837-1870', in *The Old Limerick Journal*, Winter

Edition 1996; Margaret C. Scully, *Galway Schooling and the Presentation Sisters: An Account of the Work of a Religious Body in the Practice of Education* (1815–1873), unpublished MEd thesis).

13. Fahey, 'Nuns in the Catholic Church' in Cullen (ed.), *Girls Don't Do Honours*, 7.

14. M.G. Jones, *The Charity School Movement A Study of Eighteenth Century Puritanism in Action* (Cambridge: Cambridge University Press, 1938).

15. Walsh, *Nano Nagle*, 23–34.

16. Mother Clare Callaghan to Bishop Coppinger, n.d., in Walsh, *Nano Nagle*, 381–3; Walsh, *Nano Nagle*, 38–43

17. Walsh, *Nano Nagle*, 44–7.

18. Ibid.; see also Walsh, *Nano Nagle*, 45–8; Consedine, *Listening Journey*, 44–5.

19. Nano Nagle to Miss Fitzsimons, 17 July 1769, in Walsh, *Nano Nagle* 345; Walsh, *Nano Nagle*, 45–8; Consedine, *Listening Journey*, 44–5.

20. Walsh, *Nano Nagle*, 47–8; O'Farrell, *Woman of the Gospel*, 77–8. The *petites écoles* were the ordinary means of education for poor children in the towns of France and dated back to 1357.

21. Nagle to Fitzsimons, in Walsh, *Nano Nagle*, 346.

22. Ibid.

23. Walsh, *Nano Nagle*, 50; Consedine, *Listening Journey*, 51; O'Farrell, *Woman of the Gospel*, 93–4.

24. O'Farrell, *Woman of the Gospel*, 103.

25. JoAnn Kay McNamara, *Sisters in Arms: Catholic Nuns Through Two Millennia*, (Cambridge, Massachusetts & London: Harvard University Press, 1998), 460–65; Walsh, *Nano Nagle*, 58, 168–9; Caitríona Clear, *Nuns in Nineteenth-Century Ireland* (Dublin: Gill and Macmillan, 1987), 45.

26. Walsh, *Nano Nagle*, 55–93. Nano Nagle to Miss Mulally, 29 September 1776, in Walsh, *Nano Nagle*, 357.

27. Walsh, *Nano Nagle*, 87–100; O'Farrell, *Woman of the Gospel*, 144–50. Francis Moylan was ordained as a priest for the diocese of Cork at the Irish College of Toulouse. He returned to Cork in 1763 and became an important figure in the revival of Catholic education. The three women who began their novitiates with Nano were Mary Fouhy, Elizabeth Burke and Mary Ann Collins.

28. Nagle to Mulally, 24 August 1778, in Walsh *Nano Nagle*, 359; South Presentation Convent Cork Archives (hereafter SPC) Annals, in Consedine, *Listening Journey*, 73.

29. Walsh, *Nano Nagle*, 101; O'Farrell, *Woman of the Gospel*, 158.

30. Walsh, *Nano Nagle*, 130–1; O'Farrell, *Woman of the Gospel*, 177–8. Mother Angela Collins and Sr Jospehine Fouhy had been joined by Margaret Tobin (Sr Francis) and Mother Angela's sister Margaret (Sr Monica).

31. Mother Angela Collins to Joseph Nagle, 12 June 1800, in Walsh, *Nano Nagle*, 376–8; Walsh, *Nano Nagle and the Presentation Sisters*, 131–43; O'Farrell, *Woman of the Gospel*, 175, 187. David and Jospeh Nagle, Nano's brothers, were executors of the will. They appointed Thomas Roche, their agent in Cork, to act as administrator.

32. Walsh, *Nano Nagle*, 145–6; O'Farrell, *Woman of the Gospel*, 190.

33. O'Farrell, *Woman of the Gospel*, 192–3.

34. Walsh, *Nano Nagle*, 132.

35. O'Farrell, *Woman of the Gospel*, 199; Walsh, *Nano Nagle*, 133–5.

36. 'Letter of the Sacred Congregation, Rome, to Bishop Moylan, 6 August 1791' and '*Decretum Laudis*, 3 September 1791', in O'Farrell, *Breaking of Morn*, 158–66; O'Farrell, *Woman of the Gospel*, 209–10.

37. Walsh, *Nano Nagle*, 102, 130–9; O'Farrell, *Woman of the Gospel*, 199–212. The title relates to the Presentation of the Blessed Virgin Mary in the Temple the feast of which is marked on 21 November. Members of the Institute are often recorded as PBVMs.38. Walsh, *Nano Nagle*, 160–1; O'Farrell, *Woman of the Gospel*, 217.

39. Walsh, *Nano Nagle*, 173–5.

40. 'Final Approbation, 9 April 1805', in O'Farrell, *Breaking of Morn*, 275–6; Walsh, *Nano Nagle*, 175–81; O'Farrell, *Woman of the Gospel*, 226–36.

41. Nano Nagle to Miss Mulally, AL 29 September 1776, in Walsh, *Nano Nagle*, 357.

42. Walsh, *Nano Nagle*, 146.

43. 'Conspectus of the Presentation Order from its foundation in 1777 to the year 1875', in *Nano Nagle: Her Life*; 'Presentation Development Chart', in Walsh, *Nano Nagle*.

44. Roland Burke Savage, *A Valiant Dublin Woman: The Story of George's Hill (1766–1940)* (Dublin: M.H. Gill & Son, Ltd., 1940), 221–2.; Consedine, *Listening Journey*, 216.

45. Burke Savage, *A Valiant Dublin Woman*, 222–32; 'Conspectus', in Hutch, *Nano Nagle: Her Life*; 'Presentation Development Chart', in Walsh, *Nano Nagle*.

46. Hutch, *Nano Nagle: Her Life*, 167–80; 'Presentation Development Chart', in Walsh, *Nano Nagle*.

47. Hutch, *Nano Nagle: Her Life*, 326–33.

48. Walsh, *Nano Nagle*, 159; Hutch, *Nano Nagle: Her Life*, 173–98; 'Presentation Development Chart', in Walsh, *Nano Nagle*; Consedine, *Listening Journey*, 144. The International Presentation Association (IPA) is an umbrella organisation for the worldwide community of Presentation Sisters.

49. 'Conspectus', in Hutch, *Nano Nagle: Her Life*; *Nano Nagle Seminars July–August 1984* (Cork: Nano Nagle House, Douglas Street, 1984), 38–41.

50. Within the wider context of institutes of women religious in Ireland, Presentation convents accounted for 55 per cent of all convents in 1840. By 1900 Presentation and Mercy congregations together made up 58 per cent of all Irish convents. (Clear, *Nuns*, 52).

51. Ibid.

52. *Second Report of the Commissioners of Education Inquiry, (Abstract of Returns in 1824, from the Protestant and Roman Catholic Clergy in Ireland, of the state of Education in their respective parishes)*; 1826–27 (12.) XII. 1, 6-18.

53. O'Farrell, *Woman of the Gospel*, 262.

54. *Rules and Constitutions of the Institute of the Religious Sisterhood of the Presentation of the Ever Blessed Virgin Mary* (Dublin: M. J. Elwood, 1872), 10–13.

55. Ibid., 13–6; see also Walsh, *Nano Nagle*, 206.

56. The Stanley Letter in *Royal Commission of Inquiry into Primary Education (Ireland), Vol. I Pt. I: Report of the Commissioners; with an appendix*, pt. i., 22–26.

57. Ibid.

58. Donald H. Akenson, *The Irish Education Experiment; The National System of Education in the Nineteenth Century* (London: Routledge & Kegan Paul, 1970). See also Norman Atkinson, *Irish Education: A History of Educational Institutions* (Dublin: Allen Figgis, 1969); John Coolahan, *Irish Education: History and Structure* (Dublin: Institute of Public Administration, 1981); Áine Hyland and Kenneth Milne (eds), *Irish Educational Documents, Vol. I* (Dublin: CICE, 1987).

59. James Kavanagh, *Mixed Education, The Catholic Case Stated; or, Principles, Working, and Results of the System of National Education; with suggestions for the settlement of the education question. Most respectfully dedicated to the Catholic Archbishops and Bishops of Ireland* (Dublin: John Mullany, 1859), 233.

60. *Appendix to Twentieth Report..., for the year 1853,* (1834), H.C. 1854, XXX, pt. i, 319; *Appendix to Twenty-fourth Report..., for the year 1857,* (2456-1), H.C. 1859, VII, 252–5; *Appendix to Thirty-first Report..., for the year 1864,* (3496), H.C. 1865, XIX, 262–5; *Appendix to Thirty-seventh Report..., for the year 1870,* 656–9.

61. Walsh, *Nano Nagle,* 209–18.

62. Burke Savage, *A Valiant Dublin Woman,* 235–8; Walsh, *Nano Nagle,* 217.

63. Walsh, *Nano Nagle,* 215.

64. Kavanagh, *Mixed Education,* 237–41; Walsh, *Nano Nagle,* 215–6.

65. *Rules and Constitutions, Chapter 2,* quoted in Consedine, *Listening Journey,* 407–8.

66. Consedine, *Listening Journey,* 219–22.

67. Ibid., 221.

68. *A Directory for the Religious of the Presentation Order According to the Practices of The Parent House, Founded in the Year 1775 By the Venerable Mother Nano Nagle, in Douglas Street, Cork,* (Cork: Wm. Hurley, 1850), 13.

69. *Rules and Constitutions,* Chapter 2, quoted in Consedine, *Listening Journey,* 407; *Presentation Directory,* 13.

70. Ibid., 13–14.

71. *Presentation Directory,* 14. The recommendation was that if possible, the clock should strike once every half hour.

72. National Archives of Ireland (hereafter NAI), ED 1, MS Files on Application.

73. *Appendix to Twenty-second Report..., for the year 1855,* (2142-11), H.C. 1856, XXVII, pt. ii, 42≠9. The General Lesson was a statement of the benign neighbourliness that should exist between Christians, compiled from the Scriptures by Dr. Richard Whately, the Anglican Archbishop of Dublin and a member of the Board of Commissioners until his resignation in 1853. The Commissioners required that the principles of the Lesson, or a Lesson of similar import approved by them, be strictly inculcated during the hours of combined instruction and a copy of the Lesson be hung up in each school. (Walsh, *Nano Nagle,* 211).

74. *Appendix to Twenty-second Report..., for the year 1855,* 42–9.

75. *Presentation Directory,* 20.

76. Ibid., 24–5.

77. Ibid., 41–2.

78. Ibid., 45–53.

79. *Appendix to Twenty-second Report ..., for the year 1855,* 122–26.

80. *Appendix to the Twenty-fifth Report ..., for the year 1858,* 168.

81. *Appendix to the Twenty-sixth Report ..., for the year 1859,* Vol. II, 136–37.

82. *Appendix to the Twenty-second Report ..., for the year 1855,* 122–26.

83. Ibid.

84. Ibid.

85. *Appendix to Twenty-eighth Report ..., for the year 1861,* 4.

86. *Presentation Directory,* 30–3.

87. Ibid., 41–2.

88. Ibid., 42–5. All writing materials were supplied by the Sisters.

89. Ibid., 45–7. The numbers in the groups depended on the size of the school.

90. Ibid.

91. Ibid.

92. Ibid., 48. The author noted that whilst the new skills may be more difficult, they were not more necessary.

93. Ibid., 48–9.

3

PART THREE
EDUCATION POLICY AND
CHANGE IN THE
TWENTIETH CENTURY

8 THE CHURCH OF IRELAND, THE STATE AND EDUCATION IN IRISH LANGUAGE AND IRISH HISTORY, 1920s-1950s

MARTINA RELIHAN

After the concession of Irish independence from Britain in 1922, the southern membership of the Church of Ireland was consigned to its new status as the alienated remainder of an erstwhile ascendancy class. The majority of its co-religionists were located in the northern six-county area which was to retain its links with Britain. In this radically changed political landscape in which the newly-established Irish Free State consciously presented itself as Catholic and Gaelic, the Church of Ireland found it incumbent upon itself to engage with the educational system of the new Irish state and specifically with its emphasis on the Irish language, the teaching of which was made compulsory in schools from the early 1920s.[1]

The Irish language was afforded a dominant curricular status that extended well beyond the mere teaching of it as one school subject.[2] A high standard of Irish was required for students wishing to enter the State's teacher training colleges and a sustained concentration on the language was maintained throughout the period of the student's training.[3] School textbooks of the period frequently presented material which reflected the new State's cultural and political agenda.[4]

While the difficulties which the Irish language policy posed for Protestant secondary schools were not as acute as those experienced in the primary sector, Protestant second-level establishments frequently articulated a strong antipathy towards the language policy and particularly resented the compulsory status afforded the language in State examinations from the late 1920s and the coupling of the study of it with the payment of capitation grants to schools. The Church of Ireland authorities perceived the cumulative effect of these policies as threatening to the identity of their schools at both primary and secondary levels.

Intermittent clashes persisted between the State and the Church of Ireland authorities on these issues until the mid-century period. Tensions gradually eased during the succeeding decades as the government began to relax its position on the role of the Irish language in the schools and the religious minority concomitantly became more comfortable with its position in the new Irish state.

The virulence of the language policy being pursued by the government was also intermittently contested by the Irish National Teachers' Organisation (INTO), which expressed its particular disquiet at the use of Irish as a teaching medium in the schools during the late 1930s–1940s.[5] Groups of Catholic parents, notably in the west of Ireland, articulated their concern at the implications of the policy for the teaching of the English language, a high competency in which they considered vital for the large proportion of their children who were destined to emigrate to Great Britain and the United States of America.[6] However, the policy presented particular difficulties for the Church of Ireland and for the smaller Protestant Churches, notably the Presbyterian Church. While a small minority of Irish Protestants actively participated in the Irish language revival movement, the great majority 'found it difficult to adapt to the narrow concept of nationalism cultivated around the language and which presented Irish as an exclusively Catholic-nationalist appendage.'[7] This chapter will focus on the position of the Church of Ireland as much the dominant of the Protestant Churches in the newly-independent Irish state, while making occasional reference to schools under Presbyterian management. Aspects of the difficulties encountered by the Church of Ireland and the other Protestant Churches in relation to the education system have been dealt with in works by Donald H. Akenson and Adrian Kelly.[8] Detailed studies of the implications of the State's Irish language policy for the Church of Ireland Training College (hereafter the CITC) have been undertaken by Susan Parkes and Valerie Jones.[9]

The chapter endeavours to provide an analysis of the engagement between the Church of Ireland and the State authorities in relation to a range of educational issues during the 1920s to 1950s.[10] It will, however, concentrate on the Church's reaction to the State's Irish language policy, which was the aspect of curricular policy destined to provide 'an early test of [Protestant] willingness and capacity to adjust to the new political regime.'[11] The analysis will also focus on the content and style of the arguments used by the Church of Ireland authorities in the presentation of their case to the State on the Irish language policy and related curricular questions. The State's response to these representations will be assessed in the light of the Church's approach. The degree to which the State accommodated Church of Ireland concerns will be evaluated through a critical examination of relevant primary and secondary source material.[12]

THE IRISH LANGUAGE POLICY OF THE IRISH FREE STATE AND THE NATIONAL PROGRAMME CONFERENCE, 1925–26

The Irish Free State assumed formal control over education on 1 February 1922. It proceeded immediately to prioritise the Irish language in the school curriculum. On that day, it issued a public notice, which was to take effect from the succeeding St. Patrick's Day, concerning the teaching of the Irish language in national schools. The language was to be taught for at least one full hour a day in all schools where there was a teacher competent to teach it. Schools that experienced difficulties in the implementation of the provision, were to communicate these difficulties to the Inspector of Irish Instruction in the National Education Office.

A New Programme of Instruction in National Schools was introduced at the beginning of the school year 1922–23. In response to earlier criticisms of what was regarded as the unwieldy nature of the school curriculum which had been introduced into schools by the National Board of Education in 1900, the new programme eliminated as compulsory subjects, drawing, elementary science, cookery and laundry, hygiene and nature study. Especially controversial was the stipulation that the work of the infant classes was to be conducted entirely through the medium of the Irish language.[13] While there was official acceptance that it would not be feasible to implement the latter measure immediately in a large proportion of schools, all schools were obliged to introduce the teaching of Irish for at least one hour per day.

In 1923 the religious minority succeeded in electing fourteen deputies to the national parliament, Dáil Éireann, out of a total of 153.[14] Thus parliament provided a potential forum for the Protestant members to express their reaction to the Irish language policy. They were diffident about utilising it for this purpose, however. Bowen (1983) depicts their initial stance in the Dáil as one of 'indignant marginality [which] rapidly evolved into one of indifference, estrangement and apathy.'[15] Deputy Thrift, who represented Trinity College Dublin, was relatively forthright in expressing his reservations about the compulsory Irish policy in a Dáil debate in 1924. He took issue with the notion 'that the development of Irish everywhere is necessary for the development of the national life.'[16] He opined that the policy of compulsion would have the effect of subverting 'the growing national demand of people throughout the country for an education which will fit them for their place in life combined with the mental and moral development which education ought to give them.'[17]

The following year, the religious minority was afforded an opportunity to articulate its position on the compulsory Irish issue and related educational questions when the Minister for Education, Eoin MacNeill (1867–1945), convened a National Programme Conference (NPC) of educational stakeholders in order to review the operation of the new education programme.[18] Representatives to the NPC were nominated on behalf of the school managers, the INTO, the General Council of County Councils, and the Irish language revival organisation, the Gaelic League, together with public representatives and school inspectors. The body was also to receive written submissions from individuals and interest groups and to conduct oral examinations of nineteen selected witnesses including the Professors of Education at Trinity College and University College Dublin, Edward P. Culverwell and Timothy J. Corcoran respectively. The most prominent Church of Ireland participant at the NPC was Rev. Kingsmill Moore, the principal of the CITC then located in Kildare Street in Dublin. He had held the position for the previous forty years and was widely regarded as the most influential figure of his generation in Church of Ireland education. While Kingsmill Moore attended the conference in his capacity as a school manager rather than as a representative of the Church of Ireland authorities *per se*, his attendance nonetheless constituted an opportunity for the Church to present its view of education policy to an important government-appointed forum. Initially he was a reluctant participant, baulking at the prospect of being, as he put it, 'among some twenty-five others whose aspirations and ideals promised the widest divergence of opinion', amongst whom he was destined to form 'a minority of one' for voting purposes.[19] These reservations proved to be unfounded, however, as the other conference delegates appeared to be able to ingratiate themselves with him with little difficulty. As he later recounted in his memoirs, 'from the first, in some inexplainable [*sic*] way, I found myself at home.'[20] His status as elder statesman was acknowledged by his being seated to the right of the chairman throughout the proceedings, except for one very cold day when it was suggested to him that he might be more comfortable being seated by the fire.[21]

Kingsmill Moore, notwithstanding the courtesy of his treatment at the conference, made no more than a perfunctory attempt at representing Church of Ireland concerns in relation to the Irish language policy in the schools at the NPC. This policy was copper-fastened at the conference. Its implementation was to have uncomfortable implications both for CITC and the Church of Ireland's network of primary schools. The controversial stipulation that infant classes were to be conducted entirely through the medium of Irish was slightly moderated at Kingsmill Moore's instigation and the teaching of English for a half-hour per day (before 10.30am) in the infant classes was permitted. Protestant bodies who presented written submissions to the conference indicated strong antipathy to the measure. The Protestant Teachers' Union proposed that it be 'eliminated' while the Church's Archbishop of Dublin, Dr Gregg, suggested that 'Infants should be taught in Irish only in Irish-speaking districts.'[22]

The other contentious provision of the new school programme (which emanated originally from the first NPC which had been convened by the INTO in 1920) was the stipulation that 'in the case of schools where the majority of the parents of the children object to having either Irish or English taught as an obligatory subject, their wishes should be complied with.'[23] The rationale for this stipulation was, in the opinion of the Chairman, Rev. McKenna, that 'there was a good probability that the schools in Ulster would be under the Department [of Education] and that the majority of these schools would object to Irish and could not be coerced into teaching it.'[24] In the interim, the report of the Boundary Commission of 1925 had confirmed the partition of the country along the lines of the Anglo-Irish Treaty of 1921. Antipathy towards the teaching of Irish was concentrated in Protestant schools in counties Cavan, Monaghan and Donegal, which straddled the Free State/Northern Ireland border.[25] Some forty of these schools had since 1922 utilised the provision in order to opt out of teaching Irish. The majority of the members of the NPC were unenthusiastic at the prospect of immediately abolishing the rule, settling instead for a continuation of the 'privilege' afforded to such schools 'during the tenure of office of the present teachers or for a period of ten years whichever be the longer period.'[26] The wording of this provision was far from watertight. Its loopholes, such as the calculation of the date on which a particular school had opted out of the teaching of Irish and which obviously determined the date of the commencement of the ten-year period stipulated in the revised rule, were exploited by a number of Protestant schools during the late 1920s and 1930s.[27]

The position of the Irish language pervaded the discussion on virtually all other subject areas of the curriculum and had the effect of limiting curricular scope in order to maximise the time provided for the teaching of Irish. This trend had been clearly established by the programme issued in 1922. The programme had drastically curtailed the number of obligatory subjects from that which had pertained since the introduction of the revised curriculum for schools in 1900. The consideration of the course content of the remaining subjects was also undertaken with a view to determining the degree to which subject material could be manipulated in order to further national aims. This was notably the case in relation to music, history and geography. One conference member was adamant that only Irish music should be taught in the schools as an antidote to the contemporary obsession with the 'foreign and jazz-like' and deplored the prospect that any 'loophole should be left for the introduction of Music-Hall singing.'[28]

Nationalist considerations heavily infiltrated the discussion as to whether history and geography should be included as obligatory subjects in the curriculum. One school inspector was in favour of the inclusion of geography as an obligatory subject so long as the course content excluded countries outside Ireland.[29] In the case of history, Brother Kelleher, representing the Christian Brothers, considered the inclusion of history as an obligatory subject essential as it was 'on a par almost with the language.'[30] The approach to be adopted towards the teaching of the subject was clearly one of some sensitivity for the Church of Ireland authorities. In written submissions to the conference they expressed concern that history could be utilised to facilitate a narrowly understood (Catholic) nationalist agenda with the consequent exclusion of other dimensions of Irish history. For example, the Limerick Diocesan Education Board, in its submission, contended that '...the history of Ireland cannot be truthfully taught without reference to the lives and achievements of men of all races who during past centuries have made Ireland their home...'[31] It was finally agreed that history should be included as an obligatory subject in all schools of two or more qualified teachers. The State's singular failure to reconcile 'the dichotomies of the good Irishman and the evil Englishman, the poor tenant and the cruel landlord'[32] in the version of Irish history which it subsequently presented in the schools was to be a source of unease to the Church of Ireland authorities during the succeeding decades.

Kingsmill Moore served as a member of the sub-committee which was charged with the formulation of the final report of the conference. At one of the concluding sessions of the NPC he proposed an effusive vote of thanks to the chairman. He noted, 'I myself having signed the Report have done something which I could not imagine possible some time ago.'[33] He did not elaborate on the reason for this *volte-face*. While the Church of Ireland was not afforded specific representation at the NPC Conference, its most powerful educational figure, Kingsmill Moore, was presented with an effective opportunity to enter into dialogue with representatives of the majority tradition on educational questions. He did not, however, proffer a consciously articulated view of the Irish language issue from the perspective of the religious minority. His approach contrasted with that of the IPTU and the Church of Ireland Boards of Education, all of whom were significantly less diffident in their written communications with the NPC.

The report of the second NPC was adopted by the government in May 1926. In 1932, the Fianna Fáil party, under the leadership of Éamon de Valera, assumed office and remained in power for an uninterrupted period of sixteen years. Coolahan (1981) notes the commitment of the new Minister for Education, Thomas Derrig, 'to school programmes in which the Irish language and history would combine to foster a patriotic and Gaelic outlook' and his 'impatience with the rate of progress in the promotion of Irish in the schools.'[34] Accordingly, he issued *The Revised Programme of Primary Instruction* which became operative in the schools from September 1934. Under its terms the concession agreed by the NPC that English could be taught for half an hour per day in the infant classes was dropped, with the study of English as a school subject rendered 'optional' in First Class. The syllabus in mathematics was restricted in order to facilitate 'more rapid progress and more effective work in the teaching of Irish and in the development of teaching through Irish.'[35] It could be reasonably argued that Derrig's approach as reflected in the revised programme constituted no more than a tightening of the policy which had been introduced during the Free State era in this regard.

The Board of Education of the Church of Ireland lost little time in expressing its unease in relation to the revised programme, especially the stipulation concerning the teaching of infant classes entirely through the medium of Irish. Representatives of the board held a meeting with the minister in January 1935 and he endeavoured to give 'due consideration' to the views of the deputation while emphasising the unique position of the language in the country, one which was 'without precedent in the history of education in other countries.'[36]

Some five years later, the Board of Education decided to conduct an inquiry in relation to the use of Irish in its schools, with replies received from almost all its schools in the south of Ireland, which numbered just under 500. The board's report of 1942 noted that the 'great majority' of its teachers were 'highly qualified' in Irish. Nonetheless dissatisfaction was expressed that 'the teaching of Irish [had] rendered the work of the school as a whole less efficient', with parents generally hostile towards the subject and with the vast majority of school managers opposed to the teaching of Irish 'on the present compulsory basis.'[37] The INTO was at this time also reflecting the disquiet of its membership towards the government's language policy. The Minister for Education was similarly unwilling to entertain the organisation's misgivings.[38]

The educational authorities of the Church of Ireland were clearly unhappy with the dominant position of Irish in the school curriculum. Ó Buachalla (1988) contends that, in their attempts to dilute the policy, 'the Protestant Churches were totally unsuccessful with the Fianna Fáil governments of the forties.'[39]

CHURCH OF IRELAND PRIMARY SCHOOLS AND TEACHER TRAINING

In 1927 there were 516 primary schools within the Irish Free State jurisdiction under Church of Ireland management, with just under half of them catering for less than twenty pupils.[40] By 1950, a mere 6 per cent of these schools had in excess of fifty pupils on roll. The Church of Ireland authorities viewed the maintenance of this network of schools as essential to its very survival as a distinct entity in the south of the country and to its capacity to act as a counter to the State's representation of itself as a Catholic/Gaelic nation.[41]

From 1928, the Board of Education of the General Synod of the Church of Ireland became actively involved with the issue of facilitating the transportation of Protestant schoolchildren to their nearest Protestant school. The authorities feared that those living in remote areas far from such an establishment would be left with no choice but to attend a Catholic school, where they would encounter 'Roman Catholic doctrine and practices which are not in accordance with [their] reformed faith.'[42]

By 1931, the board had quantified the problem and calculated that there were some 1,500 Protestant children outside reasonable walking distance of a

Protestant school. In its opinion it behoved the government to help subvent a school transport scheme and emphasised '…the paramount duty…of training up the children…in the faith of their fathers and of providing daily teaching in the word of God and the doctrines of the Church of Ireland.'[43] A member of the Board, Canon Pratt, appealed to the generosity of the government and found it unthinkable that it would 'treat in niggardly fashion the appeal of a law-abiding and deserving minority.'[44] Canon Pratt's confidence was not misplaced. The Department of Education had already been providing boat and van services for children of all denominations who were living in island and/or remote locations. In 1934, it established a specific transport scheme for Protestant children. Under its terms the department was to contribute £5 annually per child subject to an average daily number of at least five eligible children in a particular location. The Church of Ireland authorities were to contribute a minimum of £1500 per annum towards the running of the scheme.[45] By 1936, the department was grant-aiding a total of sixty-one van services for Protestant children, thirteen of which were operating in County Cork, eight in County Wicklow, with the remainder scattered throughout the country.[46]

The priority which the Church afforded the issue is reflected by its commitment to fund a further twenty-three schemes exclusively from its own resources with grants being advanced for the provision of bus and rail fares and, where necessary, accommodation near the schools concerned. These schemes were funded from a combination of parochial, diocesan and central Church sources. The Board of Education Report of 1937 noted that the cumulative effect of the schemes being funded either solely by the Church itself, or in partnership with the Department of Education, was enabling the provision of a Protestant education for some 800 children in schools under Church of Ireland management, in the process rescuing an estimated twenty schools from possible closure.[47]

While the Department of Education normally required an enrolment of twenty pupils in order to recognise a school, it deemed ten pupils to be sufficient if a child did not have reasonable access to a school of his/her denomination. In practice it continued to fund schools unless average enrolment fell below seven pupils. Akenson (1975) views the concession as one which '…reinforce[d] the tendency for Protestant schools to be small, inadequate, one-teacher institutions, even while it simultaneously relieved some of the dangers to the religious identity of the Protestant children.'[48] It is nonetheless difficult to argue with Milne's (2006) contention that the government-subsidised transport scheme was advantageous to the Protestant community in the Free State as Protestant children '… attended schools consistent in ethos with their homes, yet within the state system, providing them as it were with a congenial arc to carry them through the somewhat perilous waters of political and cultural change.'[49] The government-subsidised transport scheme was a crucial element in the consolidation of the position of Church of Ireland primary schools in the new Irish state.

The dominant position of the Irish language in the school curriculum constituted a more intractable problem for Church of Ireland schools. As mentioned above, opposition to the measure was unsurprisingly concentrated in schools located in the northern counties of Cavan, Monaghan and Donegal. Both proximity to the border with Northern Ireland and the relative strength of their numbers in these areas combined to embolden Protestants to articulate their position on the issue in unequivocal terms. Organised protests from groups of parents and school managers against the teaching of Irish in their schools received a consistently measured response from school inspectors, who were in the main successful in encouraging them to adopt an incremental approach to the introduction of the language.[50] Protests by groups of Catholic parents to the language question were by contrast isolated affairs which were easily fended off by the Department of Education. One such protest was initiated by a group of parents in a school in the Connemara Gaeltacht area who regarded 'a sound English education' as a prerequisite for the majority of the pupils whose destiny was emigration to America or Britain.[51] A similar protest by parents of pupils of a Catholic school in Newmarket, County Cork was more concerted. The parents signed a plebiscite against the teaching of Irish and visited the school as a group while insisting that Irish should not be taught to their children 'whether the Government sanctioned it or not.'[52] In a communication to the Department of Education they noted that 'the school [was] a small little school in the middle of a bog', the pupils of which were destined 'either to go out in service or go to America to help us …. so we want as little Irish as possible.'[53]

Protestant parental opposition to the teaching of the language tended to emphasise perceived practical problems in relation to their children learning Irish. One parent from County Donegal informed the Department of Education that, 'I do not wish my children to learn Irish as it will be of no use to them in any country they may go and very little in this country.'[54] However, one unusually forthright school manager in County Monaghan informed the department that it 'would never make any success of the policy of trying to force people to learn Irish, and there is not a Protestant in my district in favour of it, and you will please remember, this is a Protestant school.'[55] There were also isolated examples of similar protests outside the border counties, notably in Cork city and Wicklow town, both of which had relatively significant Protestant populations.[56]

The departmental response to this disquiet was carefully measured. While formal derogations from the Irish language policy were not proffered by the officials and school inspectors, the policy was in practice diluted in Protestant schools. Schools were typically cajoled into accepting the introduction of Irish for a half an hour per day. Subsequently, gentle pressure was exerted to extend this to one hour per day. This incremental approach towards the implementation of the policy facilitated the gradual easing of Protestant schools into the language programme.[57] In the process, confrontation with parents, managers and teachers was minimised. While teachers were required to obtain a 'Bilingual Certificate' which qualified them to teach general school subjects through the medium of Irish, department officials adopted a relaxed approach to the provision for Protestant teachers, usually allowing them protracted periods of time to obtain the qualification.[58]

The Irish language issue was the area of government education policy which was the source of most contention between the State authorities and the religious minority. There is considerable evidence to suggest that in relation to the implementation of the policy in Protestant primary schools, the State was prepared to make significant practical concessions towards the convictions of the religious minority and to treat it with a measure of both tolerance and sensitivity.[59]

The CITC, which was located in Kildare Place in central Dublin, found itself caught off-guard in its dealings with the new Irish language requirements. In tandem with its curricular emphasis on the Irish language, the new state introduced stringent Irish language requirements for entry into the teacher training colleges.[60] The colleges had been 'gaelicised' by the late 1920s, with all subjects being taught through the medium of the language at St Patrick's Training College in Dublin by the 1930s.[61] While the stringency of these requirements impacted on the Catholic-managed colleges,[62] difficulties at the CITC were particularly acute owing to its inattention to the language during the preceding decades and the dilatory nature of its response to the issue during the early 1920s. The college was at this time also attempting to grapple with the abrupt loss of over half of its student body following the failure of its attempt to retain its cohort of students from Northern Ireland in the immediate post-independence period.[63]

The tardiness of the college's response to the exigencies of the new situation was undoubtedly compounded, if not actually largely determined, by the approach of its principal, Kingsmill Moore. He was coming to the close of his long tenure in office and was grappling with adapting to the college's dramatically altered position within an independent Irish state.[64]

The situation was ameliorated with the appointment of E.C. Hodges in 1928. The new appointee clearly realised the urgency of dealing with the Irish language issue in a realistic fashion. He accepted the imperative that the college should provide a steady stream of teachers suitably qualified to teach the Irish language as an essential component in the survival of the Church of Ireland's network of primary schools.[65] This emphasis on the language was grounded in pragmatism as it was incumbent on the college to adjust to the Irish language requirements if it was to survive as an educational establishment.

The college was greatly facilitated in its endeavours to comply with the Irish language requirements with the foundation by the State under the management of the Church of Ireland of the 'preparatory college', Colaiste Moibhi. This functioned as an effective feeder-school for CITC from the early 1930s. It was established by the State under the patronage of the Church of Ireland Archbishop of Dublin in 1927. Over the succeeding decades, until its closure in the mid-1990s, it was destined to become a mainstay for CITC in the provision of candidates suitably qualified in the Irish language. The college was established, along with six other Catholic-managed institutions, as part of a government scheme of what were styled 'preparatory colleges.'[66] These colleges were secondary schools conducted entirely through the medium of Irish and demanded a very high standard of Irish from entrants. Most were located at or near Gaeltacht/Irish-speaking areas in the west of Ireland. They were designed to provide the teacher training colleges with a supply of fluent Irish-speaking students. Entry requirements were diluted for those applying for Colaiste Moibhi, which was initially located in Moibhi Road, Glasnevin, in north Dublin. Candidates for the college were granted concessions by the Department of Education until well into the 1930s and unlike the Catholic-managed colleges the entrance examination papers were presented in English. While the Church of Ireland Archbishop of Dublin, Dr. Gregg, was entirely supportive of the establishment of the college, his endorsement of it was not grounded in any new-found enthusiasm for the study of the language. He encouraged Church of Ireland children to study Irish 'whatever might be their private feelings …because this was a government regulation and they could not secure posts without it.'[67]

As the college established itself over the succeeding years, it attracted fulsome praise from the unlikely quarter of *The Irish Times* newspaper, which had heretofore adopted a negative editorial stance on the effect of the Irish language policy on Protestant schools. In 1926 the paper actually recommended the withdrawal of Church of Ireland schools from government control if it failed to negotiate an alternative to 'the tyranny of compulsion.'[68] In an article published in 1938, however, the paper lauded the work of the college and referred to its students as 'the Reconcilers of the Present and the Past.'[69] In another article on the topic, the same writer waxed lyrical about a visit to the college and noted the 'happy, clever-looking girls in their pretty uniform… [who] soon become fluent in Irish, the language used in college life, and can presently say, as one of them expressed it, "all we need to say and more".'[70] While there was undoubtedly some hyperbole in the depiction of Colaiste Moibhi as a Gaelic haven for Protestants, the college clearly succeeded in providing the CITC with significant numbers of students who were proficient in the Irish language, which helped to surmount the difficulties which the latter college had been experiencing in this regard.

SCHOOL TEXTBOOKS AND PROTESTANT SCHOOLS

The Board of Education of the General Synod had appreciable difficulty in reaching an accommodation with the Irish state in relation to school textbooks during the decades following the 1922 political settlement. Disagreement revolved around such issues as the tendency of many school textbooks to unquestioningly equate Irish nationality, language revival and Catholicism; allusions of a negative nature to 'England' and the perceived role of 'England' in Irish affairs; and the use of a historical narrative which relied exclusively on the Catholic-nationalist perspective of Irish history while by implication denigrating or ignoring the Protestant conception of the issue.[71]

The suitability of Irish language textbooks for Protestant schools concentrated the minds of the Church of Ireland authorities from the early 1920s. In its report to the General Synod of 1923, the Board of Education noted that '…there are expressions in the Irish textbooks now in use in National Schools which violate the principles hitherto recognized in National Schools that there should be no interference with the religious beliefs of any child attending them…'[72]

Jones (1992) summarises some of the aspects of the content of textbooks which offended Protestant susceptibilities, such as 'frequent references to the departed in Irish' as they regarded the practice of 'praying for the dead in Purgatory as "unscriptural", together with incidental references to Mass, Confession and Holy Communion.[73]

The Minister for Education, Eoin MacNeill, reassured the Church authorities that school inspectors would not expect Protestant schools to teach any material deemed to be in contravention of Protestant beliefs. In the event of books, used either in the schools or in the training college, being regarded as unacceptable to the Protestant authorities, he would see to it that equivalent acceptable books were substituted. The Board of Education exhorted their school managers to encourage the teachers in their schools to be vigilant in ensuring the omission from their lessons of '…any teaching or phrases they may meet not in accordance with Protestant beliefs.'[74] While Minister MacNeill's reassurances had the immediate effect of placating the Board of Education, the practical issue of the provision of textbooks considered suitable for this small minority of pupils was not meaningfully addressed by his department. Thus, the provision of textbooks which the Church deemed suitable for use in its schools was an issue which was destined to perturb the Board of Education for a further period of some thirty years.

By 1932 the Department of Education had formulated its general procedures in relation to the sanctioning of school textbooks. It envisaged the compilation of three separate lists of such books, the first of which catered for all schools with the other two catering for exclusively Catholic or Protestant establishments. The Church of Ireland authorities experienced practical difficulties in relation to the implementation of this policy. During the 1930s, the department acceded to the board's request to permit it to recommend books for use in its schools which were not included in the official lists. The board was, however, obliged to apply on an annual basis to the department for renewal of the concession. The board continued to engage the department in relation to the issue throughout the 1940s and noted that 'some of the books in the existing list do not commend themselves on religious grounds.'[75] It would appear that the department acceded to Church requests without argument, with the exercise being somewhat perfunctorily referred to in the Board of Education reports of the 1930s and 1940s.

The issue of the provision of a suitable history textbook for use in Protestant schools was a source of specific difficulty for the Church authorities throughout this period. The Protestant authorities vented their disquiet with the state policy of sanctioning textbooks which presented 'versions of the past designed to serve present needs.'[76] In the late 1930s, frustration with the Catholic/nationalist slant of the officially sanctioned textbooks culminated in a Board of Education decision to hold a competition for such a textbook suitable for use in Protestant schools. The competition was advertised in the national press and offered a prize of one hundred guineas to the winning entry.[77] The textbook chosen, entitled *A History of Ireland*, was written by a Dublin-based secondary school teacher, Dora Casserley, and was published in 1941.[78] The textbook was widely used in Protestant schools and had achieved sales of 26,000 by 1947.[79]

A sense of mutual unease in relation to the textbook issue persisted between the Church and the department with the latter body conceding in 1950 that there were 'undoubtedly some grounds for grievances in relation to the textbooks as 'the tone and outlook of many of them was undoubtedly Catholic.'[80]Canon Harvey, the Rector of Sandford Parish, Dublin, controversially opined to the General Synod of that year that school textbooks contained 'a flood of undiluted nationalism.'[81]

It could be argued that the Department of Education failed to coherently define its attitude towards the question of the sanctioning of suitable textbooks for Protestant schools during the early decades of the independent Irish state. It delivered *ad hoc* responses to specific issues which were raised by the Church of Ireland authorities, notably difficulties relating to Irish and history textbooks. Departmental officials seemed to perceive the unacceptability of certain material in textbooks solely in terms of possible offence to the specific religious tenets of Protestantism. Some of the material contained in Irish, English and history textbooks casually equated gaelicisation, nationalism and Catholicism and portrayed England's historical role in Ireland in exclusively pejorative terms.[82] The Board of Education, for its part, sought either specific textbooks for Protestant schools or, alternatively, books which had been sanctioned for general use in schools which were purged of references which they considered offensive. Thus, the Church of Ireland authorities sought to position themselves in isolation from the pervasive cultural influences of the Irish state rather than encouraging a process of dialogue with it. Akenson (1975) contends that the Protestants of the State were variously 'treated with great generosity' and 'hectored, bullied or ignored' in their position as a religious and cultural minority.[83] In the State's dealings with the minority on the school textbook issue, it is possible to discern elements of all of these characteristics. Generosity was certainly in evidence at the level of rhetoric, especially during the 1920s, but the department did sanction a significant amount of material that the religious minority regarded as unacceptable. As Protestants constituted such a small minority of the school-going population, a mere 2 per cent by the late 1940s, they could ultimately be ignored in respect of the provision of textbooks which the Church of Ireland Board of Education deemed to be suitable for use in its schools.

THE POSITION OF PROTESTANT SECOND-LEVEL SCHOOLS

In tandem with the situation pertaining in its national schools, many of the Free State's fifty-five Protestant secondary schools were too small to be viable. This situation was compounded by the absence of a centralised administrative structure for the schools. The Incorporated Society for the Promotion of Protestant Schools in Ireland controlled a total of eleven schools, with the Erasmus Smith Board controlling a further three. The schools catered for a total student body of some 3,700, but over half of these were tiny establishments with less than forty students on roll.[84] The schools were funded mainly through an unwieldy system of endowments the administration of which was placed under the control of the Minister for Education in the early 1920s.[85] White (1975) depicts Protestant secondary schools as '…a haphazard growth of private academies and charitable foundations, [which] were far too miscellaneous to be called a system of education…'[86] The 'benevolent founders' of these schools established them with 'the twin purposes of preserving the reformed faith and redeeming the little papists from superstition and witchcraft.'[87]

The majority of the pupils attended Dublin-based schools such as St. Andrew's College on St. Stephen's Green, which was under Presbyterian management and had a total of 181 pupils in 1932.[88]The High School in Harcourt St, under Church of Ireland management, had 206 pupils in 1928.[89]The schools had operated within self-contained worlds of Anglo-Irish privilege, which rendered them unprepared for the political upheavals of the 1920s. The writer Dorothy Macardle, who was a pupil at Alexandra College during the pre-World War I period, describes it as a 'microcosm of that world of the Anglo-Irish ascendancy, with all its extraordinary privilege, with its talent and creativeness, its social conscience, its grace, vigour and charm.'[90] It was, however, oblivious to the 'tide of change' and the 'surge of revolution' which was 'beating about the walls.'[91] Journalist Mary Manning (1905–1999), who attended Alexandra College in the height of the political turmoil of the early 1920s, recalls how as students they 'rode (their) bicycles through ambushes and got pushed into shelters when the bullets were flying, and heard the British tanks patrolling the streets at night and paid no heed.'[92] Even more dramatically, the principal of the college, in her report for the 1922–23 school year, noted that the 'breaking up party' held at the end of June 'unfortunately coincided with the blowing up of the Four Courts which kept away a great many of our guests.'[93]

The management bodies of Protestant secondary schools responded slowly to the Free State's curricular emphasis on the Irish language. At a meeting held in May 1922, the Governors of the Erasmus Smith schools decided that any consideration of the matter of the teaching of Irish in their schools should be postponed.[94] No particular sense of urgency attended their deliberations on the issue at their meeting the following month when it was resolved 'that the headmaster should consult the parents of the pupils in order to ascertain their wishes on the matter.'[95] The authorities at Alexandra College adopted a similarly dilatory approach. In June 1923, the head mistress informed the council that Irish had been introduced as an optional subject in the college, with the college's governing council noting that it would require 'further consideration before including it in the obligatory curriculum.'[96]

Unsurprisingly, such prevarication on the part of the schools' authorities was reflected in their level of participation in the state examinations in Irish during this period. At a time when Catholic secondary schools presented virtually all of their students for examination in the subject, the results of the Intermediate Examination of 1925 as published by the Department of Education for male students showed that none of the pupils of the Protestant schools listed attempted Irish.

From 1928, Irish was made a compulsory subject for the Intermediate Certificate examination, thus forcing Protestant school authorities to tackle the issue with more urgency. The Chairman of the Board of Governors of the High School, the Bishop of Cashel, Rev. Robert Miller, responded to the measure with a singular lack of enthusiasm. On the occasion of the school's annual prize-giving in 1926, he ruefully contemplated the school's situation. He noted that failure of students to comply with the new regulations meant their effective exclusion from the examination, thus precluding them from any prospect of obtaining a scholarship. Facilities would be provided for those children wishing to learn 'modern Irish' but Rev. Miller noted that 'as the mouthpiece of the parents I have not failed to make it quite clear to the authorities and to the public that our parents most emphatically do not wish for compulsory Irish.'[97] Their children 'must in large numbers at the present time look forward to earning their living elsewhere than in the Free State' while parents looked to '... the great Commonwealth of Nations to which we are proud to belong and (to) other undeveloped countries of the world (for) opportunities for their children for which a knowledge of Irish is of no advantage...'[98]

Wallace (2004) refers to the Protestant 'aversion to compulsory Irish', which he regards as 'probably also a symptom of a deeper sense of alienation from the new state', with Protestant authorities compelled into a reluctant acceptance of the new political reality.[99] The uneasy response to this reality was encapsulated in a circular letter from the principal of the High School to the parents of pupils in 1933. Mr. Bennett was careful to emphasise that according to school rules no boy would be compelled to learn Irish. He also pointed out, however, the perilous implications for the school of significant numbers of pupils taking this decision, as state grants would only be paid in respect of 'recognised' pupils and only pupils attempting Irish would be so 'recognised.'[100] The level of the grants received also impacted on teachers' pensions. He notes that boys refusing to take Irish were in effect saving the present government money and in the event of all parents refusing to allow their children to study the subject, the school would either have to cease operations or charge significantly increased fees. Bennett noted the futility of any attempt at exercising political influence as 'the government is quite indifferent to arguments and protests from us.'[101] He was careful to reassure parents that the Irish teacher 'is an old pupil of this school' and that he had found 'that those who take Irish are not in any way behind the others.'[102]

The performance of Protestant students in Irish at the state examinations was lacklustre. While all sixteen candidates who attempted the Intermediate Examination in the King's Hospital School in 1930 presented Irish, only two of them were successful. Five years later, the situation showed marked improvement with twenty-three out of twenty-five students succeeding in the examination. Meaningful engagement with the subject was singularly limited in some Protestant schools. While the High School presented all its twenty-one Intermediate Certificate candidates for the Irish examination in 1935, only five of them were successful.[103] It would appear that in most of the schools the effort to introduce Irish was motivated more by the necessity to comply with the department's regulations than by a genuine desire to develop the study of the language in their schools.

In 1950 the Department of Education presented an internal report on the state of the Irish language in Protestant secondary schools to the then minister, Richard Mulcahy. The report viewed the standard of Irish as being contingent on the attitude towards the subject of the manager of the relevant school.[104] The headmaster at St. Andrew's received favourable mention as, though he was an Englishman, '... he decided on his appointment as headmaster to give Irish a secure place in the programme and took immediate steps to place the teaching of the language in competent hands...'[105]Others were 'frankly hostile to Irish.' Notable in this regard was the management of Glengara Park School in Dun Laoghaire, Co. Dublin. The headmistress there was concerned lest the study of the language should spoil 'the good English accent' of the students and she was also of the view that teachers of Irish were 'socially very much inferior to the pupils.'[106] While she unsurprisingly changed Irish teachers with 'amazing rapidity', she felt obliged for financial reasons to maintain her connection with the department.[107]

The report attributed the chief weakness in the system as regards the standard of Irish to the poor competence of pupils in the language on entry to the schools. This was especially the case when pupils had received their elementary schooling in private schools or from governesses or private tutors who had perhaps come from Northern Ireland, England or further afield. The report emphasised the relative independence of most Protestant schools in respect of the state examinations. The language was not required for entry to Trinity College or the College of Surgeons. Pupils could secure positions 'in the big commercial houses and in industry', without any knowledge of Irish. The 'armed forces of the British Crown' was another career option which students could pursue independently of the Irish requirement. The report concluded by noting that, while the Protestant population was not large, it was 'extremely powerful financially and (was) able to provide for its own young people irrespective of Irish not only in this country but also overseas.'[108]

The management bodies of Protestant secondary schools were placed in an invidious position by the political settlement of 1922. Their loyalty towards the new state was at best equivocal. This situation was exacerbated by the State's Irish language policy.[109]While their response to the introduction of the language into their schools during the 1920s was dilatory, it became incumbent upon them to grapple with the issue thereafter as Irish became compulsory for state examinations and school funding was based on capitation grants which were contingent on pupils studying Irish.[110] Throughout the 1930s and 1940s, Protestant secondary schools presented substantially increased numbers of their pupils for the state examinations in Irish. Nonetheless, the Department of Education in its report on the position of Protestant secondary schools of 1950 was generally unimpressed with the progress achieved by the schools in relation to the language. It was at pains to emphasise the relative prosperity of the Protestant community and its ability to encourage its young people towards career choices that could be pursued independently of the study of Irish.[111]

CONCLUSION

Early in 1922, the newly appointed chief executive of the Irish Free State's education system, Patrick Bradley, disbanded the National Board of Education Commissioners who had administered the system under the British administration. He carefully noted that, while the new administration was fully committed to furthering the indigenous Irish culture and language in the schools, it would actively welcome the advice of the religious minority which the National Board was mainly seen to represent, in assessing '...schemes of education...' which might prove difficult for this minority, while they may '...fully commend themselves to the majority of the population...'[112] In fact the new administration pursued 'schemes of education' with scant regard for the susceptibilities of Irish Protestants. The focus of its education policy was reflected in its single-minded pursuit of a narrow Catholic/nationalist agenda.

This paper has endeavoured to probe the relationship of the Church of Ireland and the Irish Free State within the context of the fractious socio-political climate in Ireland during the period 1922-1950. Akenson (1975) contends that the Church was favourably treated by the government in relation to freedom of religious practice but insensitively dealt with as regards its broader cultural concerns.[113] This dichotomy was clearly reflected in the State's handling of the issue of the provision of textbooks deemed suitable by the Church of Ireland authorities for use in their schools. The State was satisfied once the Church was not required to use material which was contrary to the tenets of its religious beliefs. It displayed little awareness of Protestant sensitivities in relation to a significant proportion of material in Irish, English and history textbooks which sometimes promoted a virulent form of Catholic/Irish nationalism, made disparaging references to England as a country or made frequent incidental references to Catholic Church practices.[114]

The State's Irish language policy was implemented with particular vigour in the country's national schools. Many Protestant schools located near the border with Northern Ireland, in counties Cavan, Monaghan and Donegal, actively contested the policy. Protestant resistance outside of these areas was isolated and sporadic. School inspectors and department officials were circumspect in their dealings with the managers, parents and teachers of these schools and implemented the language policy in them incrementally.[115] The government insistence on a high standard of Irish both for entry into the teacher training colleges and in the teacher training courses themselves created difficulties for the Church of Ireland managed college, the CITC. The situation was ameliorated from the late 1920s with the foundation by the government in 1927 of the 'preparatory college', Colaiste Moibhi, and by the Irish language policy pursued in the college by E.C. Hodges who served as principal from 1928.[116]Protestant secondary schools were not as acutely affected by the language policy. Nonetheless, the State's stipulations in 1928 and 1934 respectively that Irish was compulsory for passing state examinations and the coupling of capitation grants for secondary schools with the numbers of pupils studying Irish during the same period was widely resented by the management of these schools.[117]

The Church of Ireland was consistently vigilant to couch its arguments on the language policy in terms which emphasised its objections to it on specifically pedagogical grounds. For example, it complained that aspects of the policy such as the teaching of the infant classes more or less exclusively through Irish and the teaching of general school subjects through the medium of the language in national schools, were pedagogically unsound. At second-level the language was regarded as having little value as regards a pupil's future career prospects. The Church authorities were, however, unwilling to articulate their difficulties with the policy on the basis of the inability of a religious and cultural minority with a qualified loyalty to the new State to identify with the Irish language. Farren (1995) notes that the Protestant authorities presented their case on the language policy 'on educational and practical grounds rather than on political or sectarian grounds.'[118] He speculates as to whether objections predicated purely on the political or sectarian aspects of the policy 'would have won any sympathy let alone any concessions whatever.'[119]

The State's educational policies were heavily concentrated on the utilisation of the schools to revive the Irish language as the vernacular language of the people. The language was also to function as a talisman for the independent Irish State. It was closely associated with an exclusive definition of Irish identity as Catholic/Gaelic. In the light of these associations, it was unsurprising that the prominence afforded the language by the State was viewed as provocative by most Protestants. The consequent interaction between the Church of Ireland authorities and the State on this question constitutes something of a litmus test by which to assess the treatment of Protestants in the Free State during this era.

Such an investigation of the Protestant position cannot be confined to a narrow consideration of the impact of what became popularly known as the compulsory Irish policy. In formulating the curricular policy for the new Irish state, the Government was acutely conscious of utilising the education system as a means of binding the citizenry to a Catholic/Gaelic concept of the new entity. Thus, the content of the various school subjects, notably English and history, was infused with a sense of national fervour and teachers were actively encouraged by school inspectors to foster a Gaelic atmosphere in their classrooms.

Conciliatory rhetoric was certainly in evidence. The State was seen to behave generously towards the minority notably in the provision of state-subsidised transport for Church of Ireland national schools in remote locations and the establishment of a dedicated Protestant 'preparatory college', Colaiste Moibhi. While the State was, for its part, conciliatory in its approach towards individual Protestant schools and teachers in relation to the implementation of the Irish language policy, it refused either to alter the policy or to offer the Church of Ireland authorities any formal derogation from it. The approach of the latter consisted predominantly in seeking to effect a dilution or alteration to aspects of the language policy, neither of which the Government was prepared to concede.

In the period immediately succeeding the establishment of the Irish state, the Church of Ireland community was a beleaguered and bewildered minority. While it largely retained its socio-economic privileges, it was shorn of the trappings of ascendancy power, and shocked by its abrupt fall from grace.[120] In this regard, it is difficult to disagree with the view of White (1975) that '... the Catholic [found] that the presumptions [were] in his favour. He acquire[d] membership of the nation by being born into the majority, and he [could] suit himself about the other conditions.'[121] In the decades succeeding the foundation of the Irish state, it was a luxury which was not afforded the Protestant minority, which was involved in a frequently painful attempt at defining its position in relation to the new entity. This adaptation was especially problematic in the area of education, as the State embarked upon an ill-fated attempt at the gaelicisation of the schools while in the process displaying no more than a sporadic and perfunctory regard for the perceived interests of its Protestant population.

NOTES

1. The teaching of Irish was made compulsory in all national schools for at least one hour per day from St Patrick's Day, 1922. The new Programme of Instruction in National Schools was introduced at the beginning of the school year, 1922–23. See Áine Hyland & Kenneth Milne (eds), *Irish Educational Documents Volume II* (Dublin: CICE, 1992), 86–96.
2. Martina Relihan, 'The Church of Ireland and its Relationship with the Irish Education System, 1922–1950 with Particular Reference to the Irish Language and Gaelic Culture' (unpublished PhD Thesis, University College Dublin, 2008), 94–97.
3. Adrian Kelly, *Compulsory Irish – Language and Education in Ireland 1870s–1970s* (Dublin: Irish Academic Press, 2002), 65–86.
4. Relihan, 'The Church of Ireland', 255–323.
5. Kelly, *Compulsory Irish*, 49–53.
6. ED/File No. 20930 Box 457, National Archives of Ireland (NAI).
7. Kelly, *Compulsory Irish*, 29. Ernest Blythe, the Minister for Finance in the Free State government 1922–1932, and the playwright Sean O'Casey were amongst the most prominent members of the Church of Ireland active in the Irish revival movement, the Gaelic League.
8. Donald H. Akenson, *A Mirror to Kathleen's Face* (Montreal: McGill-Queen's University Press, 1975); Kelly, *Compulsory Irish*.
9. Susan Parkes, *Kildare Place: The History of the Church of Ireland Training College 1811–1969* (Dublin: Church of Ireland College of Education, 1984); Valerie Jones, 'Recruitment and Formation of Students into the Church of Ireland Training College 1922–1961', (unpublished MLitt thesis, Trinity College Dublin, 1989).
10. Relihan, 'The Church of Ireland'.
11. Sean Farren, *The Politics of Irish Education 1920–65* (Belfast: Queen's University, 1995), 115.
12. Minutes of the National Programme Conference (1925–26), which finalised curricular policy during the Free State period, and Department of Education files together with reports of the Board of Education of the General Synod of the Church of Ireland for the 1920s–1950s period have been extensively consulted for this study.
13. Maura O'Connor, *The Development of Infant Education in Ireland, 1838–1948*, (Oxford: Peter Lang, 2010), 187–197.
14. Kurt Bowen, *Protestants in a Catholic State– Ireland's Privileged Minority* (Quebec: McGill-Queen's University Press, 1983), 48.
15. Ibid., 58.
16. Dáil Debates, Vol. 8, 7 July 1924, col. 595.
17. Ibid., col. 596.
18. A National Programme Conference had been convened at the instigation of the Irish National Teachers' Organisation (INTO) in 1921. The recommendations of the body heavily influenced the programme which was introduced into the schools the following year.
19. Henry Kingsmill Moore, *Reminiscences and Reflections from Some Sixty Years of Life in Ireland* (London: Longmans, Green & Co. Ltd., 1930), 289.
20. Ibid.

21. Ibid.
22. Written submission to NPC ED/File No. 12850 Box 245, NAI.
23. Report of the first NPC (1921–22) in Áine Hyland and Kenneth Milne, *Irish Educational Documents, Vol. II* (Dublin: Church of Ireland College of Education, 1992), 92.
24. Minutes of the NPC, ED/File No. 12848 Box 245, NAI.
25. Relihan, 'The Church of Ireland', 145–152.
26. Minutes of NPC 25 November 1925, ED/File No. 12848 Box 245, NAI.
27. Relihan, 'The Church of Ireland', 88–91.
28. The contribution was made by 'An Seabhac', pen-name of the West Kerry writer which translates as 'The Hawk'. He was a representative of the General Council of County Councils at the NPC. Minutes of meeting of NPC 4 March 1926. ED/File No. 12847 Box 244, NAI.
29. Minutes of meeting of NPC, 19 November 1925, ED/File No. 12848, Box 245, NAI.
30. Minutes of NPC, 17 November 1925, ED/File No. 12848, Box 245, NAI.
31. Written submission to NPC ED/File No.12850, Box 245, NAI.
32. John O'Callaghan, *Teaching Irish Independence: History in Irish Schools* (Cambridge Scholars' Publishing, 2009), 52.
33. Minutes of meeting of the Report Subcommittee of the NPC, 5 March 1926, ED/File No. 12847 Box 244, NAI.
34. John Coolahan, *Irish Education–History and Structure* (Dublin: Institute of Public Administration, 1981), 42.
35. Quoted in Hyland and Milne, *Irish Educational Documents, Vol. II*, 114.
36. Report of the Board of Education of the General Synod 1935, 228.
37. Report of the Board of Education of the General Synod 1942, 210.
38. Kelly, *Compulsory Irish*, 49–53.
39. Séamas Ó Buachalla, *Education Policy in Twentieth Century Ireland* (Dublin: Wolfhound Press, 1988), 245.
40. Quoted in Ó Buachalla, *Education Policy in Twentieth Century Ireland*, 249.
41. Relihan, 'The Church of Ireland', 128–193.
42. Report of the Board of Education of the General Synod, 1928.
43. Report of the Board of Education of the General Synod, 1931.
44. *Church of Ireland Gazette*, 19 May 1933.
45. Annual Report of the Department of Education 1934–35, 8.
46. Annual Report of the Department of Education 1935–36, 6–7.
47. Report of the Board of Education of the General Synod, 1937.
48. Akenson, *A Mirror to Kathleen's Face*, 116.
49. Kenneth Milne, 'The Clergy and the Schools', in Toby C. Barnard and William G. Neely (eds), *The Clergy and the Church of Ireland, 1000-2000: Messengers, Watchmen and Stewards* (Dublin: Four Courts Press, 2006), 229.
50. Relihan, 'The Church of Ireland', 156–161.
51. Ed/File No.20930, Box 457, NAI.
52. Ed/File No.22161, Box 491, NAI.
53. Ibid.
54. ED/File No 15655, NAI.
55. Ibid.
56. Relihan, 'The Church of Ireland', 152–154.

57. Ibid., 145–193.
58. Ibid.
59. Relihan, 'The Church of Ireland', 145–193.
60. The State's other teacher training colleges were located in Dublin, Waterford and Limerick and were all under the management of the Catholic Church.
61. Kelly, *Compulsory Irish*, 68.
62. Relihan, 'The Church of Ireland', 225–226.
63. Parkes, *Kildare Place – A History*, 145.
64. Relihan, 'The Church of Ireland', 222; Parkes, *Kildare Place – A History*, 151; Jones, 'Recruitment and Formation', 68–69.
65. Annual Reports, CITC 1928-9; 1929–30.
66. Valerie Jones, *A Gaelic Experiment:the Preparatory System 1926–61 and Colaiste Moibhi* (Dublin: Woodfield Press, 2006).
67. Quoted in George Seaver, *John Allen Fitzgerald Gregg, Archbishop* (London: The Faith Press, 1963), 190.
68. Anonymous, *The Irish Times*, 18 November 1926.
69. Anonymous, *The Irish Times*, 26 February 1938.
70. Anonymous, *The Irish Times*, 14 February 1938.
71. For a comprehensive analysis of the way in which a Catholic-nationalist perspective was reflected in Irish, English and History textbooks of the 1920s and 1930s, see Relihan, 'The Church of Ireland', 255–323.
72. Report of the Board of Education of the General Synod, 1923.
73. Valerie Jones, 'The Attitude of the Church of Ireland Board of Education to Textbooks in National Schools, 1922-1967', *Irish Educational Studies*, vol. 11, 1992, 73.
74. Report of the Board of Education of the General Synod, 1923.
75. Report of the Board of Education of the General Synod, 1944.
76. O'Callaghan, *Teaching Irish Independence*, 58.
77. Report of the Board of Education of the General Synod, 1939.
78. Dora Casserley, *History of Ireland* (Dublin: Church of Ireland, 1941).
79. Jones, 'The Attitudes of the Church of Ireland Board of Education to Textbooks in National Schools, 1922-1967', 72–81.
80. Mulcahy Papers, P7/C/152, UCD archive.
81. Comments quoted in *The Irish Times*, 11 May 1950.
82. Relihan, 'The Church of Ireland', 255–323.
83. Akenson, *A Mirror to Kathleen's Face*, 134.
84. *The Church of Ireland A.D. 432–1932* (Dublin: Church of Ireland Printing and Publishing, 1932), 224.
85. Ibid.
86. Jack White, *Minority Report: the Protestant Community in the Irish Republic* (Dublin: Gill and Macmillan, 1975), 146.
87. Ibid.
88. Georgina Fitzpatrick, *St Andrew's College, 1894–1994* (Dublin: St. Andrew's College, 1994), 112.
89. W.J.R. Wallace, *Faithful to Our Trust- A History of the Erasmus Smith Trust and the High School Dublin* (Dublin: Columba Press, 2004), 215.

90. *Alexandra College Magazine*, Summer 1952, 6–9. See also Anne V. O'Connor & Susan M. Parkes, *Gladly Learn and Gladly Teach: Alexandra College and School 1866–1966* (Dublin: Blackwater Press, 1983).
91. Ibid.
92. Article by Mary Manning, 'The School girls of Alexandra', published as part of a supplement to *The Irish Times*, 3 June 1978.
93. Annual Report of the Lady Principal to Alexandra College Council 1922–23. The Four Courts is a complex of buildings at Inns Quay, Dublin which is now the centre of the Irish court system. The buildings were seized by the IRA in April 1922. They were subsequently bombarded by the Free State government in June of that year, an act which marked the beginning of the Civil War.
94. Minutes of meeting of the Governors of Erasmus Smith Schools, 12 May 1922, Erasmus Smith Archive BG/1014.
95. Ibid., 23 June 1922.
96. Minutes of Meeting of Alexandra College Council, 27 June 1923.
97. *The Erasmian*, December 1926.
98. Ibid.
99. Wallace, *Faithful to Our Trust*, 192–193.
100. Circular letter from principal of The High School to parents who refused to allow their children to learn Irish. Erasmus Smith Archive GS/119.
101. Ibid.
102. Ibid.
103. Department of Education 'Pass Lists' for the relevant years.
104. Mulcahy Papers, P7/C/152, UCD Archive.
105. Ibid.
106. Ibid.
107. Ibid.
108. Ibid.
109. Relihan, 'The Church of Ireland', 359–373.
110. Ibid.
111. Mulcahy Papers, P7/C/152, UCD Archive.
112. Speech quoted in *The Irish Times*, 1 February 1922.
113. Akenson, *A Mirror to Kathleen's Face*, 109–134.
114. Relihan, 'The Church of Ireland', 255–323.
115. Ibid., 145–152.
116. Ibid., 222–238.
117. Ibid., 376–383.
118. Farren, *The Politics of Irish Education*, 122.
119. Ibid.
120. Bowen, *Protestants in a Catholic State*.
121. White, *Minority Report*, 185.

9 THE MODERNISATION OF THE RECRUIT TRAINING AND EDUCATION POLICIES OF THE GARDA SÍOCHÁNA, 1922–1985

BRIAN McCARTHY

Following the ratification of the Anglo-Irish Treaty by Dáil Éireann in January 1922, the newly-established Provisional Government, under the Chairmanship of Michael Collins, accepted responsibility for the governing of Southern Ireland. As civil war loomed, Collins urgently required the restoration of law and order in a country debilitated in the wake of the War of Independence. Collins took the pragmatic decision to establish a new police force, the Civic Guard (renamed the Garda Síochána in 1923),[1] and implement almost an identical system of recruit training to that of its predecessor, the Royal Irish Constabulary (RIC).

Between 1836 and 1922, the RIC held the responsibility of policing Ireland with the exception of Dublin city which had its own police force, the Dublin Metropolitan Police (DMP). The lower ranks of the force had been largely reserved for men of the native lower agrarian classes. The force had generally enjoyed positive relations with the public except at times of agrarian and political unrest when the RIC was identified by nationalists as the protectors of British rule in Ireland.[2] The RIC had the distinction of being the only armed police force in the United Kingdom and it implemented a training regime which was revered within the British Empire to the extent that, in 1907, the Colonial Office in London obliged the RIC to assume responsibility for training all colonial police officers of commissioned rank within the confines of the RIC's training depot at the Phoenix Park in Dublin.[3] However, the position of the RIC became untenable when confronted with the guerrilla war campaign initiated by the

Irish Republican Army (IRA) during the War of Independence (1919–1921). In response to IRA attacks on RIC barracks, the British government completed the militarisation of the force through the provision of military paraphernalia and the enlistment of former military personnel to support the police during the IRA campaign of violence against Crown Forces.[4] Consequently, the RIC lost public acceptance as a police force and were disbanded on the creation of the new state in 1922.

The recruit training programme of the Garda Síochána, which had been effectively inherited from the RIC, would remain largely unchanged up to the early 1960s. As the bulk of the force was recruited in the 1920s, recruitment and training considerations were not of particular relevance to the authorities until mass retirements from the force commenced in the early 1960s. Such an exodus from the Garda Síochána depleted it of experienced members and led to a 'wastage crisis' within the force. Despite the inevitability of mass retirements, the authorities were ill-prepared and indecisive about confronting the issue to the extent that government leaders were divided over the proposal to decentralise the training depot in order to facilitate training large batches of recruits.

Notwithstanding significant societal shifts within Ireland in the 1960s, the antiquated training programme of the force remained largely intact and inattentive to international police training advancements. Despite numerous appeals by Garda representative bodies for higher educational entry standards and for the restructuring of the training programme, the government only acceded to a comprehensive overhaul of the training regime following the publication of the Walsh Report in 1985. This chapter assesses the factors which contributed to the government delay in replacing the systems of recruitment and training which had become increasingly unsuitable to the needs of Irish society in the late twentieth century.

THE CIVIC GUARD

In early February 1922, Collins personally selected an organising committee composed of RIC, DMP and IRA men to assist in the formation of a new police force. He granted the members a mere three weeks to present their report to the Provisional Government. A month later, the Civic Guard had been established as an armed force which would be trained along the lines of the RIC.[5] However, the exclusive recruitment of pro-Treaty IRA men[6] to the lower ranks of the force would prove detrimental to the force within a matter of weeks.

On 15 May 1922, approximately 1,000 recruits of the new Civic Guard broke ranks at the General Parade in Kildare Barracks and raided the armoury in an outright act of defiance against the first commissioner of the Civic Guard, Michael Staines. The recruits were particularly incensed that Staines had appointed former RIC men to the majority of the senior positions within the headquarters staff.[7] On the evacuation of Staines and his staff from the depot, the armed recruits defiantly remained in a state of mutiny for almost seven weeks. Following a commission of enquiry into the events, the Provisional Government accepted Staines's resignation, disarmed the Civic Guard and appointed the formidable IRA leader General Eoin O'Duffy in his place.

O'DUFFY'S LEGACY

In the wake of the mutiny and in the midst of civil war, the earliest recruits were constantly transferred to a variety of temporary depots and only afforded a modest and abbreviated training which was delivered in an erratic and haphazard manner. O'Duffy was openly reliant upon his cousin, Assistant Commissioner Patrick Walsh, a highly experienced disbanded RIC District Inspector.[8] Under the direction of Walsh, O'Duffy established a training programme for the Civic Guard. In an effort to distinguish the new force from its predecessors, O'Duffy demanded that all members be fluent in the Irish language within four years of joining the force.[9] O'Duffy's eleven-year tenure enshrined a system of recruit training that would remain 'virtually unchanged for the next thirty years'[10] as he embraced the former RIC policy of favouring the recruitment of physically strong men from the lower agrarian class. He wrote that 'the son of the peasant is the backbone of the Force.'[11] The pragmatic decision to employ the RIC methods of recruitment and training up to the 1960s was not particularly conspicuous in a country which had remained largely agrarian and economically stagnant. Arguably, the Garda Síochána was not intentionally conservative in its policy of implementing RIC policies until the 1960s and instead could be perceived as a microcosm of Irish society in that the force 'reflected the religion, occupation and education of the vast majority of the people of the state. The Garda authorities tended to recruit members who were almost identical to those recruited by the RIC, with regard to age, height, marital status and county of origin.'[12]

Despite the unarming of the new force, O'Duffy continued to emphasise the semi-military practices of the RIC tradition. He insisted that all recruits were to be awoken to the sound of a bugle-call at 6.30am, and were to immediately make up their beds before shaving and washing in cold water.[13] Breakfast could only be consumed on completion of drilling exercises for the duration of three-quarters of an hour. Daily inspection followed breakfast and recruits retreated to their dormitories to set about their designated duties, which included dry-scrubbing floors, brushing down stairways and attending to every detail of their uniforms.[14] Following the daily inspection, the bugle sounded the call for the recruits to attend parades and drills until 10.00am. Thereafter, recruits were occupied with lectures in police duties, law and Irish classes. Intermittently, recruits were ordered to return to the square for additional parades and drilling. These activities were only interrupted with an hour for dinner and continued until tea-time at 5.15pm. Between 6pm and the Roll Call at 10pm, recruits were at liberty to spend time in the canteen or games-room, or to leave the grounds of the depot in the Phoenix Park, which was within walking distance of Dublin's city centre.

The evolution of training in the Garda Síochána was also severely compromised by the bitter legacy of the Irish Civil War which ravaged the country between June 1922 and May 1923. Thereafter, the political landscape was essentially divided into two opposing parties, Fine Gael (following the merger of Cumann na nGaedheal, the National Centre Party and the National Guard in 1933) and Fianna Fáil.[15] On entering government at various junctures, both political parties grappled with the realities of low economic productivity during the 1930s and 1940s. On 3 March 1938, Commissioner Eamonn Broy wrote a four-page memorandum imploring the Secretary of the Department of Justice to appreciate the increasing demands placed on the Garda Síochána notwithstanding a temporary ban on recruitment to the force. According to Broy, the 'extra duties added every year by fresh legislation' to those already being performed by the force had placed an intolerable workload on members of the Garda Síochána. The commissioner was exasperated that the training of recruits was being suspended at a time of an increase of population in the capital city which was stretching the limited resources of the force: '…in the case of the [Dublin] Metropolitan Division, I stand in daily fear of the collapse of the police machine altogether. Meanwhile, most precious time, which could be devoted to the training of recruits to relieve the strain, is being lost forever.'[16]

As the increase of population in urban areas continued during the early 1950s, the government persisted with restrictions on recruitment. In 1951, Daniel Morrisey, the Minister for Justice, expressed his dissatisfaction with the government's reluctance to strengthen the force in response to the growth of cities and towns, and asked Patrick McGilligan, the Minister for Finance, to reopen recruitment immediately as the force was increasingly incapable of carrying out its duties: 'Indictable crime in Dublin during the first quarter of this year has increased substantially and the police say that with the strength at present available they are able to pay little or no attention to some new housing estates notably the big colony at Ballyfermot.'[17] Despite such appeals, the government did not increase recruitment and continued to preserve a training programme originally designed to cater for the needs of an agrarian based society of the early twentieth century. Therefore, duties concerning the prevention and investigation of larceny, damage to property and illicit distillation were of primary importance to recruits in the training depot.[18]

THE RECRUITMENT OF WOMEN

By the late 1950s, the government finally relented to an intensive and prolonged media campaign for the recruitment of women to the Garda Síochána. In June 1957, *The Irish Times* published an article that openly criticised the Minister for Justice, Oscar Traynor, for procrastinating on the matter: 'Is another 25 years to pass by before the requisite action is undertaken, and a deficiency supplied which gives this country an unenviable distinction among her more forward-looking neighbours?'[19] Three months later, Traynor formally announced his approval for the admission of women into the Garda Síochána:

> The Minister for Justice feels that the time has come when the appointment of policewomen cannot be further delayed if this country is not to be accused of falling behind in the humanitarian treatment of women and children … His intention is to have merely an experimental force, of, say, twelve policewomen who will be allocated to the Dublin Metropolitan Division.[20]

However, within the confines of the Department of Justice, Traynor was not particularly supportive of women entering the force and requested senior civil servants not to continue inconveniencing him about drafting the necessary legislation as 'My own belief is that the careers of these young women will be, perhaps, no longer than those of Air Hostesses and the other type of uniformed glamour girls.'[21] In August 1958, the Department of Justice placed advertisements in the national newspapers for the recruitment of policewomen.

Following consultation between the Department of Justice and the Garda authorities, it was proposed that women police or 'Ban Ghardaí' would complete the same six-month training programme already in operation for male recruits and that they be assigned the same duties as normally carried out by the Garda Síochána: 'This work will include beat and point duty, checking of street offences, investigating complaints from the public, interviewing witnesses and taking statements from them, giving evidence in court etc.'[22] In addition, it was envisaged that Ban Ghardaí would be particularly involved in the investigation of crimes concerning women and children either as injured parties or as suspects. It was further proposed that the selection board favour women who possessed character, self-respect and self-discipline associated with a good family background: 'She must be interested in people, reasonably well-educated and intelligent above the average. Whilst a high standard of education is an asset, the essential requirements are intelligence and an informed mind.'[23] Finally, it was recommended that the selection board appoint women who were considered to be 'of pleasing appearance and personality ... The masculine woman, we are informed, does not make a good policewoman.'[24]

The first batch of twelve female recruits commenced their training in July 1959 at the Training Depot in the Phoenix Park. The women were particularly incensed on their arrival to learn that they were required, unlike their male counterparts, to pay for lodgings outside the confines of the Phoenix Park due to the lack of accommodation for recruits in the dilapidated buildings of the depot.[25] Four months into the training of the first batch of female recruits, a dispute ensued between the women and the Garda authorities which received prominent attention in the newspapers. On Sunday 18 October 1959, the front page of the *Sunday Review* announced that the twelve recruits had issued Commissioner Daniel Costigan with an ultimatum, 'Give-us-more-money-or-we'll-look-for-other-jobs',[26] while *The Sunday Independent* published an article entitled 'Increase Our Pay Or We'll Resign'.[27] Prior to notifying the press of their distress, all twelve recruits signed a letter addressed to Costigan on 14 October 1959, which expressed their dissatisfaction with their lower rates of pay in comparison with men and their living-out allowances, which they considered to be totally inadequate. Despite their initial stance, women in the Garda Síochána would continue to receive lower pay and were required to resign their positions on marriage until the late 1970s.[28] Furthermore, female members of the force were not appointed to specialised units until 1976.[29] As the intake of women increased during the mid-1970s, the prominence of women in various roles gradually became more evident and by 1997, women represented 8 per cent of the entire force.[30]

A NEW DEPOT

In March 1960, representatives of the Department of Finance, Department of Justice, Garda Síochána and Office of Public Works met to discuss the accommodation crisis in the Training Depot. Thomas Coyne of the Department of Justice stated that, since the foundation of the State in 1922, the problem of providing suitable buildings to the Garda Síochána had continuously presented itself and that the inadequate accommodation accepted by the force was not owed entirely to 'patriotic fervour', but was largely attributable to the fact that the recruits tended to be drawn from 'the poorer section of the agricultural community.'[31] According to Coyne, the buildings inhabited by the Garda Síochána had not received the required renovation to offset damage 'caused by the ravages of time' to the extent that Garda buildings were in a poorer state 'than thirty-five years ago.' Coyne informed the various representatives that a shortage of personnel within the force was imminent as almost half of the 6,000 members of the Garda Síochána would be eligible to retire over the next five years. It was anticipated that the replenishment of the force would require the training of at least 600 recruits per year. However, the existing facilities in the Phoenix Park were only capable of training a maximum of 400 per year and therefore, the Minister for Justice, Oscar Traynor, favoured building a new Garda Síochána headquarters in order to provide additional facilities and accommodation for the expected increased numbers of recruits.

Between 1961 and February 1964, the provision of a new training depot in Co. Tipperary was undertaken with the conversion of the former 150-year-old British army barracks at Templemore. On opening tenders for the project, civil servants in the Department of Finance expected quotations to be in the region of £250,000 and were surprised that construction companies were instead quoting almost £500,000. Although the Parliamentary Secretary to the Minister for Justice, Charles Haughey TD, was appalled by the quotations, he strongly urged Traynor to continue with the building project for fear that its cancellation had the potential to harm the popularity of the Fianna Fáil parliamentary party: 'The results of any such decision would be very bad politically for the Government and would have very serious psychological repercussions in rural Ireland generally.'[32] Haughey's determination to support the Templemore project was illustrated by his suggestion to Traynor that recruits could be dispatched in small batches for training to Templemore prior to the completion of building work. Both Traynor and Commissioner Costigan expressed their wish to cancel the project largely due to the implications that the expenditure would necessitate extensive cost-cutting of facilities for recruits and declared their preference for the renovation of the depot in the Phoenix Park.[33] In a memorandum to his Government colleagues, Traynor announced that 'The Minister for Justice considers that, in the light of the estimated cost, the proposal to transfer the Training Centre to Templemore Barracks should be rescinded. It would, in his view, be wasteful to spend such a considerable sum on the conversion of an old building, especially for a short-term need.'[34] A day after Traynor issued the memorandum, the Taoiseach, Seán Lemass, wrote to him and extinguished any possibility that the project could be cancelled. In an abrupt tone, Lemass asserted: 'I consider that a reversal of the decision to transfer the Garda Training Centre to Templemore is out of the question at this stage.'[35] The deflated Traynor informed a senior civil servant that the decision to renovate Templemore Barracks appeared to be final and that matters had been further exacerbated by the imposition of considerable cost reductions on the project: 'It is the operation of the old tag of "being penny wise and pound foolish". I have tried my best to change that attitude in respect to these so-called savings but without result. Time alone will show whose views were correct. I'm afraid I can do no more.'[36]

Notwithstanding the reduced expenditure available for the renovation of Templemore, the opening of the training depot in February 1964 facilitated the implementation of new training procedures for recruits. Henceforth, Part I of the course required recruits to complete eighteen weeks of theory, including police duties, law enforcement and powers of arrest. Recruits were also instructed in first-aid, life-saving and the use of firearms. After the sixth, tenth and thirteenth weeks of training, recruits sat an examination with a pass mark of 50 per cent. Those failing to reach the pass mark were relegated to the next class of recruits studying for the relevant examination. The final four weeks of Part I involved recruits being allocated to a Garda station and placed under the supervision of a sergeant. On completion of Part I, recruits were dispatched to another station for a year and then returned to Templemore to undergo Part II of the training course. Such an alteration to the original training programme was considered necessary by the Garda authorities on the basis that particular modules should be introduced to recruits only after they had grasped a practical understanding of their duties. Part II of the training course immediately commenced with an examination on their return to Templemore.[37] In his published recollections as a 19-year-old recruit in 1966, Tim Doyle offers a valuable insight into the modified training programme at Templemore and the experiences encountered by recruits during their work placement at designated Garda stations.[38] The analysis of the training programme by Doyle is particularly relevant as he became professionally involved in the training of recruits later in his career. On entering Templemore, Doyle was disappointed by the almost hostile reception awaiting the latest batch of recruits on their first day:

> No this. No that. No nothing. And they droned on with what seemed an endless list of rules about order, decorum, personal cleanliness, rooms, time to go to bed, to get up, to eat, to pray, to study, to stay alive … My mind trailed away from this deluge and I began to consider my fate. First impressions were not encouraging. There would be no smiles here. Our instructions would be inflicted rather than imparted.[39]

Apart from his dissatisfaction with the austere style of training in Templemore, Doyle was further disheartened by his experiences during the work placement. He soon found serious shortfalls in learning large tracts of police duties off by heart and attempting to apply them in his daily routine of police work: 'I looked at the lectures in the suitcase on top of my locker. They were undisturbed since my arrival, becoming more and more irrelevant. What a sham! The job was nowhere near the words contained in them.'[40] He felt particularly exasperated by the prospect of being released on the public without receiving proper instructions or guidance from his experienced colleagues and superiors: "This job was too serious to be taught by trial and error. There had to be a better way.'[41] On remembering his second day as a recruit in Dublin, Doyle was patrolling a street on his own when he was suddenly called upon to request an ambulance by a woman who had witnessed an accident in which a man was injured. The guileless recruit entered the nearest telephone box and immediately realised that he did not possess sufficient communication skills to operate a phone and request an ambulance:

> I turned away and noticed a long-haired youth with his nose pressed against the glass. This was my chance.'Come here.' 'Yes,

mistah.' Get in there and ring an ambulance.' Soon I had him imprisoned in the kiosk. This was my first introduction to the power of the uniform. It felt good. 'Do you know how to use this phone?' 'I do,' he said, obviously amazed at the question. 'Well then,' I directed, 'ring an ambulance.' He put his hand on top of the receiver and turned the handle a few times. 'I'm off,' he said. 'Hey, what kind of bleedin' guard are you? Did you ever hear of 999?'[42]

THE DEMAND FOR HIGHER EDUCATIONAL STANDARDS

In 1963 a pay claim was advanced by the Representative Body for Guards (RBG) seeking parity for guards with particular grades of civil service clerks. The claim was declined on the basis that the cited grades of clerks required the attainment of the Leaving Certificate to enter the civil service. In contrast, the entrance examination for potential recruits to the Garda Síochána remained at fifth or sixth class standard in national school as originally implemented by the RIC up to 1922. Consequently, the RBG sought to enhance their claim for a pay increase by clamouring for higher educational qualifications for entrance into the force. In June 1964, Commissioner Daniel Costigan informed Peter Berry, the Secretary of the Department of Justice, that he had discussed the possibility of raising the standard of the entrance examination with the Civil Service Commission (CSC). While the Commissioner was generally in favour of raising the standard, he was wary that any substantial change 'may have the effect of failing to qualify the large number of recruits who are at present required and might result in the exclusion of many highly intelligent young men who have not had the opportunity of receiving Secondary Education.'[43] Costigan stressed that the entrance examination which consisted of four tests in English, Irish, Arithmetic and Geography, should not be perceived as a means of assessing educational attainment, but instead as a test of intelligence:

> It should be remembered that there are many young men who have received only a national school education, but who have more natural ability and intelligence than many young men who have passed the Leaving Certificate. Such men are likely to make first class Guards and with private study can fit themselves for the highest rank.[44]

A month later, representatives from the Department of Justice, Garda authorities and CSC attended a meeting to discuss the standard of the entrance examination. The existing system required candidates to attain at least a pass mark of 33.3 per cent in the subjects of Irish (300 marks) English (300 marks), Arithmetic (300 marks), and Geography (150 marks). An aggregate score of 525 marks was also required. Following the conference, it was agreed to include additional questions in the English and Arithmetic examinations, and replace the Geography with a General Knowledge examination. Henceforth, candidates were required to achieve at least a pass mark of 40 per cent and attain an aggregate score of no less than 525 marks in the four subjects of Irish, English, Arithmetic and General Knowledge.[45] However, by November 1965, senior civil servants within the Department of Justice were perturbed by the low percentage of candidates deemed to have qualified in the last three entrance examinations which had dropped from the typical rate of 68 per cent to a disturbingly inadequate 48 per cent. In an internal memorandum, it was noted that a serious recruitment problem would ensue if such a trend was allowed to continue as approximately one third of candidates called for the medical examination would normally fail.[46] Three days later, Berry wrote to the Secretary of the CSC, Noel Duggan, to express the Minister's dissatisfaction with the latest statistics for candidates deemed to have qualified in the entrance examination. Berry asserted that the results of the last two examinations would jeopardise the prospects of candidates in possession of a national school education:

> The duties of the Force are such as make it peculiarly suitable that candidates with a good primary education should form the bulk of the Force at all times. We are satisfied that it would not be in the public interest that the standard of the examination should be raised so as to put it out of reach of candidates with a good primary education.[47]

In response, Duggan denied that there had been 'any stiffening in the standard of marking or in the standard of the papers set, by comparison with the last such examination' and claimed that the disappointing results were 'due to the poor quality of many of the candidates'. Duggan also informed Berry that the examiners were national school teachers who appreciated the expected standard of answering from candidates and were 'unlikely to set too high a standard in marking the papers.'[48]

THE CONROY REPORT, 1970

In September 1968, Minister for Justice, Micheál Ó Móráin, appointed Judge John C. Conroy as the chairman of a committee which was to investigate the issues of Garda pay and conditions in response to threats of industrial action by members of the force. The committee was established to placate the Garda representative bodies following an unpopular ruling a month earlier by the Labour Court. During 1969, the committee interviewed delegates from the representative bodies of the Garda Síochána and conducted tours of inspection of other police forces in Britain, Holland, Denmark and Sweden.[49] In the published report of January 1970, Conroy made fifty-two recommendations regarding such areas as pay, accommodation, recruitment, promotion, discipline, education and training. Conroy made particular reference to the educational standards of entry into the force. The report stated that the decision to raise the educational entrance standards in 1964 had altered the composition of recruits in terms of academic ability:

> In theory a person with a good primary education should be able to qualify in this examination. In practice it is becoming increasingly difficult for a person to do so. In the six-year period from 1962 to 1967, 45% of the recruits held an Intermediate Certificate, and 31% of the recruits had the Matriculation or Leaving Certificate.[50]

Conroy speculated that the introduction of 'free education' by the Department of Education for post-primary students in 1967 would ensure that the typical recruit entering the force would possess even higher educational standards than his or her contemporary counterpart. Consequently, Conroy anticipated 'the availability of free secondary education will provide a bigger quota of recruits holding certificates from secondary school examinations.'[51]

In a separate section of the report, Conroy commended the present recruitment standards which 'have given a highly efficient force at all levels,' yet he advised against raising the educational entry standards of the force as 'it may bar persons who, though they lack formal post-primary education, are excellent material for a career in the Garda Síochána. Educational levels should be related to the standard required for a satisfactory performance of the job.' Conroy feared that a higher educational standard of entry for recruits would only serve to facilitate the employment of personnel who would become tired of the dreary and dull duties associated with the position. Consequently, Conroy warned that 'if the educational level is too high it may lead to job dissatisfaction.'[52]

> In practice the number of applicants who had post primary education, and who hold Intermediate Certificates or higher, is increasing. In the six year period 1950 to 1955, of the 1,413 men appointed, 376 or 27% had the Intermediate Certificate or higher. In the six year period 1956 to 1961, of the 1,967 persons who were appointed, 711, or 36%, had the Intermediate Certificate or higher. The figures for the six year period 1962 to 1967 were 2,205 appointed and 1,000 or 45.3% with Secondary Certificates.[53]

In their submission to the Commission, the Garda authorities also expressed the opinion that it would not be right to deprive a young person with a good primary education of an opportunity of competing for entry into the Garda Síochána. Furthermore, the authorities claimed that such recruits lacking formal educational qualifications were well capable of completing the training programme and advancing through the ranks. The authorities expressed their satisfaction with the current system of recruitment which generally provided the force with an abundance of candidates to choose from and feared that any adjustment in favour of recruiting highly qualified individuals would be counterproductive:

> Over-qualification is as serious a problem as under-qualification. The duties of a Garda involve a lot of monotonous routine duty. A substantial percentage of the men cannot hope for promotion. An overly qualified person might well get discontented in his job and this would be bad for the morale of himself and his companions.[54]

Following the publication of the Conroy Report (1970), an article was published in the *Sunday Independent* entitled 'The Garda Revolt'. The article claimed that the report had not done enough to persuade a proportion of young and well educated members of the force to remain in the Garda Síochána.[55] Young Gardaí, it was argued, who had attained their Leaving Certificate felt frustrated that they were required to perform mundane duties. According to a recently attested member of the force stationed at Donnybrook, Dublin, young guards felt aggrieved at the low level of professionalism associated with their positions: 'Most of the young men like me feel that we are nothing more than night watchmen and are not getting much of a chance to become professional lawmen.'[56]

Minister Ó Móráin also spoke about the lack of professionalism in the force and asserted that the Garda Síochána could be equated to a 'machine that was outdated, outmoded, and inefficient … [the Garda Síochána] belonged to the horse and buggy days at every level … I immediately acceded to the Garda Representative Body's request to establish the Conroy Commission. I did this because I was utterly dissatisfied with the lack of efficiency I found in the force.'[57] Although the minister acknowledged that the commission had done a 'fairly good job', he was dissatisfied with the existing training system: 'I am appalled at the number of "nuts" being released on the public … I am amazed that so many of them are left in the force for so long. I feel a great deal more care should be taken in selecting recruits at the application stage … I believe the unsuitable ones should be weeded out at the Templemore stage.'[58] Despite his remarks, the existing recruitment and training policies continued to be upheld by successive Ministers for Justice for another fifteen years.

THE RYAN REPORT, 1979

In October 1978, the issue of pay again threatened discipline within the ranks of the Garda Síochána. The Minister for Justice, Gerard Collins, diverted threats of industrial action through the establishment of a committee of inquiry into the issue of pay. In November 1978, Dr Louden Ryan, professor of political economy at Trinity College, Dublin (TCD), was appointed as chairman of the five-person review committee. As Ryan and his committee prepared to meet, Garda Jack Marrinan, General Secretary of the recently established Garda Representative Association (GRA) and editor of the *Garda Review*, wrote a series of editorials referring to the need for the new commission of inquiry to consider raising the educational entrance criteria for applicants, which continued to compromise the position of the GRA in negotiating pay deals with the government:

> We will accept and indeed we are urging, the introduction of higher educational standards for entry into the force. We realise that our recruit-intake must be geared toward the filling of the highest ranks within the force in the years ahead. We will not deny our own dissatisfaction in this respect at present. We frankly

admit that we are not getting the best of the school leavers and we are as anxious as anyone else to have the situation rectified.[59]

The General Secretary of the Association of Garda Sergeants and Inspectors (AGSI), Sergeant Derek Nally, followed Marrinan's example and publicly criticised the existing recruitment and training procedures. Nally claimed that a career in the Garda Síochána was perceived as being stagnant and it was unfortunate that 'the right kind of young men and women leaving our schools today' were being deterred by the rates of remuneration and the lack of promotion opportunities. In addition, Nally identified the training programmes within the force as requiring 'radical reassessment and overhaul.'[60]

Ryan and his committee furnished the Minister for Justice with their findings in April 1979 following consultations with the commissioner, representatives from the Department of Justice and the various Garda representative bodies. The report drew attention to the fact that successful candidates entering the force were aware from the commencement of their careers that the majority of members within the Garda Síochána would remain at the basic rank of Garda until retirement. Therefore, the report noted that such a proposition attracted a significant number of unenthusiastic individuals with no desire to further their career. The report also expressed its concern about the recent practice of immediately dispatching recruits to security duty at the border with Northern Ireland on their completion of twenty-two weeks at Templemore. Such a policy effectively prevented recruits from completing the prescribed six months work experience in a Garda station and was criticised for generating a negative image of the force among potential candidates with higher qualifications. In their concluding comments, the committee stated that during their inquiry, the issue of training had been outside the original terms of reference and strongly urged the government to consider investigating the matter. The report was particularly critical of the existing training regime for recruits, which it considered 'inadequate' and incapable of providing a meaningful assessment of their progress. It was suggested that the government should review training programmes for all ranks 'as a matter of urgency.'[61]

Although the Ryan Report was published in April 1979, its unequivocal recommendation that an evaluation of the recruit training course should be undertaken was arguably impeded by a period of political instability as a succession of minority and coalition governments failed to complete a full term of office. Four different Ministers for Justice served between the publication of the Ryan Report and December 1982. Marrinan wrote of his impatience for the authorities to immediately address the issue of training in the force. He was outspoken in his criticism of the authorities who had little difficulty in attracting suitable recruits during harsh economic periods of the previous decades, but with the advent of a more affluent society, had been remiss in devising a strategy to ensure an adequate supply of appropriate recruits:

> Let us be blunt about it; that time HAS come; but, unfortunately, the parallel development of a proper personnel policy has not taken place. Conroy stated it baldly. Ryan has reiterated it and has called for extensive and far reaching changes in recruitment and training procedures.[62]

Although Marrinan conceded that the force continued to attract 'many fine young recruits', he claimed in a forthright manner that the recruitment policy of the Garda Síochána facilitated the enrolment of totally inept individuals:

> We are also getting some sorry base characters; rejects from organisations whose standards have been lifted higher in keeping with the rising educational profile of the community; we are getting young men whose personal lives are in such a mess that a well-paid and secure place in the police is seen as a refuge from their problems; we are getting – frankly young men who will not be had anywhere else and whom our selection system is unable to catch when they turn up at their local Garda station possessed of the right physical requirements and a certain basic level of education.[63]

A selection of recommendations in the report was embraced by Collins. He duly amended the entrance regulations in May 1981, including the lowering of the minimum age from nineteen to eighteen years of age and the establishment of a competitive half-hour interview for candidates who satisfied the educational entrance examination. Although the Ryan Report accepted 'the desirability of seeking recruits with educational qualifications higher than Leaving Certificate at pass level', the amended regulations went beyond the expressed sentiments of the committee by exempting candidates in possession of the Leaving Certificate or a similar educational qualification from sitting the qualifying educational examination.

THE WALSH REPORT, 1985

In late 1984, the government finally responded to the criticisms of the recruit training programme as identified by the Ryan Report. It was announced that a Garda training committee was to be established with extensive terms of reference: 'To examine all training in the Garda Síochána from Recruit intake stage up to and including courses at the Garda College, and to make recommendations.'[64]

In December 1985, the Garda training committee submitted its first commissioned report to the government, 'Report on Probationer Training'. The report dealt exclusively with selection and training of recruits. The committee was predominantly academic in its composition. The chairman of the ten-person committee, Dr Tom Walsh, was previously employed as a third-level lecturer and a founding member of the National Council for Educational Awards (NCEA) and served as its chairman between 1976 and 1984. Former deputy commissioner E.J. Doherty was the only committee member to have served with the Garda Síochána and was a central figure in the establishment of the training headquarters at Templemore in 1964.

Between January and December 1985, the committee undertook a substantial and extensive investigation into education and training of recruits. The appraisal of the recruit training programme was organised through a variety of activities which included administering a sizeable survey among a large proportion of Garda personnel, the establishment of sub-committees, the arrangement of meetings with the training staff at Templemore and the conduct of an international comparative study of recruitment and training policies in use by a variety of forces, including: the London Metropolitan Police, the Essex Police, the Scottish Police, the Danish Police, Royal Canadian Mounted Police, Ottawa Police Force, Baltimore Police, Pennsylvania Police, San-Jose Police, New York City Police and New Zealand Police. Between September and November 1985, deputations from the committee undertook an ambitious itinerary, visiting Tulliallan Police College and Strathclyde University in Scotland, three training centres in Denmark, five police study centres in Holland, four training centres in England, two police academies in the United States of America and one police college in Canada.

In their report on probationer training, the committee recommended replacing the term 'recruits' with either 'students' or 'probationers', depending on the stage of training being undertaken by the trainee. The committee clearly asserted the need for the training programme to reflect significant changes in Irish society on the basis that 'the history of the Garda Síochána is the history of the Irish people, since the origins and developments of the Garda Síochána are inseparably bound to the evolutionary process of the State as a whole.'[65] Previously, the force employed the technique of preventative policing 'with the emphasis on a strong presence on the street and contact with the community, for the purpose of having a good local knowledge.' As Irish society became increasingly urbanised, the committee claimed that 'the strength of the family as a unit of social control had been reduced' and consequently, Irish society became reliant on the Garda Síochána 'as guardians of social order', which in turn required the force to provide additional departments to serve the public. Notwithstanding significant social changes in Ireland, the committee commented 'there has been little change in the approach to basic training over the years.' Hence, the committee was adamant that the contemporary complexities of Irish society required an immediate overhaul of education and training policies within the force: 'Education/Training reform is necessary in order to prepare the personnel required to service the multitude of posts in this complex system and, more specifically, to manage the organisation at its various levels and in its various areas of activity.'[66]

From the outset, the committee argued that policing could be regarded as an occupation in which technical knowledge was attained through prescribed and extensive training.[67] Accordingly, the efficiency of the force was largely determined by the selection of students capable of dedicating themselves to their professional position and their responsibilities. Moreover, the committee maintained that the training of students to perform their professional duties also required course modules in 'personal development' as the role of the guard could vary from being impersonal, for example when enforcing the Road Traffic Acts, to being sympathetic and compassionate when informing the spouse of the death of a partner. The committee argued that the existing training programme did not sufficiently instruct recruits on the vast range of duties which would be assigned to them during the course of their profession. Therefore, three fundamental changes to the ethos of the training programme were proposed. Firstly, the report was concerned with the issue of 'discipline' as an integral part of the training programme. It was noted that 'the present training period is dominated by an over-emphasis on the extensive range of rules and regulations.' Such a preoccupation with discipline was considered to be counterproductive as a proportion of students who possessed undesirable traits for a career in the force were not easily identifiable in training because they adhered to the discipline regulations without displaying their normal standard of behaviour:

> The atmosphere should therefore be more relaxed with less specific rules and regulations. The aim should be to lay down broad guidelines for behaviour and encourage trainees to reach standards of behaviour befitting their role as police officers… There should be no hesitation in dismissing trainees who are either unwilling or unable to meet the desired standards.[68]

Secondly, the committee identified 'social skills' as an area requiring further emphasis within Templemore. Through the promotion of sporting, social, cultural and recreational activities, the committee anticipated that positive relations between students and their instructors would be fostered. Furthermore, involvement in such activities 'would provide a more relaxed atmosphere in the college' and enable students to equip themselves with the necessary social skills to 'integrate with local communities on allocation to their stations and to organise such facilities in areas where they do not already exist thus contributing to Garda-Community relations.'[69]

Thirdly, the committee suggested that the personal development of students could be enhanced through the provision of leadership training: 'Ideally, Gardaí should be in a position to exercise leadership skills amongst the community where they serve and their education/training should prepare them for this role.'[70] In addition to the inclusion of a leadership course of training, the committee recommended that leadership qualities could be promoted by assigning roles of responsibility to students, which would include the rotation of class representatives and organisers of leisure-time activities at the Garda College outside official training hours.

In their assessment of college accommodation, the committee was disappointed to report that the buildings in Templemore were being shared with the army. In addition, it noted that the 'standard of accommodation is deplorable as a national training centre of young men/women.'[71] The Garda authorities were advised to make the necessary arrangements to acquire complete control of the training centre. It was reported that the classrooms within the main building had been converted into dormitories and consequently classes were held in one of the twenty 'unsuitable' prefabricated buildings. The report recommended that the former classrooms be utilised for their original function after refurbishment and redecoration. The allocation of a further twelve classrooms would be required for the full implementation of the report and an additional seven rooms for specialist classes in such areas as first aid, communications and technical instruction. The provision of a lecture theatre was also identified by the report as necessary to accommodate large numbers of students on occasions of lectures by guest speakers.[72] On inspecting the grounds of Templemore, the committee reported that the physical education facilities only included a gymnasium, swimming pool, handball alleys, basketball courts and playing pitches for GAA games and soccer. It was proposed that trainees should also be provided with a multi-purpose sports hall (equipped to play volleyball, netball and basketball), squash courts and tennis courts. Furthermore, it was suggested that the playing fields should also cater for the sport of rugby.[73]

Walsh and his committee were particularly critical of the training arrangements in operation at Templemore and noted 'that the current Training Course is inadequately structured to enable its objectives to be properly achieved. We are particularly concerned at the absence of proper integration between the programme at Templemore and the on-the-job training.'[74] The empirical research conducted by the committee consisted of surveys and structured interviews. It led Walsh and his colleagues to a variety of negative conclusions. In the first instance, the committee asserted that the training course was too short, crammed, abstract and examination-oriented. The course was criticised for failing to prepare the trainees sufficiently for the various duties to be thrust upon them, especially relating to the social role of the Garda in Irish society. The findings of the research also clearly identified the 'on-the-job training programme' as 'not organised, directed, supervised or monitored.'[75] The committee proposed revising the programme through the implementation of six particular measures. First, 'elements of theory and knowledge' within the programme would be studied over longer duration. Second, the programme would be 'more practically orientated and provide for more simulated exercises, role-playing, case studies and class discussions.'[76] Third, modules in the social sciences would be included in the programme. Fourth, emphasis would be placed on developing the students' interpersonal skills through the provision of communication classes. Fifth, a structured on-the-job training programme would be devised to 'ensure the integration of theory and practice' under the direction of full-time training sergeants. In their final recommendation, the committee suggested that the training programme should be completed over two years and based on five integrated phases:

Phase 1   28 weeks at Templemore Garda College followed by two weeks leave of absence.

Phase 2   20 weeks at a selected station, under supervision, followed by two weeks leave of absence.

Phase 3   10 weeks at Templemore Garda College.

Phase 4   26 weeks at a selected station followed by four weeks leave of absence.

Phase 5   12 weeks at Templemore Garda College.[77]

The committee was adamant that the success of the proposed modular training programme was heavily reliant upon the skills of the teaching staff at Templemore and the selected training sergeants and Garda tutors in the various on-the-job training stations. Therefore, the training staff would be obliged to complete a three-month training course before embarking upon a three-year period in their capacity as trainers.[78] Teachers/trainers were to serve only three years in Templemore in order to ensure that the 'credibility' of the training programme would not be undermined by employing personnel without recent experience of executing police duties. In contrast with the 'present system', the committee anticipated that the 'new system' of training Garda teachers would ensure the staff embraced and promoted the goals, aims and objectives of the proposed programme by facilitating a 'move from authoritarian lecture-type situations to demonstrations, actual and simulated exercises, the full use of audio-visual technology and individualised instruction, all designed to encourage active participation by students.' According to the committee, the realisation of such a training policy would require financial expenditure in terms of allocating the necessary equipment and provision of sufficient in-service training to the new staff.

Although Walsh submitted his report on probationer training to the Department of Justice in 1985, the contents of the report were unavailable for some time, much to the displeasure of government and opposition members of Dáil Éireann. In April 1986, the Minister for Justice, Alan Dukes, refused to divulge a date for publication of the report 'as the committee are still working on some additions they wish to make to the report'.[79] In November 1986, Dukes was accused by Dr Michael Woods in Dáil Éireann of 'shelving' the report and having 'no intention of pursuing the recommendations' of the Walsh Report.[80] Dukes vehemently denied the accusations and responded that he had decided to further delay the publication of the report on the basis that it was the subject of discussion among representative bodies of the Garda Síochána.[81] In May 1987, the Minister for Justice, Gerard Collins, was similarly questioned about the lack of progress in the implementation of the Walsh Report. Collins responded that the buildings in Templemore were not fit for purpose and were 'in very bad repair. The Walsh report on Garda training has come out very strongly on this issue. Because of that I have established [a committee] … to advise on how best we can improve the buildings having regard to what is required, and we will see where we are going from here.'[82]

In February 1988, Minister Collins announced in Dáil Éireann that the recommendations of the Walsh Report would be implemented for the next batch of recruits to enter Templemore. Collins stated that the new educational qualifications for applicants required candidates to achieve at least grade D in five subjects, including Irish, English and mathematics in the Leaving Certificate. He announced that in the new programme, 'there will be an emphasis during training on the development of practical policing skills' and that recruits would be studying 'the basics of criminology, behavioural science, psychology, public relations, communications, social science and management skills.'[83] The announcement by Collins of a new progressive era in the training and education of the Garda Síochána attained cross-party support within Dáil Éireann. Henceforth, students entering Templemore would be provided with structured on-the-job training opportunities and would be formally supported by a dedicated staff of Garda tutors and training sergeants. It was envisaged that the new training programme would apply the theoretical learning of the classroom to the actual daily experiences of the guard. The overhaul of the training programme was designed to equip 'students/probationers' with sufficient means to accept the responsibilities of the position in a competent and professional manner. The Walsh Report terminated the outmoded practices of Garda training and reinvigorated the status of the force by demanding candidates of a higher educational standard and establishing an organised student/probationer training programme which required constant monitoring and assessment from professionally trained members of the force.

CONCLUSION

At the turn of the twentieth century, the recruit training regime at the Phoenix Park was revered as the model police training course of the British Empire. By 1922, the Irish Free State was reliant upon the RIC methods of training in its efforts to establish a new police force in the midst of civil war. However, the convenience of inheriting the RIC training programme provided the Garda Síochána with little impetus to develop its own training regime in tandem with changes in Irish society. As almost the entire force was trained during the 1920s, the necessity to review and augment the course was largely ignored until mass retirements from the force commenced in the early 1960s. In essence, the recruitment of large batches of recruits in the 1920s ensured that only small numbers of men were required at intervening junctures to maintain the strength of the force. Consequently, the entrance requirements and the training programme were not prioritised by the Garda authorities until the wastage crisis caused by retirements forced their urgent consideration. By the late 1950s and early 1960s, the deficiencies of the outdated training course were partly addressed by the transfer of training to the incomplete buildings at Templemore.

It is significant that the Secretary of the Department of Justice, T.C. Coyne, argued that dilapidated training buildings were not a cause of concern to recruits largely drawn from the poorer sections of Irish agrarian society. Indeed, the availability of a wide pool of applicants with a national school education and few other employment possibilities encouraged the Garda authorities to persist with a training programme that promoted physical prowess over educational attainment. However, with the introduction of free second-level education in the 1960s, potential applicants began to seek alternative sources of employment and courses of study owing to the rates of remuneration and lack of career advancement in the Garda Síochána.

While the transfer of training to Templemore provided the Garda authorities with the opportunity to modestly expand and revise the training programme to include a placement module in a Garda station, a comprehensive analysis of recruitment and training did not happen for a further four decades. The eventual overhaul of recruit training was inadvertently instigated by a series of unproductive pay claims. Consequently, the Conroy Report and Ryan Report were established to placate the demands of the representative bodies, which in turn strongly recommended the need for a comprehensive review of Garda recruitment and training, and ultimately culminated in the publication of the

Walsh Report. Although the appraisal of Garda training was commissioned some sixty years after the force was established, the Walsh Report provided detailed recommendations which ensured the new programme reflected the educational and societal shifts which had occurred in the interim. Furthermore, the dominance of academics on the committee required the Garda authorities to convert Templemore into a third level campus, primarily in terms of accommodation, lecturing style, library facilities and extracurricular activities. In 2005, a defining moment in the history of Garda education and training was realised with the announcement that the two-year training programme as set out by Walsh and his committee would be accredited as a BA in Police Studies.

NOTES

1. Civic Guard Bill introduced by Minister Kevin O'Higgins in July 1923 to authorise the permanent implementation of the force. During the committee stage of the bill, an amendment was accepted which proposed to change the name of the force from the 'Civic Guard' to 'Garda Síochána'.
2. See Seamus Breathnach, *The Irish Police: From Earliest Times to the Present Day* (Dublin: Anvil Books, 1970), 59.
3. R.V. Vernon, Under Secretary of State, Colonial Office to the Secretary of State, Colonial Office, London, 11 May 1905, *Report on the training and organisation of the Royal Irish Constabulary* (NAUK, CO 884/9/3), 3.
4. See Charles Townshend, *The British Campaign in Ireland, 1919-1921* (Oxford: Clarendon Press, 1975), 94.
5. 'Civic Guard – Organisation Scheme,' February 1922 (NAI, D/J, H/99).
6. Conor Brady, *Guardians of the Peace* (Dublin: Gill and Macmillan, 1974), 47.
7. Evidence of Commissioner Michael Staines, 14 July, 1922, in Minutes of evidence to mutiny enquiry (NAI, D/J, H235/329).
8. Brady, *Guardians of the Peace*, 74.
9. Commissioner Eoin O'Duffy to the Secretary of the Department of Justice, Henry O'Frighill, no date, 'Garda Síochána: Use of Irish, 1923-34, Part I' (NAI, D/J, 4/31).
10. Liam McNiffe, *A History of the Garda Síochána* (Dublin: Wolfhound Press, 1997), 58.
11. Commissioner Eoin O'Duffy, 'Recruitment of the Garda Síochána', *Garda Review* 4.6 (May 1929): 541–542.
12. McNiffe, *A History of the Garda Síochána*, 51.
13. Commissioner Eoin O'Duffy, 'Policemen in the Making', *Garda Review* 4.7 (June 1929): 656.
14. Ibid.
15. Cumann na nGaedheal was renamed Fine Gael in September 1933.
16. Broy to Roche, 3 March 1938, TLS, 'Garda Síochána Recruitment Part I, 1922-1948' (NAI, D/J, 4/107).
17. Daniel Morrisey, Minister for Justice, to Patrick McGilligan, Minister for Finance, 18 April 1951, TLS, 'Garda Síochána Recruitment, Part II, 1951–1961' (NAI, D/J, 4/107).
18. McNiffe, *A History of the Garda Síochána*, 65.

19. *The Irish Times*, 25 June 1957.
20. Department of Justice, 'Recruitment of Ban Ghardaí, 1952–1962', 16 September 1957, (NAI, D/J, 4/62/2).
21. Traynor to Coyne, 17 April 1958, ALS, 'Recruitment of Ban Ghardaí, 1952–1962' (NAI, D/J, 4/62/2).
22. Assistant Commissioner Thomas Woods to Coyne, Secretary of Department of Justice (DJ), Typed Letter Signed (TLS), 16 September, 1958, File Number 4/62/2, Recruitment of Ban Ghardaí, 1952-1962, National Archives of Ireland (NAI).
23. Ibid.
24. Ibid.
25. Ann Marie Burke, Female Recruit No. 2W, to Costigan, 14 October 1959, TLS, 'Recruitment of Ban Ghardaí, 1952-1962' (NAI, D/J, 4/62/2).
26. *Sunday Review*, 18 October 1959.
27. *Sunday Independent*, 18 October 1959.
28. See McNiffe, *A History of the Garda Síochána*, 166.
29. Superintendent Catherine Clancy, 'The Role of Women', *Communique*, June 1997, 33.
30. Ibid.
31. Department of Justice, *Report from Conference in the Department of Finance*, 11 March 1960, 'Transfer of Training Centre for Garda Recruits to Templemore' (NAI, Department of Justice, 4/48/3).
32. Charles Haughey, Parliamentary Secretary to Minister for Justice, to Traynor, 25 February 1961, TLS, 'Transfer of Training Centre for Garda Recruits to Templemore' (NAI, D/J, 4/48/3).
33. Department of Justice, memorandum to each member of the Government, 1 March 1961, TD, 'Transfer of Training Centre for Garda Recruits to Templemore' (NAI, D/J, 4/48/3)
34. Department of Justice, draft copy of memorandum to each member of the Government, 1 March 1961, TD, 'Transfer of Training Centre for Garda Recruits to Templemore' (NAI, D/J, 4/48/3)
35. Seán Lemass, Taoiseach, to Traynor, 2 March 1961, TLS, 'Transfer of Training Centre for Garda Recruits to Templemore' (NAI, D/J, 4/48/3).
36. Traynor to Peter Berry, Secretary of Department of Justice (appointed to the position following death of T.J. Coyne in February 1961), 21 April 1961, ALS, 'Transfer of Training Centre for Garda Recruits to Templemore' (NAI, D/J, 4/48/3).
37. *Commission on the Garda Síochána: Report on Remuneration and Conditions of Service* [hereafter *Conroy Report*] (Dublin: Government Publications, 1970), 38.
38. Tim Doyle, *Peaks and Valleys: The ups and downs of a young garda* (Dublin: TJD Publications, 1997).
39. Ibid., 33.
40. Ibid., 102.
41. Ibid., 66.
42. Ibid., 77.
43. Commissioner Daniel Costigan to Peter Berry, Secretary of the Department of Justice, 15 June 1964, TLS, 'Garda recruitment, contents of and special examinations, 1962-1964' (NAI, D/J, 2005/147/77).
44. Ibid.

45. *Conroy Report*, 112.
46. John Griffin, Assistant Secretary of Department of Justice, to Berry, 23 November 1965, TLS, 'Garda recruitment, contents of and special examinations, 1962–1969' (NAI, D/J, 2005/147/77).
47. Berry to Noel Duggan, Secretary of Civil Service Commissioners, 26 November 1965, TLS, 'Garda recruitment, contents of and special examinations, 1962–1969' (NAI, D/J, 2005/147/77).
48. Duggan to Berry, 1 December 1965, TLS, 'Garda recruitment, contents of and special examinations, 1962-1969' (NAI, D/J, 2005/147/77).
49. *Commission on the Garda Síochána: Report on Remuneration and Conditions of Service* [hereafter *Conroy Report*] (Dublin: Government Publications, 1970), 3.
50. Ibid., 38–38.
51. Ibid.
52. Ibid., 43.
53. Ibid., 113.
54. Ibid.
55. *Sunday Independent*, 10 October 1971, 4.
56. Ibid.
57. Ibid.
58. Ibid.
59. Jack Marrinan, 'Editorial', *Garda Review* 6.12 (December 1978): 1.
60. Ibid., 15.
61. *Ryan Report*, 111.
62. Jack Marrinan, 'Editorial', *Garda Review*, 8.1 (January 1980): 1.
63. Ibid.
64. *Garda Training Committee: Report on Probationer Training* [hereafter *Walsh Report*] (Dublin: Government Publications, 1985), 15.
65. Ibid., 21.
66. Ibid., 22.
67. Ibid., 32.
68. Ibid., 35.
69. Ibid.
70. Ibid.
71. Ibid., 178.
72. Ibid., 194.
73. Ibid., 204.
74. Ibid., 43.
75. Ibid.
76. Ibid., 44.
77. Ibid., 45.
78. Ibid., 66.
79. Dáil Éireann Debates, 9 April 1986 (vol. 365, col. 43).
80. Dáil Éireann Debates, 19 November 1986 (vol. 369, col. 382).
81. Ibid.
82. Dáil Éireann Debates, 13 May 1987 (vol. 372, col. 1763).
83. Dáil Éireann Debates, 18 February 1988 (vol. 378, col. 419).

10 THE IMPLEMENTATION OF THE GREATER SCHOOLS CO-OPERATION POLICY AND VOCATIONAL EDUCATION COMMITTEES IN 1960s IRELAND

MARIE CLARKE

This chapter examines the policy initiative of the State, which sought to achieve greater schools co-operation between the secondary school authorities and the vocational education committees (hereafter VECs) in the Irish education system during the 1960s. The State sought to realise this ambition through the introduction of the Common Intermediate Certificate, a three-year junior cycle programme, which would be offered by both systems. Many authors who have focused on education policy formation during this period have ignored the implications of macro policies on micro contexts, particularly with reference to the role played by the VECs. The result is an incomplete analysis. This chapter seeks to redress this imbalance by highlighting the tensions between local actors addressing these proposed changes in the Irish education system, using four counties (Co. Dublin, Co. Leitrim, Co. Monaghan and North Tipperary) as case studies. The chapter contributes to the historiography of the period and provides a new dimension through which Irish education policy can be understood now.

Kogan suggests that it would be comforting and intellectually satisfying to be able to make clear generalisations about the relationships between the development of educational policy and local implementation.[1] The reality is much more complex. Unfortunately, in the field of educational history, local policies generally have been poorly regarded, holding an altogether subordinate position to national and indeed international circumstances. It is not always possible to see an automatic and easy correspondence between the politics of the community, the workings of local authorities and the formation of national policies.[2]

The introduction of any educational policy must be considered at its implementation stage before any judgements can be made about its success.[3] This includes the institutional and policy contexts at both national and local levels. Previous scholarship on educational policy-making in 1960's Ireland, particularly with reference to greater schools co-operation and the introduction of the Common Intermediate Certificate, has highlighted the diverse sectional national interest groups involved,[4] while implementation at local level has been ignored. In order to examine the response of local VECs to the introduction of the greater schools co-operation policy a case study approach was employed. Previously unused source material from the minutes of four county Vocational Education Committees (VECs) was examined. The counties under review, Co. Leitrim, Co. Dublin, North Tipperary and Co. Monaghan were very different in terms of the administrative areas that they served during the period under review. This diversity makes the local study during this period all the more valuable. Co. Leitrim and North Tipperary VEC were rural in orientation. Co. Monaghan VEC and Co. Dublin VEC were both urban and rural in their provision. The chapter employs the source material from the VECs as this evidence has not been analysed to date by historians of education with reference to these specific policies.

The difficulties surrounding the implementation of government policy at local level is clearly reflected in the case studies. It is not claimed that these case studies are representative of all areas where these policies were attempted, but the in-depth analysis that they facilitate underscores the important contribution of education micro politics to historical inquiry. What matters most to macro policy outcomes is local capacity. This chapter contends that the greater schools co-operation policy developed by the Department of Education officials was inconsistently implemented in local contexts.

CREATING A UNIFIED SECOND-LEVEL SYSTEM: THE MACRO CONTEXT

The issue of the costs and benefits of education has been central to educational policy-making for decades.[5] Educational thinking in Ireland during the 1960s focused on the role of education in economic development, and debate about educational change centred on the economic advantages accruing from a highly educated workforce. The two were regarded as being very closely inter-linked, and the main emphasis of government policy was placed on developing technology and related skills. However, this was a difficult goal to achieve.[6] At the beginning of 1963 there were two types of post-primary school in Ireland.[7] There were private fee-paying secondary schools, in the main run by the Churches, with an academic curriculum which prepared pupils for the Intermediate Certificate, the Leaving Certificate, and entry to university and the professions. The secondary schools were private and elite.[8] The core subjects on the syllabus in these schools were religion, Irish, English, and mathematics. In addition other subjects included history and geography, science and another language, usually Latin in the case of boys and French in the case of girls.[9] O'Donoghue argues that the secondary school programme of study – a grammar-type curriculum with a strong literary-classical emphasis – was rationalised in terms of personal and moral development.[10] The *Report of the Council of Education on the Curriculum of the Secondary School*, published in 1962, stated that the ultimate purpose of education was the overall development (religious, moral, intellectual and physical) of the person.[11]

The VECs, local authority structures operating within a system of local government, were introduced under the 1930 Vocational Education Act. They had responsibility under the legislation for the development of technical education. They built and ran vocational schools, which were free.[12] At the start of the 1960s the vocational school offered nothing beyond a two-year Day Vocational Group Certificate. The two-year Day Vocational Group Certificate, introduced to the vocational sector in 1947, had 20 different subjects on its syllabus. Few schools had every subject; the majority provided arithmetic, commerce, domestic economy, English, Irish, mechanical drawing, religion, typewriting and woodwork. In larger urban schools, subjects such as art, French or German were offered.[13] Most of those who attended vocational school intended to seek manual employment as soon as the law released them from the obligation to attend school. The educational attainment by participants was perceived as being poor.[14] The VECs also offered a range of adult and community education programmes, which made their profile and presence very important in local communities.[15] At the *Symposium on Investment in Education* in 1965 reference was made to the fact that, in 1964, 30,000 full-time pupils were enrolled in vocational schools and average attendance in vocational schools fell as low as 76 per cent of the enrolment.[16] Many vocational schools were rural in orientation and contained only one or two rooms. This also attracted much criticism at the *Symposium on Investment in Education*. By continental standards vocational schools in Ireland were very limited. While they had classrooms, they did not typically have specialised rooms to cater for a variety of skills.

The 1960s in the Republic of Ireland has been considered a period of great change, economically, socially and culturally.[17] Reform in education during the period is generally considered within this broad framework.[18] In 1961, the OECD had arranged the Washington Policy Conference on 'Economic growth and investment in Education'. Ireland participated in this conference and volunteered for a co-ordinated examination of the Irish education system. The survey team that worked between 1962 and 1965 concentrated on a number of issues in their final report entitled *Investment in Education*.[19] They considered the lack of educational statistics available in Ireland about the system and devised methods of securing the relevant data pertinent to their inquiry.[20] They also recommended the setting up of a Development Branch within the Department of Education. Differences in education participation in the various socio-economic groups and in different geographical areas were analysed.[21] In 1963, the survey team found that while 42 per cent of that year's primary school leavers transferred into secondary school and another 29 per cent transferred into vocational school, 29 per cent had already finished their schooling and had entered the labour market. Eight thousand of the cohort had left the primary school before reaching the end of sixth class.[22] Emerging from the data was the reality that existing school provision was not adequate to meet the needs of the existing school-going population.

While the OECD was conducting its analysis, the Minister for Education, Patrick Hillery set up a committee of civil servants from the Department of Education in 1962 to study the education system and to advise on required changes. The report asserted that a set period of post-primary education, reasonably well planned and adequately provided for, was a national necessity from a social and economic point of view. The authors recommended that the school leaving age be raised to 15 years initially, and after a period of ten years it should be raised to 16 years. They were unhappy with the divide between secondary and vocational schools and concluded that the distinction should disappear and a common programme of study at junior cycle be provided over three years in both school types.[23] O'Sullivan argues that *Investment in Education* shifted the prevailing view of secondary education, which focused on cultural and religious transmission, to one where the overall development of the person included preparation for economic participation.[24]

George Colley was appointed Minister for Education in 1965 and he championed the introduction of the greater schools co-operation policy and the Common Intermediate Certificate.[25] In his estimate speech of June 1965, he announced the establishment of the Development Branch in the Department of Education, which would carry out surveys to establish the need for school provision within each county. He appealed for co-operation and harmony on education issues amongst all sectors, pointing out that the uncoordinated building of schools could not continue indefinitely.[26] Prior to his term of office, both the secondary and vocational systems built new schools with scant regard to the actual needs of a particular area. From the VEC perspective schools were often built at the request of local residents who viewed the location of these schools as an important addition, particularly in remote parts of rural Ireland.[27] Co-operation had been minimal between the various branches of education and each sector felt threatened by the minister's proposals for co-operation. O'Connor makes the point that Colley's policies met with much opposition in 1965.[28] The school building programme was suspended until these surveys were completed. Some applications were refused on the grounds that there were enough schools in the area to meet the necessary requirements. Under Colley's proposals, if one school had facilities not available to another then he wanted them to share those resources.[29] Colley requested that a series of meetings take place between local providers to advance this proposal in each county, attended by VEC representatives, secondary school representatives and an inspector from the Department of Education. The inspector would assist the post-primary school authorities in considering the issues raised by the minister and would transmit any proposed arrangements for collaboration to the department.[30] The Irish Vocational Education Association (IVEA) and the Vocational Teachers Association (VTA) welcomed the proposals for co-operation between the secondary and vocational authorities at local level. Secondary school managers and the Catholic bishops were less enthusiastic.[31]

Walsh argues that Colley's proposal for wide-ranging collaboration between the secondary and vocational schools was one of the most radical educational initiatives undertaken by any minister since the foundation of the state.[32] He also suggests that the planning meetings, which were initiated following Colley's request, generally proved unproductive, as secondary school managers were willing to use practical problems as a means of delaying any significant changes. Other factors at both national and local level contributed to the lack of progress. O'Sullivan argues that the State's initiatives were often diluted and that its own commitment varied over time and across the range of policies that it had proclaimed.[33]

A key element of the greater schools co-operation policy was the introduction of the Common Intermediate Certificate, a three-year broad course of post primary education for all students. As Walsh suggests, Colley and the senior officials in the Department of Education were well aware that a broad curriculum, including academic and vocational elements, could be achieved only through collaboration between the secondary and vocational systems.[34] After a series of subject committee meetings between December 1965 and May 1966, the revised programme was approved and Circular M27/66 provided for the introduction of the Common Intermediate Certificate examination in secondary and vocational schools, starting in September 1966.[35] This added 342 schools to the existing 585 secondary schools that were already making such provision.[36]

IMPLEMENTING GREATER SCHOOL CO-OPERATION AT LOCAL LEVEL: CHALLENGES FOR VECs

The Co. Dublin VEC approved of Minister Colley's plans for greater co-operation between vocational and secondary schools.[37] Before meeting with local secondary school authorities, Co. Dublin VEC conducted its own survey and ascertained the number of secondary schools in each locality. When that task was completed meetings were called between secondary and vocational schools in an attempt to implement the minister's recommendations. However, the VEC encountered a number of difficulties with the Department of Education in relation to this policy. The Department of Education did not inform Co. Dublin VEC when a local primary school had decided to open a 'secondary top' school.[38] Secondary top schools were, in the main, Catholic Church-managed national schools, that offered the secondary school curriculum. This development seriously threatened enrolment at the local vocational school in the area.[39] Ms E. Dempsey, Principal of Dundrum Vocational School, informed the VEC that the Principal of Our Lady's Primary School, Columbanus Road, Dundrum had told her that an application had been made to the Department of Education for permission to open a secondary top school.[40] Ms Dempsey pointed out that a high proportion of the students who attended the vocational school had received their education at that primary school. Obviously the opening of such a school would have had a negative impact on Dundrum Vocational School. There were four established Catholic secondary schools in the area: St. Anne's, Milltown; Notre Dame, Churchtown Rd; Our Lady's Grove, Goatstown Rd; and Mount Anville, Dundrum. As Co. Dublin VEC had built a new vocational school for girls in the Dundrum area the previous year, it had accommodation for 75 new students. From the point of view of the VEC, the opening of a secondary top school actually duplicated the services in the area, which in its opinion was contrary to the policy of schools co-operation. The Department of Education refused to meet representatives from Co. Dublin VEC to discuss the matter. Similar difficulties arose in Co. Leitrim.

A meeting took place during April 1966 in the Department of Education about co-operation between schools in Co. Leitrim.[41] It was attended by a number of personnel from the Department of Education. These officers represented the three branches in the Department of Education, the Secondary, the Technical and the newly-formed Development Branch. Fr. McLoughlin, who was the Headmaster of Scoil Mhanchain, Mohill, and the CEO of Co. Leitrim VEC also attended the meeting. The Development Branch Officers outlined the current and projected enrolment figures for the Mohill area, which showed that the potential annual intake of first year post-primary pupils in the Mohill district was 100, leading to an enrolment of 300 pupils in the three-year course leading to the Common Intermediate Certificate. Based on the assumption that 30 per cent of those followed on to Leaving Certificate, it was assumed that some 400 pupils would receive post primary education in Mohill. From those figures, the Department of Education believed that there was little justification for more than two post-primary schools in the area. They suggested that the policy of co-operation be pursued *via* the retention of the local convent school and the promotion of greater co-operation between Scoil Mhanchain and the local VEC school. The provision of post-primary courses in the convent school would remain as it currently existed. Similar courses were to be provided for boys and girls in the vocational school. The Department of Education suggested that staff in the vocational school would also include the headmaster and other teachers from the secondary school. The headmaster and the secondary school teachers were to be appointed, supervised and paid by the Secondary School branch of the Department of Education.[42] The officials suggested that a committee of three be appointed to direct the school. Membership of this committee would include the headmaster of the secondary school, the headmaster of the vocational school and one other. The title 'vocational school' was to disappear and be replaced by a new title, which was not to be a comprehensive school. The CEO was not entitled to supervise or direct in any way classes conducted by secondary teachers in the school. The headmaster of the secondary school was proposed as vice-principal of the new school and consequently he was responsible for the time tabling of courses and discipline. Teachers in the school appointed by the VEC were subject to VEC conditions and answerable to the CEO.[43]

The meeting was significant in relation to the policy of closer co-operation between schools as envisaged for Co. Leitrim. The local convent school was to be kept intact, and staff members were to remain working in their respective sectors. The control of the school was left in the hands of a committee, with no clarification as to who the third person would be and the removal of the title vocational school caused the VEC in Co. Leitrim much unease. Neither side was happy with the proposals made by the Department of Education personnel.[44] The CEO expressed doubts about the notion of dual control. The headmaster of the secondary school stated that he would make no decision until a new bishop was appointed to the diocese. The CEO enquired about the position of students who were unable to complete the new Common Intermediate Certificate programme but who would benefit from the Day Group Certificate. It was pointed out that the Day Group Certificate would not be conducted in the school. From the perspective of the VEC a central tenet of the vocational school programme was removed. In reality, this meant that pupils whose parents, because of financial circumstances, wanted them to follow a Day Group Certificate two-year course in order to gain employment could not do so. It would have been difficult for the VEC to agree to such a proposal and the CEO pointed this out. Towards the end of the meeting the headmaster of the secondary school stated that his preference was for an amalgamation with the local convent secondary school rather than with the vocational school.[45] This highlights the divisions that existed between the various sectors in education at local level. This reality was also mirrored in Co. Monaghan.

The Co. Monaghan VEC had intended to build a new vocational school in the Clones area. The VEC received a letter from the President of St Tiernach's Secondary School Clones about the policy of greater schools co-operation. The President of St. Tiernach's stated that with the provision of a metal and woodwork room, comprehensive education could be provided in the area at a fraction of the cost of building a new vocational school.[46] In September 1967,

Mr. E. Cassidy, a member of the VEC, voiced the opinion that the people of Clones believed that two post-primary schools could not be sustained in the area. He recommended that the VEC co-operate with St. Tiernach's secondary school. Another member of the VEC, Mr Gillanders, supported this view. The majority of members on the committee disagreed. The Co. Monaghan VEC had a long association with the Clones area. The majority of members argued that part of the responsibility of the VEC was to make arrangements for the continued development of vocational education in Clones and they refused to co-operate with St. Tiernach's secondary school. The Department of Education eventually agreed to the building of a new vocational school in the area.[47]

North Tipperary VEC for its part never considered greater schools co-operation as a realistic policy for its administrative area.[48] In Thurles, there was no accommodation to cater for extra students. In Nenagh, there was no accommodation and no facilities in the boys' secondary school for the interchange of classes. In Roscrea accommodation was full. Four teachers already interchanged with the secondary schools in the local area. North Tipperary VEC wanted extra teaching services to be provided for an expected increase in girls' classes. They expected an increase in this enrolment because the 'secondary top' part of the local convent national school had closed. In Borrisokane, accommodation in the building was insufficient and there was no secondary school in the area to cater for post-primary education. In Newport, as there was no post-primary school for boys in the town, the question of interchange of classes or teachers did not arise. In Templemore there was no accommodation available in the vocational school or in the local boys' and girls' secondary schools for the policy of co-operation to work.[49] Therefore there was very little room to facilitate national policy. The introduction of the greater schools co-operation policy was also influenced by responses at local level to the introduction of the Common Intermediate Certificate programme.

THE INTRODUCTION OF THE COMMON INTERMEDIATE CERTIFICATE PROGRAMME IN VECs

The introduction of the Common Intermediate Certificate programme in vocational schools was undermined by a number of issues. Two years after the proposal was first made, the VECs under study considered that they did not have enough information about the new programme.[50] They had received no instructions about what students could be entered for the examination.

Many VECs did not have the required staff to provide various elements of the course. For some VECs, the introduction of the programme impacted upon their evening classes, as staff would be timetabled to teach day-time courses. For many attending VEC schools, the Day Group Certificate was never completed within the two-year official time frame but took three years and this also impacted on their capacity to provide the Common Intermediate Certificate programme. Pupils in vocational schools were obliged under the new programme to take English, Irish, maths, mechanical drawing or art or home economics or commerce. They also had to take not less than two other subjects from the approved list with civics. The list of approved subjects that were optional included manual training (later metalwork and woodwork), science (later general and rural science), Latin, Greek, French, German, Italian, Spanish, music and history and geography.

Some VECs had not wanted to introduce this new course, arguing the introduction of this programme took away from the purpose and aim of vocational education. Members of Co. Leitrim VEC[51] expressed concerns that only a minority of pupils in the vocational system would actually benefit from the Common Intermediate Certificate over a three-year cycle. They were fearful that this would be to the detriment of students who were unable to meet programme requirements. The introduction of Irish, English and maths at Common Intermediate Certificate standard to the core group of practical subjects in the Group Certificate was in the opinion of members of Co. Leitrim VEC a dilution of the distinctive character and purpose of the day vocational schools.[52] The principal of Mohill Vocational School was quite positive about the new policy and submitted a report to the VEC which showed that it was possible to introduce the new programme into his school with only a few changes.[53] He wanted permission to rent a local building to provide extra accommodation and he also wanted to employ teachers of languages, history and geography. With these extra resources he had planned a first year Common Intermediate Certificate course including Irish, English, maths, science, Latin, French or history or geography, mechanical drawing, woodwork, metalwork, commerce, home economics, christian doctrine and civics. Canon McLoughlin, a member of Leitrim VEC, opposed this proposal on the grounds that the board of management of An Scoil Mhanchain, a local secondary school, did not want the Common Intermediate Certificate introduced in the local vocational school.[54] Another priest who served on Co. Leitrim VEC, Canon McNiffe, explained to the committee that the parents of the children who had attended An Scoil

Mhanchain had expressed the view that as time had to be devoted to practical subjects, sufficient hours could not be devoted to literary subjects to bring the pupils to the Common Intermediate Certificate standard, unless the standard of the examination was lowered. This was a very powerful argument. The views of the parents were very important to the politicians who served on the VECs and who did not want to be associated with unpopular decisions. Indeed, Deputy P.J. Reynolds TD expressed the opinion that in order to preserve the good relationship between the public and Mohill Vocational School, it was unwise for the VEC to take any steps that might run counter to the wishes of the parents. Personal votes were much more important than becoming embroiled in a row with the Catholic Church over the introduction of the Common Intermediate Certificate in a vocational school.

Mr. S.P. O'Buachalla acted as the minister's representative with the task of encouraging co-operation between vocational and secondary schools in offering the Common Intermediate Certificate. He attended a meeting of Co. Leitrim VEC in November 1965, where he outlined the minister's policy on second-level education.[55] Mr. O'Buachalla informed the meeting that an Intermediate Certificate secured through courses in a vocational school was of the same standard and value as that secured through a secondary school. Canon McNiffe, when he spoke to O'Buachalla, took a different line of argument than he had at the previous VEC meeting when he outlined his objections. He argued that the introduction of the Common Intermediate Certificate in vocational schools would result in a lowering of the standard in practical subjects in the Group Certificate. Consequently pupils would not receive the high standard of training that they had got in those subjects. He also argued that with an increased number of subjects fewer teaching hours could then be devoted to practical subjects. He felt that this was unacceptable and that the standards of practical training should not be lowered. These arguments, though different in emphasis, illustrate further the opposition of the local clergy to the introduction of the Common Intermediate Certificate in vocational schools and highlighted the unwillingness of the Catholic hierarchy on a national level to engage in the process of greater co-operation.[56]

North Tipperary VEC decided that a comprehensive educational programme to cater for both vocational and secondary students should be provided to fulfil the needs of the locality. This entailed the provision of extra teachers for classical or continental languages, history and geography. It proposed the introduction of a day school programme that would have enabled students to sit for the Day Group Certificate examination after two years and the Common Intermediate Certificate examination after three years. They also wanted to provide night classes in English and arithmetic for students in employment who possessed only primary school standards of education. These plans could not be implemented effectively, however, because the VEC was not in a position to allocate staffing and resources due to the lack of information received from the Department of Education about the proposed programme. Despite these difficulties the programme got underway in the vocational schools in North Tipperary. The introduction of the Common Intermediate Certificate caused a strain between the VECs and the Catholic Church in a local context. This was very evident at some VEC meetings where a local priest usually held the position of chairman of the VEC.

CONCLUSION

The evidence from the VEC minutes contextualises the impact of national policy at local level and suggests that a number of tensions existed between the macro policy of greater schools co-operation and the micro reality in terms of its implementation. While no general claims are made from the case studies presented in this chapter, nevertheless this source material provides perspectives not captured previously in relation to the analysis of national policy in local contexts. While the Minister for Education was committed to the policy and advocated a new approach with reference to wide consultation, it is clear from the case studies that such an approach did not work at local level. Meetings between officials from the Department of Education and local interest groups indicate that representatives from the department acceded to local opposition when confronted, supporting O'Sullivan's contention that policy implementation, at macro level, during this period was inconsistent.

From the negotiations that took place at local level in the case of Co. Leitrim, the solution offered by the officials actually undermined the local vocational school, did not facilitate a comprehensive school and promoted a new entity, which would be controlled by a committee. In Co. Dublin, the Department of Education facilitated the opening of a new secondary top school despite the negative impact that this would have on the local vocational school enrolments and on the policy of greater schools co-operation in the area. In Co. Monaghan departmental officials agreed to the building of a new vocational school, when the VEC did not support the policy of greater schools cooperation in the area.

The challenge of linking curricular change to facilitate school provision is evident in the local context. It is clear at national level that the minister and departmental officials sought to achieve greater schools co-operation through the introduction of the Common Intermediate Certificate. At national level the reconfiguration of the existing programme was achieved in a very short space of time. The education system at that juncture was comprised of two very different systems: the VECs on the one hand which had a poor track record with reference to educational attainment but nevertheless were an important presence in local communities and the secondary schools which were academic in orientation and catered for a more affluent social class. The proposals for a unified junior cycle reflected an academic bias on the part of the Department of Education as many of the vocationally oriented subjects were optional, despite the intention in 1962 to seek a more equal balance between academic and vocational subjects in the system. The relationship between the Day Group Certificate and the new three-year Common Intermediate Certificate was not given detailed consideration, given the fact that the Group Certificate which was offered by vocational schools was rarely completed within its official two-year time frame. In the case of Co. Leitrim, it was clear that the officials from the Department wanted the Day Group Certificate to be discontinued.

The introduction of the Common Intermediate Certificate programme did not achieve greater schools co-operation. Tensions existed between VEC members and principals in local areas. In the case of Co. Leitrim VEC, the Principal of Mohill Vocational School indicated that he could implement the new programme but this was rejected by the VEC. In Co. Monaghan the principal of the local secondary school indicated that a common programme could be provided without building a new vocational school yet the Department of Education sanctioned a new vocational school. The proposed reforms with reference to the provision of a common curriculum at junior cycle and greater schools cooperation highlighted the deep divisions that existed among the providers of Irish education at local level. It is also clear from the local evidence available that departmental policy was not consistent around the country in relation to the introduction of a unified junior cycle and the greater schools cooperation policy. The decisions made and the resulting tensions at local level impacted upon the Irish education system for many decades to come.

NOTES

1. Maurice Kogan (assisted by Katherine Bowden), *Educational Policy-Making: A Study of Interest Groups and Parliament* (London: Allen and Unwin, 1975), 129.
2. Kogan, *Educational Policy-Making*, 129.
3. Ibid.
4. Noël Barber, *Comprehensive Schooling in Ireland* (Dublin: ESRI, 1989); Imelda Bonel-Elliott, 'Lessons from the Sixties: Reviewing Dr Hillery's Educational Reform', *Irish Educational Studies* 13, no. 1 (1994): 32–45; John Coolahan, *Irish Education: History and Structure* (Dublin: Institute of Public Administration, 1981); Séamas Ó Buachalla, *Education Policy in Twentieth-Century Ireland* (Dublin: Wolfhound Press, 1988); John Walsh, *The Politics of Expansion: the transformation of educational policy in the Republic of Ireland, 1957–72* (Manchester: Manchester University Press, 2009).
5. Tom Woodin, Gary McCulloch and Steven Cowan, 'Raising the participation age in historical perspective: policy learning from the past?', *British Educational Research Journal* (2012), iFirst DOI 10.1080/01411926.2012.668871, 5.
6. Ó Buachalla, *Education Policy in Twentieth Century Ireland*, 71.
7. Bonel-Elliott, 'Lessons from the Sixties', 32–45.
8. John Logan, 'All the children: economic development, social change and education 1958–1994', in John Logan (ed.), *Teachers' Union: The TUI and its Forerunners 1899-1994* (Dublin: A. & A. Farmar, 1999), 277.
9. Logan, 'All the children: economic development, social change and education 1958–1994', 277.
10. Thomas A. O'Donoghue, *The Catholic Church and the Secondary School Curriculum in Ireland, 1922–1962* (New York: Peter Lang, 1999), 89.
11. Denis O'Sullivan, *Cultural Politics and Irish Education since the 1950s: Policy, Paradigms and Power* (Dublin: Institute of Public Administration, 2005), 133.
12. Bonel-Elliott, 'Lessons from the Sixties: Reviewing Dr Hillery's Educational Reform', 34.
13. Logan, 'All the children: economic development, social change and education 1958–1994', 282.
14. Áine Hyland, 'The Curriculum of Vocational Education 1930–1966', in John Logan (ed.), *Teachers' Union: The TUI and its Forerunners 1899-1994* (Dublin: A. & A. Farmar, 1999), 153.
15. Marie Clarke, 'Vocational Education in a local context 1930–1998' (unpublished PhD thesis, University College Dublin, 1999), 152.
16. Patrick Cannon, 'Analysis of Educational Policies in the 1960s, Symposium on Investment in Education', *Journal of Statistical and Social Inquiry*, 119, 1 (965/6), 77.
17. Paul Bew and Henry Patterson, *Sean Lemass and the Making of the New Ireland* (Dublin: Gill and Macmillan, 1982); Terence Brown, *Ireland: A Social and Cultural History, 1922–85* (London: Fontana, 1985), John Cooney, *John Charles McQuaid: Ruler of Catholic Ireland* (Dublin: O Brien Press, 1999); Joe Lee, *Ireland 1912–1985, Politics and Society* (Cambridge: Cambridge University Press, 1989); Brian Girvin, *Between Two Worlds: Politics and Economy in Independent Ireland* (Dublin: Gill and Macmillan, 1989); Roy Foster, *Modern Ireland, 1600–1972* (London: Allen Lane, 1988); Áine

Hyland and Kenneth Milne, *Irish Educational Documents Vol. 2* (Dublin: Church of Ireland College of Education, 1992); Kieran Kennedy and Brian Dowling, *Economic Growth in Ireland: The Experience Since 1947* (Dublin: Gill and Macmillan, 1975); John Horgan, *Sean Lemass: The Enigmatic Patriot* (Dublin: Gill and Macmillan, 1997); Brian Nolan, Patrick O'Connell and Christopher Whelan, *The Irish Experience of Growth and Inequality* (Dublin: IPA, 2000); John Sheehan, 'Education and Society in Ireland, 1945–70' in Joseph Lee (ed.), *Ireland 1945–70* (Dublin: Gill and Macmillan, 1979), 61–72.

18. Imelda Bonel-Elliott, 'The role of the Duggan Report (1962) in the Reform of the Irish Education System', *Administration*, 44 (1996): 42-60; Coolahan, *Irish Education; Sheelagh Drudy and Kathleen Lynch, *Schools and Society in Ireland* (Dublin: Gill and Macmillan, 1993); Tom Garvin, *Preventing the Future: Why was Ireland so poor for so long?* (Dublin: Gill and Macmillan, 2004); Peter Murray, "'Can I write to you about Ireland?": John Vaizey, the Ford Foundation and Irish educational policy change, 1959–1962 [document study]', *Irish Educational Studies*, 31, 1 (2012), 67–75. Sean O'Connor, *A Troubled Sky: Reflections on the Irish Educational Scene* (Dublin: Educational Research Centre, 1986); Eileen Randles, *Post-Primary Education in Ireland 1957–1970* (Dublin: Veritas, 1975); John Walsh, *The Politics of Expansion: the transformation of educational policy in the Republic of Ireland, 1957–72* (Manchester and New York: Manchester University Press, 2009).

19. For a comprehensive analysis of *Investment in Education*, see O'Sullivan, *Cultural Politics and Irish Education since the 1950s: Policy, Paradigms and Power*, 128–150. Also Murray, "Can I write to you about Ireland?": provides interesting perspectives about Irish education policy development prior to the publication of *Investment in Education*.

20. Patrick Lynch, 'Societal Change and Education: Investment in Education Revisited', in Brian Farrell (ed.), *Issues in Education Changing Education, Changing Society* (Dublin: ASTI Journal, 1999), 5.

21. Lynch, 'Societal Change and Education: Investment in Education Revisited', 5.

22. Logan, 'All the children: economic development, social change and education 1958–1994', 280.

23. Hyland, 'The Curriculum of Vocational Education 1930–1966', 134.

24. O'Sullivan, *Cultural Politics and Irish Education since the 1950s*, 128-50.

25. Walsh, *The Politics of Expansion: the transformation of educational policy in the Republic of Ireland, 1957-72*, 114.

26. Ó Buachalla, *Education Policy in Twentieth-Century Ireland*, 281.

27. Clarke, 'Vocational Education in a local context 1930–1998', 153.

28. O'Connor, *A Troubled Sky: Reflections on the Irish Educational Scene*, 96.

29. Ibid., 97.

30. Walsh, *The Politics of Expansion: the transformation of educational policy in the Republic of Ireland, 1957-72*, 147.

31. Walsh, *The Politics of Expansion*, 147.

32. Ibid., 143.

33. O'Sullivan, *Cultural Politics and Irish Education since the 1950s*, 128.

34. Walsh, *The Politics of Expansion*, 141.

35. Ibid., 149.

36. Logan, 'All the children: economic development, social change and education 1958–1994', 277.

37. Minutes of Co. Dublin VEC, March 1966.
38. Ibid.
39. Ibid.
40. Ibid.
41. Minutes of Co. Leitrim VEC, August 1966.
42. Ibid.
43. Ibid.
44. Ibid.
45. Minutes of Co. Leitrim VEC, May 1966.
46. Minutes of Co. Monaghan VEC, April 1967.
47. Minutes of Co. Monaghan VEC, September 1967.
48. Minutes of North Tipperary VEC, February 1966.
49. Ibid.
50. Clarke, 'Vocational Education in a local context 1930–1998', 170.
51. Minutes of Co. Leitrim VEC, August 1966.
52. Ibid.
53. Minutes of Co. Leitrim VEC, May 1965.
54. Ibid.
55. Minutes of Co. Leitrim VEC, December 1965.
56. Coolahan, *Irish Education: History and Structure*, 194.

11 WHEN EDUCATION WAS ASKED TO COMPENSATE FOR SOCIETY: EDUCATION FOR CHANGE AND PERMANENCE IN NORTHERN IRELAND IN THE 1980s

KARIN FISCHER

In 1970, Basil Bernstein, a socio-linguist and professor in the sociology of education at the University of London Institute of Education for many years, published an article entitled 'Education cannot compensate for society', as part of a collective work entitled *Education for Democracy*.[1] The choice of title for his article was deliberately provocative, as he wanted to stress the existence of often overlooked social and cultural constraints, including those related to the organisational and educational contexts of the schools themselves.

Bernstein's main focus was on the capacity or incapacity of schools to compensate for social inequalities, but I have taken the liberty of using his title here as a backdrop to the question of the role and ability of education to ensure sociocultural cohesion or at least, more cautiously, lessen sociocultural divisions. Can education 'compensate for society' in this respect? Should it be asked to? What factors may facilitate or hinder the adoption, implementation and social impact of an educational reform?

People who are, or have been, actively engaged in education reform with the aim of social improvement have to believe that what they do will have some impact, but most are also aware of the often unfair weight of social and political expectations on education, which are themselves sometimes contradictory.

Hence the necessity of exploring these social, cultural and political constraints, and other factors that could help or hinder change, when looking back at educational reform efforts.

This chapter proposes an examination of the background, implications and consequences of the curricular reforms in Northern Ireland in the late 1970s and 1980s. A major dimension of these reforms was specific to the region, in that they were meant to make sure that schools became part of the solution, as opposed to part of the problem, in the conflict that set nationalists and unionists in opposition. Schools have been traditionally asked to effect a form of social and cultural reproduction,[2] but in the 1970s and 1980s there was a growing consensus among educationalists in Northern Ireland that education could and should have a positive social impact, and become a force for change. How this could be achieved, and what the aims of such education should be, remained a matter for debate. There was the central issue of a focus on educational structure and/or content, with content clearly winning out by the mid-1980s as far as direct government involvement and scale of implementation were concerned.

In the historical context of education in the region, these curricular reforms were seen as marking a significant evolution, both at the political and at the educational levels, as has been recognised in several publications charting their development.[3] Several reports and academic works have also been published since then, with a view to providing a tentative general assessment of their actual educational and social impact.[4] The studies and surveys that were carried out in the late 1990s to assess the impact of the cross-curricular theme of Education for Mutual Understanding (EMU) in particular led to a widespread recognition that EMU had not had a significant impact, partly as a result of the fact that it tended to be reduced in many schools to the organising of sporadic contact programmes.[5] In the field of school history, most fully explored by Alan McCully in Northern Ireland, subsequent studies of students' attitudes confirmed that 'the capacity to move beyond their own cultural allegiances to understand the past from other perspectives proved difficult. … Young men, particularly, as they grew older were more likely to draw selectively on their historical knowledge to support community oriented positions'.[6] While there was widespread recognition of the efforts of many educational practitioners, by the early 2000s the general impression was that of relative failure, which accounted for a shift in focus towards the area of citizenship education as a potential alternative around that time.[7]

As is visible in Norman Richardson's 2011 synthesis of successive reports and in his own general evaluation of the implementation and impact of Education for Mutual Understanding, beyond general caveats acknowledging the importance of external social factors, the reasons most often put forward for this perceived failure or relative lack of impact centred on the educational practitioners themselves. They ranged from the reluctance of many teachers to address controversial issues with their pupils to the low priority given to a cross-curricular theme like Education for Mutual Understanding by school principals and by the education system as a whole, above and beyond the positive rhetoric.[8] As we will see, some people, notably within the small and integrated education sector, had criticised this reform attempt as being flawed to start with.

The aim here is to revisit that particular period and explore some of the social, cultural and educational assumptions behind the development of education policy. As a rule, the curricular reforms, and especially those related to school history and to the cross-curricular subjects Cultural Heritage and Education for Mutual Understanding, have been presented as stemming directly from previous local educational projects that were driven by an underlying reconstructionist philosophy.[9] While there were indeed some obvious connections and while actors behind the reforms may have taken their inspiration from these pioneering projects, the extent of the filiation remains debatable. A focus on the structural constraints within which the late 1980s curricular reforms were developed and on the mindset that informed them may help put into question the common tendency to lay the blame for relative failure at the feet of teachers or school principals.

The main sources used for this chapter were government and Department of Education official publications (including curricula and examination programmes, but also speeches and press releases), and publications and reflections by educationalists, teachers and academics who were involved in these reforms.

FROM PERPETUATION TO RECONSTRUCTION?

Between the 1920s and the early 1970s, after a very short-lived attempt at restructuring the whole school system, at least on paper,[10] the authorities in Northern Ireland accepted the *de facto* religious segregation of schools. They tried to consolidate the pre-existing unionist position in the field of education through a certain amount of control over content, by insisting in official documents on the importance of inculcating 'habits of loyalty to the Constitution of Northern Ireland and to the British Empire'.[11] There was a stress put on the necessity of keeping a strict control on textbooks[12] and a clear emphasis on British history (with more occasional mentions of Ireland) in examination programmes at post-primary level,[13] but at the same time a subject like history was made optional in primary schools for 'a variety of reasons' (which remained unspecified, and while geography remained compulsory)[14] and the Stormont government in fact exerted relatively limited influence on Catholic schools and on their actual programmes of study.[15] These schools were then free to devote some time to the teaching of Irish and in a number of cases to a nationalist version of Irish history, especially at primary level, while most state-controlled schools followed the official directives to the letter and tended to deal with Irish history through a British lens or as it affected Britain historically. This should not be taken to mean that Catholic schools taught mostly Irish history while State schools only taught British history. The first detailed survey of what was taught in schools, which was undertaken in 1973, showed that some Irish history was in fact taught in most schools, but that even in Catholic second-level schools it only very rarely represented the bulk of the course.[16] As Jack Magee suggested, 'because of the suspicion with which Irish history was treated, Catholic teachers in many areas considered it safer not to teach the subject at all'.[17]

Although there had been concerns expressed as to this state of affairs before,[18] it was only after the eruption of violent conflict in 1969 that what was actually taught in schools in Northern Ireland came under scrutiny and was questioned with reference to its potential role in perpetuating the conflict.[19] The events and violence of the years 1969 to 1972 shocked many in Northern Ireland educational circles into both questioning previous practice and determining that formal education had a specific responsibility in such a context.[20] Inter-community initiatives multiplied within and without schools as well as through the setting up of local school projects such as the Schools' Curriculum Project and especially the Schools' Cultural Studies Project (in which history played an important role) between 1974 and 1980.[21] The segregated nature of the education system and its consequences in terms of identity-building and the perpetuation of stereotypes[22] also started to be questioned locally, with the first integrated school, Lagan College, opening its doors in 1981 despite the lack of either government or Church support (the school had to wait three years before becoming government funded).[23]

As schools, and especially school history, had been accused of perpetuating divisions in the past, there was now an attempt at turning them into laboratories for reconciliation. One of the major aims of educational reform in Northern Ireland in the mid-1970s, 1980s and early 1990s became explicitly to seek to address the challenges posed by sectarianism. While the drive towards integrated schooling remained tentative, localised and not actively supported under direct rule at least up to the 1990s[24] (and even since then the extent of active support has remained debatable),[25] the real focus was on changing schools from within, through curricular reform. After about a decade of local initiatives with some public funding, these reform efforts gained a measure of formal government support in the early 1980s through the publication of a circular entitled 'The Improvement of Community Relations: The Contribution of Schools'.[26] The Department of Education explicitly stated that it was 'not questioning the right to insist on forms of education in schools which amount to segregation', but considered that schools had a corresponding duty to play a role in improving community relations.[27] A common curriculum along the lines of the National Curriculum in Britain was eventually set up in 1989–91 but with some significant differences: Education for Mutual Understanding and Cultural Heritage existed as cross-curricular subjects only in Northern Ireland, and a specific history syllabus was also developed.

While differences of viewpoint and approach may still have existed, there was enough common ground between the more influential educational actors and policy makers at British government level by the mid-1980s, and it was this convergence – alongside the British government's decision to develop a National Curriculum for England to start with – which allowed the proposed reforms to gather momentum at the regional level. As Alan McCully put it, writing more specifically about school history, 'what emerged mirrored closely developments in England but also allowed recent local history initiatives to be officially endorsed'.[28]

The shift in the power structures in the field of education from the 1960s onwards with the development of representative bodies (teachers' unions etc.) and the creation of intermediary bodies like the Northern Ireland Council for Educational Development in 1980, replaced by the Northern Ireland Curriculum Council in 1989,[29] also largely contributed to making these changes possible by allowing for an increased input from teachers and educationalists. The use of widespread consultation in Northern Ireland schools[30] and the direct involvement of a number of teachers (in schools, in working groups or as temporary members of the five regional Education and Library Boards established in 1973) ensured the building of a relative consensus on reforms in the field of school history and the themes of Education for Mutual understanding and Cultural Heritage and made it at least more likely that the teachers themselves would take them on actively.

SOCIOCULTURAL AIMS OF EDUCATION: CONTINUITY AND CHANGE BETWEEN THE 1970s AND 1980s

Writers such as Norman Richardson who have charted evolutions in education policy pertaining to community relations have insisted on the common ground and continuity between the first local projects in the 1970s and the large-scale reforms of the mid- to late 1980s.[31] In the field of school history in particular, it should be said that much of the inspiration for the new approach actually came from an English-based Schools Council History Project[32] developed in the 1970s which undertook 'a radical re-think of the purpose and nature of school history'.[33] While some of the roots of Education for Mutual Understanding could indeed be found in the first local projects, some differences in philosophy between these and the cross-curricular themes of EMU and Cultural Heritage have arguably tended to be underplayed, and there was also a selection made between these projects. These differences may go some way towards explaining why the 1980s reforms were supported by government – and deemed politically acceptable by the main Northern Ireland parties representing the nationalist and unionist communities, as we will see – when previous local educational projects such as those headed by John Malone had received a much more muted – or even outright negative – response from government officials. According to Maurice Hayes, who chaired the new Community Relations Council from 1969 to 1972:

> [John Malone] raised hackles in the educational establishment … by his insistence that community relations work had to go far beyond the curriculum, and had to involve school structures and government and the manner in which the school engaged with the individual pupil. … his pioneering work was disgracefully ignored by the sceptical and non-practising pundits in the Ministry of Education.[34]

The main architects of the first local educational projects broadly agreed that schools could and should have a reconstructionist role – educators or educationalists like John Malone,[35] Malcolm Skilbeck and James McKernan from the mid-1970s to the early 1980s,[36] and then, among others, Carmel Gallagher[37] and at university-level David Harkness in the field of school history, more particularly in the 1980s.[38] This was based on the belief that schools could be agencies of cultural reconstruction and places of cultural renewal rather than just preserving existing culture, an approach building on the work of philosophers of education John Dewey, Theodore Brameld and Paolo Freire.[39] The new resources developed in the late 1970s to early 1980s for social and cultural study were explicitly 'designed to nurture young people as citizens who are effective at renewing and developing Northern Culture' according to the Schools' Cultural Studies Project's *Teachers' Handbook* in 1980.[40] Such an approach directly echoed that advocated by Malcolm Skilbeck in an article entitled 'Education and cultural change' in *Compass* (journal of the Irish Association for Curriculum Development) in 1976, in which he expressed the need to try and change Northern Ireland culture, which he described as otherwise 'encapsulated and fixed' – as well as 'aggressive and sectarian, though not sectarian in the strictly religious sense' – through the schools.[41] The overall project placed a significant responsibility on the shoulders of teachers and was criticised by some at the time for its potential of transforming teachers into scapegoats and forcing them to take responsibility for all social ills.[42]

Choices made for the reforms of the late 1980s included not taking up the local experiments towards integrated education at any level of the system (for an unlikely radical overhaul of the education system or even for wider-scale projects with government impetus),[43] and, in the field of curriculum reform, what may be interpreted as a watering down of the transformational scope or ambition of the 'reconstructionists' with more ambivalent social and cultural aims. We will look at these two aspects in turn as factors of permanence or change.

EDUCATIONAL STRUCTURES VERSUS EDUCATION CONTENT

In the selection of educational projects, common schooling does not seem to have ever been seriously considered by government as a potential dimension of its overall education policy in the 1980s, as was obvious in its 1982 circular, although integrated education became officially encouraged once it had already established itself as a viable, but still very much small-scale, alternative. The initiative for new schools continued to come from parents. One main argument put forward in 1985 by Nicholas Scott, the Northern Ireland Under-Secretary of State for Education to explain the government's reluctance to actively support integrated education was that they wanted to avoid any accusations of social engineering from both communities.[44] It is perhaps even more likely that the government was not prepared to take on the Catholic Church, whose hierarchy was very much attached to Catholic schools and adamantly against common schooling.[45] Ways to envisage the setting up of common schools on a region-wide scale were thus never fully explored and the whole idea rejected out of hand as unrealistic given the social and political circumstances. The desirability of common schooling in principle was, however, one of the few things on which a substantial majority of Northern Ireland inhabitants, both Catholic and Protestant, agreed, as was shown by successive opinion polls and surveys from the 1970s onwards,[46] thus making it a democratic as well as an educational issue. Despite the consistently widespread support for integrated schooling among the population, and despite the growth and success of the first few integrated schools by the mid-1980s, government support, while becoming more explicit, has not led to the development of any direct policy on the ground beyond facilitating the institutional transformation of schools when schools themselves expressed a wish to become officially integrated.

The importance of associating form and content, and of teaching by example for educational effectiveness especially in the area of values and attitudes, were highlighted from the start by educationalists and authors such as John Malone and Robert Crone in the early 1980s.[47] The potential effectiveness in educational terms of educational reforms aiming at social improvement in Northern Ireland was then first rendered problematic by the obvious contradiction between some of the main stated educational aims ('learning to live together' and learning to 'understand and appreciate diversity') and the institutional structure or context of religious segregation.

Indeed, one of the possible explanations for the failure of some educational reforms in terms of their social impact is when the discrepancy between the content of what is taught and the educational, social, cultural or political context is simply too great for this content to make any lasting impression on social perceptions and on the social fabric itself. In the context of Northern Ireland, even without looking outside the school system, it could then be argued that the educational case for a shared history and for the development of 'mutual understanding' was largely undermined from the start by the perpetuation of the segregated nature of the education system itself. This was a point made in the early 1990s notably by two principals or former principals of Lagan College, Terence Flanagan and Brian Lambkin, who argued that EMU allowed Northern Ireland society and authorities to preserve separation 'by conceding a degree of integration' or contact.[48] Socially and culturally speaking, this meant the ultimate preservation and perpetuation of separate identities, with EMU and Cultural Heritage offering 'what appear[ed] to be an acceptable way out'[49] in both political and moral terms. A growing body of studies on the segregated nature of the school system has since tended to confirm that, while schools alone 'cannot be regarded as the whole problem nor the whole solution'[50], the factor of educational separation is very much instrumental in developing or further entrenching a 'them and us' mentality among children, regardless of curriculum content.[51]

Basil Bernstein insisted on the importance of asking oneself (and education policy makers) the question: 'what is the potential for change within educational institutions as they are presently constituted?'[52] In the context of Northern Ireland, from this perspective, changes in educational content were bound to fall short of their overall purpose as they could never compete against the underlying message of largely unchanged educational and social structures.

THE GENERAL OUTLOOK OF EMU AND CULTURAL HERITAGE: SOCIOECONOMIC RENEWAL OR REPRODUCTION?

By the mid-1980s it was assumed by both the authorities and most educational circles that the vast majority of children in Northern Ireland would continue to attend separate schools on the basis of the religion of their parents for the foreseeable future.[53] Since one could expect the overall purpose of the late 1980s curricular reforms to take this assumption into account, it seems reasonable to question the extent to which the dominant educational philosophy of the reforms remained that of social and cultural reconstructionism. As we will see, an examination of educational and political documents related to the curricular changes tends to confirm that the overall aim of the reforms in cultural terms could in fact be described as ambivalent, oscillating between sociocultural renewal and reproduction.

There was indeed a certain continuity with the stated aims of the pioneering educational projects of the 1970s, as has been shown notably in the field of school history, with the aim of encouraging critical thinking and questioning myths and stereotypes through a better knowledge of Irish history and a better understanding of the historical writing process.[54] The very fact that there was a level of agreement among educational actors on the historical content to be taught (with many textbooks jointly written by teachers coming from both communities) was a new development which pointed towards significant change, in line with earlier projects. The reforms were implemented, and, from an educational perspective, they represented undeniable progress in many ways when compared with previous practice and have been described as exemplary by some international writers on conflict resolution.[55] A number of history teachers in both Catholic and state schools interviewed in the mid- to late 1990s, while often wary of any kind of social engineering through the schools, accepted to see their role as that of 'the devil's advocate' through a direct and deliberate questioning of their pupils' historical assumptions.[56] Pupils were now expected to adopt a less passive, more critical attitude towards traditional interpretations of history which may be taken for granted in their own social background. Behind the cross-curricular themes of Education for Mutual Understanding and Cultural Heritage more generally, there was still also the ultimate stated aim of social transformation, of 'learning to live together' peacefully, above and beyond continuing differences of opinion on the constitutional status of Northern Ireland.

On the other hand, the ambitious (and often difficult)[57] approach chosen for school history was counterbalanced by the use of a more neutral value-based discourse in the guidelines on Education for Mutual Understanding and Cultural Heritage, with the focus on 'understanding' and 'awareness'[58] (rather than questioning or critical thinking) as well as a focus on the respect for traditions and on the celebration of differences (to be 'appreciated') which was meant to be reassuring to potential critics from either side of the divide – and which also happened to be in line with the policy of multicultural education gaining ground in Britain at the time.[59] As Tony Gallagher has noted, dangers inherent in the 'fetishisation of difference' that has occurred in some forms of multiculturalism have since been highlighted notably by the Council of Europe.[60]

This ambivalence of sociocultural purpose could in fact also be found in the ideas put forward by Alan Robinson, last director of the Schools' Cultural

Studies Project, who insisted that 'in the process of cultural renewal, the Project would wish individuals to cherish, as well as be critical of, their own cultural tradition, and to respect others from different backgrounds who engage in the same process, and who may yet remain poles apart.' This vision, however, would have been something of a step down from the cultural rationale put forward by Malcolm Skilbeck (above), with his careful and deliberate use of the singular ('Northern Ireland culture'), which put into question the bi-cultural representation that became more frequent in the 1980s, and his strong insistence on the teacher as agent of cultural change. In this view, the teachers' critical focus on 'Northern Ireland culture' would lead to direct and deliberate questioning. This contrasts with the less demanding or more passive language of 'understanding' and 'appreciating' culture and cultural differences or diversity as necessarily legitimate and hence worthy of perpetuation.

When the government took up the proposals for reform in 1988 as part of the setting up of a National Curriculum in the various parts of the UK, Secretary of State for Education Brian Mawhinney expressed the following position:

> Several respondents [to the consultation] suggested that there should be opportunities for pupils to gain awareness of aspects of history, culture and traditions which contribute to the cultural heritage of Northern Ireland. The Government welcomes and accepts this suggestion as a positive measure aimed at lessening the ignorance which many feel contributes to the divisions in our society.[61]

He thus insisted on increased knowledge (which justified the more systematic introduction of Irish and Northern Irish history into the syllabus) as a potential tool for lessening social divisions. At the same time, notions of cultural change or cultural renewal which had been at the core of previous educational projects were subsumed under the dominant new political discourse acknowledging the existence and legitimacy of two distinct 'cultural traditions' in Northern Ireland. Phrases such as 'cultural heritage', implying a potentially all-inclusive, common heritage beyond historical and contemporary divisions, and 'cultural traditions', pointing rather to the perceived existence and permanence of (only) two distinct cultures in Northern Ireland, were inevitably politically loaded.[62]

The Cultural Traditions Group, set up with government support (through the new Central Community Relations Unit) in 1988, had in fact started out at the initiative of a number of academics, writers and artists as the Two Traditions Group in the early 1980s, as part of an effort to bring reflection and debate on cultural matters beyond academia into the public sphere in Northern Ireland.[63] In a series of conferences and productions from 1989 to 1997, many members of this group devoted a lot of time trying to break out of the simplistic bi-cultural projection the phrase 'cultural traditions' lent itself to in the Northern Ireland context and displayed an awareness of its pitfalls.[64] In spite of their efforts to avoid the double danger of political exploitation and cultural oversimplification, there were inherent contradictions in the project,[65] and the phrase did become commonly associated with the two communities.

The 'cultural traditions' discourse found its way explicitly into the definition and rationale for EMU: 'We understand education for mutual understanding to be about self-respect, and respect for others, and the improvement of relationships between people of differing cultural traditions.'[66] The authors of the first guidelines for Cultural Heritage, who were perhaps more aware of the pitfalls of this kind of formulation since they were dealing directly with the concept of culture, were careful to avoid it in their definition and in the first working documents. They also confronted the issue by stating that 'the Working Group' inclined to the view that there *is* a single community, although a community rent by bitter division', and that 'pupils should [investigate] the origin of our present discontents' and 'not shy away from a study of what is diverse and distinctive in their cultural heritage'.[67] On the other hand, the use of the word 'heritage' itself pointed to cultural transmission and reproduction rather than to any attempt at renewal or transformation: 'cultural heritage comprises all those elements of culture which are inherited'.[68] The language of 'tradition' by the same token tended to imply the transmission of unchanging patterns from one generation to the next and thus in the context of Northern Ireland the perpetuation of the two communities as distinct. Apart from the insistence on the twin importance of respect and knowledge, one basic premise behind EMU was the assumption of cultural difference (implicitly between members of the two main communities – although there was also an attempt at looking at 'the other' in a much wider sense),[69] while Cultural Heritage stressed the role of education in cultural transmission, which was a far cry from reconstructionist conceptions of education as an instrument of economic, social and cultural emancipation and change.

This may help explain why the main political representatives at the time did not feel overly threatened by the new British cultural and educational policy, since, beyond efforts to introduce a common curriculum and promote improved relationships, it effectively underscored the ethnicisation of the Northern Ireland conflict[70] and promised to respect and preserve the 'traditions' of each community (and not just their opposed political aspirations) and hence their distinct or parallel social existence.

From a political perspective, the curricular reforms may then have been facilitated precisely by the fact that alongside the discourse on a shared history there was an acceptance in the educational rationale behind the new curriculum (beyond potential differences of interpretation by educationalists involved in it) of the very idea of the existence of two distinct cultural traditions in the North and most importantly of their right to self-reproduction. This certainly helps account for the relatively low level of political hostility to the proposed reforms at the time. In 1989, the Social Democratic and Labour Party objected to the use of the word 'community' in the report of the working group on the theme of Cultural Heritage to describe Northern Ireland society, and asked 'that the people of Northern Ireland be referred to as belonging to different (cultural) traditions, beliefs, values and attitudes which are, in some respects, shared, but in others not.'[71] David Trimble of the Ulster Unionist Party expressed his own fears that differences would be watered down by the new curricula, using the first conference of the Cultural Traditions Group Conference in 1989 as a political platform and criticising as largely meaningless what he called the 'euphemism' of the two 'traditions' and calling for the 'more honest' use of the 'two nations' approach.[72] He insisted at the same time that 'any form of co-existence must acknowledge the right of each culture to exist and to perpetuate itself'.[73] At various times in the late 1980s, some members of the Free Presbyterian Church or the Democratic Unionist Party described the reforms as attempts at indoctrination.[74] These negative political reactions remained quite limited, however, to the surprise of the then Education Minister Brian Mawhinney, who was reported as saying: 'I have no idea why Unionists are not interested in education reforms. They represent thousands of parents but have made no attempt to persuade me to make any changes.'[75]

The insistence on culture and understanding in the educational reforms was perceived by some as potentially problematic. It was argued by some academic commentators at the time that the new political focus on 'cultural traditions' and 'reconciliation' actually encouraged a presentation of the conflict as the result of a lack of understanding and tolerance which ignored the continuing political disagreement and risked underplaying the historical reality of political and social discrimination.[76] More recently, Andrew Finlay among others has expressed misgivings with the temptation to view problems such as racism and sectarianism always as expressions of confusions and conflicts of cultural identity.[77] He pointed to the dangers of 'identity politics', using the Good Friday Agreement of 1998 as an illustration of this:

> … by institutionalising a 'two-communities' or 'bi-cultural' model, the GFA may be encouraging the reification or objectification of cultural identity that is evident in the renewed sectarian polarisation that has occurred since the GFA was signed.[78]

Overall, the new form of pluralism encouraged in Northern Ireland tended to rest on an essentialist vision of cultural identity. In that context, the notions of 'parity of esteem' and even 'respect for diversity' which pervaded the education policy discourse, while they may seem widely acceptable at first sight, were also revealing of a lingering ambiguity about the nature of identity and culture.[79] They tipped the scale towards a conservative, essentialist and static conception of culture related first and foremost to group identity, and away from the notion of culture as a dynamic process involving contact and change and the possibility of individual agency.[80]

CONCLUSION

The historical evolution in the field of education policy in Northern Ireland is usually presented as a continuous development from more local initiatives to the region-wide curriculum and the example of school history would be a good illustration of this (although it also stemmed from an English curriculum project), but a comparative analysis suggests that the reconstructionist philosophy was more prevalent in the first educational projects while the political discourse around the Northern Ireland curriculum and the rationale which supported it tended to tone down this reconstructionist objective, taking for granted notions such as 'parity of esteem' and 'cultural traditions' which pointed to a more essentialist view of educational objectives in the field of culture. The education reforms, while far-reaching and ambitious in many ways, were arguably undermined from the start at two levels: first because they relied on the supposed ability of existing schools which otherwise reflected the major social divide in structural terms to bring about change in Northern

Ireland culture and society; second because this measure of expected change was itself ambiguous, to the extent that the emphasis was put on both a form of cultural renewal through 'reconciliation' and on the notion of parity of esteem and respect for perceived (implicitly distinct) cultural traditions whose perpetuation was also seen as a legitimate aim of schooling.

The remaining structural, social and political constraints or contradictions on the one hand, compounded by the ambivalence of the social and cultural aims on the other hand, represent major factors to explain the perceived relative failure of the curricular reforms around Education for Mutual Understanding and Cultural Heritage in the late 1980s. In-built premises, in terms of educational structure but also, to a certain extent, content or overall direction, tended to legitimise continuing social division. Taking into account these very significant in-built limitations would help set the potential role of teachers in its overall historical context and question the heavy emphasis put in many subsequent evaluations by educationalists or academics (most of whom were involved in the reforms in some way or another) on the lack of readiness or ability of teachers to implement them and thus bring about social improvement.

This is not to say that programmes such as the new school history syllabus of 1989–1991 were not excellent ones, and the case has to be made for continued educational effort, as 'part of the solution', along the lines of Paulo Freire's much-quoted contention: 'It is true that education is not the ultimate lever for social transformation, but without it transformation cannot occur.'[81] But a wider historical perspective helps us recognise that such attempts at social improvement through education can only go so far, depending on the structural, social and political contexts, and that responsibility for failure does not necessarily lie with the teachers.

One of the aims of this chapter was thus to highlight the importance of a historical perspective, but also of a perspective which goes beyond the strictly educational, in order to better understand mechanisms of permanence and change in the fundamentally interrelated fields of education and society. Schools have often been described as microcosms of society, with its inequalities, its various forms of segregation and discrimination.[82] Such an outlook emphasises the need for the wider political and social contexts (including of course education policy and educational structures) to be taken into account in any historical (as well as contemporary) account of educational problems and evolutions. Not only is a narrow lens not able to provide a fully accurate picture of past evolutions in this field, but it is likely to distort historical interpretations of factors of permanence and change.

The discourse of political analysts on Northern Ireland since the Good Friday Agreement of 1998 has often been cautiously optimistic,[83] but this is in stark contrast with the findings of sociologists on the ground which at the very least give substance to the new catch-phrase of 'benign apartheid'.[84] It is striking that twenty years later, in 2005, government plans for a 'Shared Future' in Northern Ireland envisaged very similar educational developments (through school contacts, shared initiatives and 'help[ing] young people understand their own heritage and tradition more fully, in order to help build the community confidence and capacity to begin to look forward and engage with others'),[85] as if little had actually happened since the 1980s in the field of education. In parallel, there has been no major move towards wider-scale integrated education, despite both the continuing support of the vast majority of the population and the government's own position on segregated living as stated in *A Shared Future* in 2005: 'Separate but equal is not an option. Parallel living and the provision of parallel services are unsustainable, both morally and economically'.[86]

NOTES

1. Basil Bernstein, 'Education Cannot Compensate for Society', in David Rubinstein and Colin Stonemann (eds), *Education for Democracy* 1970 (Harmondsworth, UK: Penguin, 2nd edition 1972), 104–116.

2. Pierre Bourdieu and Jean-Claude Passeron, *Reproduction in Education, Society and Culture* (London: Sage Publications, 1977). Originally published as *La Reproduction: éléments pour une théorie du système d'enseignement* (Paris: Éditions de Minuit, 1970).

3. In particular Norman Richardson, 'Evaluating the Northern Ireland Experience', in Norman Richardson and Tony Gallagher (eds), *Education for Diversity and Mutual Understanding: The Experience of Northern Ireland* (Bern: Peter Lang, 2011), 331–352. For a wider perspective, see also Robert Osborne, Robert Cormack, Anthony Gallagher (eds), *After the Reforms: Education and Policy in Northern Ireland* (Aldershot, UK: Avebury, 1993).

4. For a list of publications of this kind from 1992 to 2009, see Norman Richardson, 'Chapter 13: Evaluating the Northern Ireland Experience', in Richardson and Gallagher (eds), *Education for Diversity*, 332.

5. Alan Smith and Alan Robinson, *Education for Mutual Understanding, The Initial Statutory Years* (Coleraine: University of Ulster, 1996).

6. Alan McCully and Fionnuala Waldron, 'A Question of Identity? Purpose, policy and practice in the teaching of history in Northern Ireland and the Republic of Ireland', *International Journal of Historical Learning, Teaching and Research* 11.2 (May 2013): 149. Some of the main studies carried out in the field of school history are: K.C. Barton and Alan McCully, 'History, identity and the school history curriculum in Northern

Ireland: an empirical study of secondary students' ideas and perspectives', *Journal of Curriculum Studies* 37.1 (2005): 85–116; K.C. Barton and Alan McCully, '"You can form your own point of view": Internally persuasive discourse in Northern Ireland students' encounters with history', *Teachers' College Record* 112.1 (2010): 142–181; J. Bell, U. Hansson and N. McCaffery, *The Troubles Aren't History Yet: Young People's Understanding of the Past* (Belfast: Community Relations Council, 2010).

7. Michael Arlow, 'Citizenship Education in a Divided Society: The Case of Northern Ireland' in Sobhi Tawil and Alexandra Harley (eds), *Education, Conflict and Social Cohesion* (Geneva: UNESCO International Bureau of Education, 2004), 255–313.

8. Also Tony Gallagher, 'The Community Relations Context', in Richardson and Gallagher (eds), *Education for Diversity and Mutual Understanding*, 78–79.

9. Norman Richardson, 'The Roots of Education for Diversity and Mutual Understanding', in Richardson and Gallagher (eds), *Education for Diversity and Mutual Understanding*, 89–119.

10. Structural recommendations of the Lynn Committee, and *Education Act*, in 1923. Sean Farren, *The Politics of Irish Education 1920–65* (Belfast: Institute of Irish Studies, Queen's University Belfast, 1995), 46–47; Donald H. Akenson, *Education and Enmity: the control of schooling in Northern Ireland, 1920–1950* (Newton Abbot: David and Charles, 1973), 111–117.

11. Ministry of Education for Northern Ireland, *Final Report of the Departmental Committee on the Educational Services in Northern Ireland* (Belfast: HMSO, 1923), 55.

12. Ibid., 53.

13. See, for example, Government of Northern Ireland, Ministry of Education, Programme of the Secondary School Certificate Examinations for 1929 (Belfast: HMSO, 1928), 7. Similar orientations are to be found in subsequent years.

14. 'Although for a variety of reasons we have recommended that History should be an optional subject in primary schools, we hope that the option in its favour will be largely exercised'. Ministry of Education for Northern Ireland, *Final Report of the Departmental Committee on the Educational Services in Northern Ireland* (Belfast: HMSO, 1923), 53.

15. Sean Farren, 'Nationalist-Catholic Reaction to Education Reform in Northern Ireland 1920–1930', *History of Education* 15.1 (March 1986): 30.

16. William Smyth, 'Irish History in Secondary Intermediate Schools in Northern Ireland – A Survey of Extent, Teaching Methods, Qualifications of Teachers and Pupil Attitudes' (unpublished MA thesis, Queen's University, Belfast, 1974).

17. Jack Magee, *The Teaching of Irish History in Irish Schools* (Belfast: The Northern Ireland Community Relations Commission, 1971, 4–5.

18. Notably Denis Barritt and Charles Carter, *The Northern Ireland Problem: A Study In Group Relations*, 1962 (London: Oxford University Press, 1972), 91–92 and 152.

19. Jack (originally John) Magee's landmark conference paper on this topic to the Irish Association at Queen's University, Belfast, in 1970 was published in *The Northern Teacher* (Belfast: Stranmillis College Publication, Winter 1970) and then republished as *The Teaching of Irish History in Irish Schools* (Belfast: The Northern Ireland Community Relations Commission, 1971).
    Jack Magee was then Head of the History Department at St Joseph's College of Education, one of the two Catholic teacher training colleges in Northern Ireland at the time.

20. As is evident in other articles published in teachers' journals, notably John Darby, 'Divisiveness in Education', *The Northern Teacher* 11.1 (Winter 1973): 3-12 and in the same issue, John Malone, 'Schools and Community Relations', 19-30 and Rex Cathcart, 'To Build Anew', 43–46.

21. For general presentations of the Schools' Cultural Studies Project by Alan Robinson (Director of the Project) and by James McKernan (Project Officer), see Alan Robinson, *The Schools' Cultural Studies Project: A Contribution to Peace in Northern Ireland – Director's Report* (Coleraine: New University of Ulster, 1981) and James McKernan, 'The Schools' Cultural Studies Project', in David Hicks (ed.), *Minorities: A Teachers' Resource Book for the Multi-Ethnic Curriculum* (London: Heinemann Educational Books, 1981), 36–45.

22. As highlighted in Dominic Murray, *Worlds Apart – Segregated Schools in Northern Ireland* (Belfast: Appletree Press, 1985).

23. For a short history of Lagan College, see http://www.lagancollege.com/college/schoolhistory.php (accessed 10 December 2012). For quotes from both government and Church sources, see, for example, 'Northern Ireland's "School of Hope" a special experiment in tolerance', *The Evening News*, 29 December 1985, 10A.

24. The *Education Reform (Northern Ireland) Order* 1989 placed a statutory duty on the Department of Education to 'encourage and facilitate' the development of integrated education (Article 64).
There was also a mention of the desirability of integrated education in the Belfast or Good Friday Agreement, 1998 (section 13).
There are now more integrated schools in Northern Ireland but development of the sector remains slow with these schools catering for around 6 per cent of the school population and almost half of integrated schools failing to meet the Department of Education criteria on the percentage of pupils from both communities in 2011. Lindsay Fergus, 'Integrated schools missing targets on balance of pupils', *Belfast Telegraph*, 24 September 2011.

25. See, for example, the debate over the Northern Ireland Department of Education's refusal to fund some integrated schools in the mid-2000s. Gerry Moriarty, Northern Editor, 'Integrated schools open in Belfast and Tyrone', *The Irish Times*, 5 September 2006; Kathryn Torney, 'Kathryn Torney meets the chair of the Integrated Education Fund, Geraldine Tigchelaar', *Belfast Telegraph*, 30 January 2007.

26. Department of Education, Northern Ireland, 'The Improvement of Community Relations: The Contribution of Schools', 1982 (Circular 1982/21).

27. Ibid., 1.

28. McCully and Waldron, 'A Question of Identity?', 147.

29. Northern Ireland Curriculum Council, *The Northern Ireland Curriculum Council – Education Reform* (Belfast: NICC, 1989).

30. Northern Ireland Curriculum Council, *Cross-curricular themes: consultation report* (Belfast: Stranmillis College, 1990).

31. Richardson, 'The Roots of Education for Diversity and Mutual Understanding', in Richardson and Gallagher (eds), *Education for Diversity*, 89–119.

32. Schools History Project website, 'About SHP', http://www.schoolshistoryproject.org.uk/AboutSHP/influence.htm (accessed 2 August 2013).

33. Alan McCully, 'The Northern Ireland Curriculum and National Identity', in David Kerr and Cliff O'Neil (eds), *Professional Preparation and Professional Development in a Climate of Change: redefining the contributions of history teacher educators*, (Lancaster: SCHTE, University College of St Martin, 1995), 13-21.

34. Maurice Hayes, *Minority Verdict - Experiences of a Catholic Public Servant* (Belfast: Blackstaff Press, 1995), 90. John Malone was a Belfast school principal. He is widely regarded as one of the main pioneers in educational developments in Northern Ireland in the early 1970s. Richardson and Gallagher (eds), *Education for Diversity*, 96-98.

35. John Malone and Robert Crone, 'Approaches to Innovation in Schools', *The Northern Teacher* 12.1 (Winter 1975-76): 16-20. Dominic Murray, 'Joint Work: A Tool for Reconstruction', *Network: the Journal of the Association of Teachers of Cultural and Social Studies* 1.2 (December 1980): 10-16.

36. Malcolm Skilbeck, 'The School and Cultural Development', *The Northern Teacher* 11.1 (Winter 1973): 13-18.

37. Carmel Gallagher, 'The Contribution of History to Education for Mutual Understanding', *Network: the Journal of the Association of Teachers of Cultural and Social Studies* 6 (Oct. 1983): 22-26. Carmel Gallagher was a history teacher in a Catholic secondary school on the Falls Road in Belfast in the 1980s. She became involved in the setting up and revising of the Northern Ireland Curriculum as NICCEA Officer for History and the cross-curricular themes of Education for Mutual Understanding and Cultural Heritage in the 1990s.

38. Karin Fischer, 'University historians and their role in the development of a "shared history" in Northern Ireland schools, 1960s-1980s: an illustration of the ambiguous social function of historians', *History of Education* 40.2 (March 2011): 247-248 and 251.

39. Malcolm Skilbeck and John Reynolds, *Culture and the Classroom* (London: Open Books, 1976), 86.

40. Schools' Cultural Studies Project, *Teachers' Handbook* (Coleraine: University of Ulster, 1980), 14.

41. Malcolm Skilbeck, 'Education and Cultural Change', *Compass, Journal of the Irish Association for Curriculum Development*, 5.2 (1976): 14-15.

42. Rosalind M.O. Pritchard, 'Reconstructionism - Strategy for a Brighter Future?', *The Northern Teacher* 12.1 (Winter 1975-76): 5-9.

43. As Norman Richardson notes, in the face of opposition from the Catholic Church hierarchy especially, the Direct Rule authorities quickly backed off from an implementation of the proposals of the Chilver Report (by the Northern Ireland Higher Education Review Group), which had advocated the merging of teacher training institutions. Norman Richardson, 'The Roots of Education for Diversity and Mutual Understanding', 109.

44. 'If the government was seen to be seizing onto integrated education as a - to put it crudely - social-engineering weapon, then I think there would be a backlash ... from both sides of the community'. Quoted in 'Northern Ireland's "School of Hope" a special experiment in tolerance', *The Evening News*, 29 December 1985, 10A.

45. Seamus Dunn, 'A Historical Context to Education and Church-State Relations in Northern Ireland', in Robert Osborne, Robert Cormack and Anthony Gallagher (eds), *After the Reforms: Education and Policy in Northern Ireland*, 26.

46. Ed Cairns, Seamus Dunn and Melanie Giles, 'Surveys of Integrated Education in Northern Ireland: A review', in Osborne *et al* (eds), *After the Reforms,* 143–160; Ulf Hansson, Una O'Connor Bones and John McCord (Children and Youth Programme, UNESCO Centre, University of Ulster), *Integrated Education: a review of policy and research evidence 1999-2012* (Belfast: Integrated Education Fund, January 2013), 31–45.

47. Robert Crone and John Malone, *The Human Curriculum: The Experience of the Northern Ireland Schools Support Service 1978–1982* (Belfast: Farset Co-operative Press, 1983), 163.

48. Terence Flanagan and Brian Lambkin, 'Religious Identity and Integrated Education', in Chris Moffat (ed.), *Education Together for a Change: Integrated Education and Community Relations in Northern Ireland* (Belfast: Fortnight Educational Trust, 1993), 197.

49. Flanagan and Lambkin, 'Religious Identity and Integrated Education', 197.

50. Paul Connolly, Alan Smith and Berni Kelly, *Too Young to Notice? The Cultural and Political Awareness of 3-6 Year Olds in Northern Ireland* (Belfast: Community Relations Council, 2002), 51, quoted in Richardson and Gallagher (eds), *Education for Diversity,* 38.

51. For a synthesis with bibliographical references and quotes, see Richardson and Gallagher (eds), *Education for Diversity,* 36–38, 73, 95. Claire McGlynn offers a more systematic review of literature on integrated and faith-based schooling in Northern Ireland: Claire McGlynn, 'Integrated and Faith-Based Schooling in Northern Ireland', *The Irish Journal of Education* 36 (2005), 49–62. Also Ulf Hansson, Una O'Connor Bones and John McCord, *Integrated Education: a review of policy and research evidence 1999-2012,* 48–58.

52. Basil Bernstein, 'Education Cannot Compensate for Society', 115.

53. Osborne *et al* (eds), *After the Reforms,* 5.

54. Carmel Gallagher, 'The Contribution of History to Education for Mutual Understanding', *Network* 6 (October 1983): 22–26.

55. Margaret Smith, *Reckoning with the Past: Teaching History in Northern Ireland* (Lanham, Maryland: Lexington Books, 2005).

56. These interviews were carried out from a qualitative sample of thirty teachers taking into account school type (Catholic or state, secondary or grammar school) and geography as part of the groundwork for a thesis: Karin Fischer, 'L'histoire irlandaise à l'école en Irlande 1922-1996' (unpublished PhD thesis, University of Caen, 2000).

57. It quickly became clear that a great many teachers in both sets of schools were still reluctant or completely unwilling to teach recent Northern Ireland history in particular, and this was reflected by the fact that this particular module became optional in the first revision of the history curriculum in the mid-1990s. Department of Education for Northern Ireland, *The Northern Ireland Curriculum Key Stages 3 and 4 – Programmes of Study and Attainment Targets: History* (Belfast: HMSO, 1996).

58. Northern Ireland Curriculum Council (Report of the Cross-Curricular Working Group on Cultural Heritage to the Parliamentary Under-Secretary of State for Education), *Cultural Heritage: A Cross-Curricular Theme* (Belfast: NICC, 1989); Northern Ireland Curriculum Council (Report of the Cross-Curricular Working Group on Education for Mutual Understanding to the Parliamentary Under-Secretary of State for Education), *Education for Mutual Understanding: A Cross-Curricular Theme* (Belfast: NICC, 1989).

59. Seamus Dunn, 'Multicultural Education in Northern Ireland', *The Irish Review* 6 (Spring 1989): 32–38.

60. Tony Gallagher, 'Final Thoughts', in Richardson and Gallagher, *Education for Diversity*, 357.

61. Department of Education for Northern Ireland, *Education Reform in Northern Ireland – The Way Forward* (Belfast: DENI, 1988), 6.

62. Richard English, '"Cultural Traditions" and Political Ambiguity', *The Irish Review* 15 (Spring 1994): 97–106; Richard Deutsch, 'Une politique culturelle britannique derrière le processus de paix anglo-irlandais?', *Études Irlandaises* (Special Issue 'L'Irlande: Identités et modernité', 1997): 103; Wesley Hutchinson, 'Le Gouvernement britannique et les 'traditions culturelles' en Irlande du Nord', *Études Irlandaises* 20.1 (1995): 174.

63. For a short history, see Jonathan Bardon, 'Cultural Routes: Ways of Approaching Diversity', in Maurna Crozier and Richard Froggatt (eds), *Cultural Diversity in Contemporary Europe – Proceedings of the Cultural Traditions Group Conference*, (Belfast: Institute of Irish Studies, The Queen's University, Belfast, 1998), 15–16.

64. Notably Maurice Hayes (then Chairman of the Cultural Traditions Group), *Whither Cultural Diversity?* 1991 (Belfast: Community Relations Council, 2nd edition 1993); Jonathan Bardon (a historian and teacher then Chairman of the Community Relations Council), 'Cultural Routes: Ways of Approaching Diversity', 17–19.

65. For a critical analysis, Alan Finlayson, 'The Problem of 'Culture' in Northern Ireland: A Critique of the Cultural Traditions Group', *The Irish Review*, 20 ('Ideas of Nationhood' – Winter-Spring 1997): 76–88.

66. Northern Ireland Curriculum Council, *Education for Mutual Understanding: A Cross-Curricular Theme* (Belfast: NICC, 1989), 5.

67. Northern Ireland Curriculum Council, *Cultural Heritage: A Cross-Curricular Theme* (Belfast: NICC, 1989), 6 ('is' in bold in the original text).

68. Northern Ireland Curriculum Council, *Cultural Heritage: A Cross-Curricular Theme* (Belfast: NICC, 1989), 5.

69. This was made more explicit in the 1997 guidance materials for EMU, which focused rather on 'learning to live with and appreciate human differences of all kinds'. Northern Ireland Council for Curriculum, Examinations and Assessment, *Mutual Understanding and Cultural Heritage: Cross-Curricular Guidance Materials* (Belfast: NICCEA, 1997), 5f. Somewhat paradoxically, the reformulated rationale for Cultural Heritage revived the 'cultural traditions' discourse, still conveying an essentialist and static conception of culture: '[Cultural Heritage] involves helping pupils to appreciate the shared and distinct characteristics of cultural traditions within Northern Ireland and further afield. … This may mean having to reflect on how aspects of our culture may be perceived differently by others'. NICCEA, *Mutual Understanding and Cultural Heritage: Cross-Curricular Guidance Materials* (Belfast: NICCEA, 1997), 5f.

70. Roy Wallis, Steve Bruce and David Taylor, *'No Surrender!' – Paisleyism and the Politics of Ethnic Identity in Northern Ireland* (Belfast: Department of Social Studies, Queen's University, Belfast, 1986). Cillian McGrattan, *Memory, Politics and Identity: Haunted by History* (Basingstoke, UK: Palgrave Macmillan, 2013), 16, 41–42.

71. Social Democratic and Labour Party, *Comments on the Cross-Curricular Theme Document on Cultural Heritage* (Belfast: SDLP, 1989).

72. Quoted in Maurna Crozier (ed.), *Cultural Traditions in Northern Ireland – Varieties of Irishness: Proceedings of the Cultural Traditions Group Conference* (Belfast: Institute of Irish Studies, 1989), 46.

73. Quoted in Crozier (ed.), *Cultural Traditions*, 48.

74. Sean Farren, 'Education, Identity and Northern Ireland', Conference paper delivered at the History of Education Society Conference on 'Education and National Identity', Birmingham, 1995.

75. Quoted in Carmel McQuaid, 'Union is Wary of Healing Role', *Times Educational Supplement* (10 November 1989), 18.

76. Dermot Keogh and Michael H. Haltzel (eds), *Northern Ireland and the Politics of Reconciliation* (Cambridge, MA: Cambridge University Press, 1993).

77. Andrew Finlay (ed.), *Nationalism and Multiculturalism – Irish Identity, Citizenship and the Peace Process* (New Brunswick (USA) and London (UK): Transaction Publishers, 2004), 2–3.

78. Finlay (ed.), *Nationalism and Multiculturalim*, 6.

79. Ibid., 21–23.

80. An illustration of the conceptual debate on culture and multiculturalism is explored in an illuminating and challenging way in Anne Phillips, *Multiculturalism without Culture* (Princeton and Oxford: Princeton University Press, 2007). For a bibliographical review and synthesis of writings on the concept of culture in historical perspective: Denys Cuche, *La notion de culture dans les sciences sociales* (Paris: La Découverte, 1996).

81. Paulo Freire, *Pedagogy of Freedom: Ethics, Democracy and Civic Courage* (Lanham, Maryland: Rowman and Littlefield, 1998), 37.

82. Gary K. Clabaugh, 'Public Schools: Our Face in the Mirror', *Educational Horizons* 75 (Summer 1997), http://www.newfoundations.com/Clabaugh/CuttingEdge/PSMirror. html (accessed 10 August 2013).

83. Paul Bew, *The Making and Remaking of the Good Friday Agreement* (Dublin: The Liffey Press, 2007); Michael Cox, Adrian Gwelke and Fiona Stephen (eds), *A Farewell to Arms? Beyond the Good Friday Agreement* (Manchester: Manchester University Press, 2nd revised edition 2006 – 1st edition 2000 entitled *A Farewell to Arms?: from long war to peace in Northern Ireland*).

84. Peter Shirlow and Brendan Murtagh, *Belfast: Segregation, Violence and the City* (London: Pluto Press, 2006); John Nagle and Mary-Alice C. Clancy, *Shared Society or Benign Apartheid?: Understanding Peace-building in Divided Societies* (London: Palgrave Macmillan, 2010).

85. Office of the First Minister and Deputy First Minister, *A Shared Future – Policy and Strategic Framework for Good Relations in Northern Ireland* (London: HMSO, March 2005, available from http://www.ofmdfmni.gov.uk/a-shared-future-strategy (accessed 14 February 2014)), section 2.4.10.

86. Office of the First Minister and Deputy First Minister, *A Shared Future*, 15.

SELECT BIBLIOGRAPHY

References to official reports, parliamentary debates, eighteenth and nineteenth-century print sources, state publications and legislation, together with archival references, are located in the chapter endnotes.

SECONDARY SOURCES

Acheson, A., *A History of the Church of Ireland 1691–2001*, 2nd revised edition (Dublin: Columba Press and APCK, 2002).

Ahern, M., 'The Quaker Schools in Clonmel', *Tipperary Historical Journal*, 1990.

Akenson, D.H., *A Mirror to Kathleen's Face* (Montreal: McGill-Queen's University Press, 1975).

_____*Education and Enmity: the Control of Schooling in Northern Ireland 1920–1950* (Newton Abbot: David and Charles, 1973).

_____*The Irish Education Experiment: The National System of Education in the Nineteenth Century* (London and Toronto: Routledge and Kegan Paul/University of Toronto Press, 1970).

Alvey, D., *Irish Education: The Case for Secular Reform* (Dublin: Athol Books, 1991).

Arlow, M., 'Citizenship Education in a Divided Society: The Case of Northern Ireland', in Sobhi Tawil and Alexandra Harley (eds), *Education, Conflict and Social Cohesion* (Geneva: UNESCO International Bureau of Education, 2004).

Atkinson, N., *Irish Education: A History of Educational Institutions* (Dublin: Allen Figgis, 1969).

Auchmuty, J.J., *Irish Education: A Historical Survey* (Dublin: Hodges Figgis, 1937).

_____ *Sir Thomas Wyse, 1791–1862: The Life and Career of an Educator and Diplomat* (London: King & Sons, 1939).

Barber, N., *Comprehensive Schooling in Ireland* (Dublin: ESRI, 1989).

Barnard, T., *A New Anatomy of Ireland: The Irish Protestants, 1649–1770* (New Haven and London: Yale University Press, 2003).

Barrett, W.F., *An Historical Sketch of the Royal College of Science from its Foundation to the Year 1900* (Dublin: John Falconer, 1907).

Barton, K.C. and A. McCully., '"You can form your own point of view": Internally persuasive discourse in Northern Ireland students' encounters with history'. *Teachers' College Record* 112.1 (2010): 142-181.

_____ 'History, identity and the school history curriculum in Northern Ireland: an empirical study of secondary students' ideas and perspectives'. *Journal of Curriculum Studies* 37.1 (2005).

Batterberry, R.P.J., *Sir Thomas Wyse 1791-1862: An Advocate of a 'Mixed Education' Policy over Ireland* (Dublin: Browne and Nolan Ltd, 1939).

Beckett, J.C., *The Making of Modern Ireland* (London: Faber and Faber, 1966).

Bell, J., U. Hansson and N. McCaffery, *The Troubles Aren't History Yet: Young People's Understanding of the Past* (Belfast: Community Relations Council, 2010).

Bernstein, B., 'Education Cannot Compensate for Society', in Rubinstein, D. and C. Stoneman (eds), *Education for Democracy* (Harmondsworth, UK: Penguin, 2nd edition, 1972).

Bew, P. and H. Patterson., *Sean Lemass and the Making of the New Ireland* (Dublin: Gill and Macmillan, 1982).

Bonel-Elliott, I., 'Lessons from the Sixties: Reviewing Dr Hillery's Educational Reform', *Irish Educational Studies* 13, no. 1 (1994).

_____ 'The role of the Duggan Report (1962) in the Reform of the Irish Education System'. *Administration*, 44 (1996).

Bourdieu, P. and J.-C. Passeron., *Reproduction: in education, society and culture* (London: Sage Publications, 1977). Originally published as *La Reproduction: éléments pour une théorie du système d'enseignement* (Paris: Éditions de Minuit, 1970).

Bowen, D., *The Protestant Crusade in Ireland, 1800–1870* (Dublin: Gill and Macmillan, 1978).

Bowen, K., *Protestants in a Catholic State: Ireland's Privileged Minority* (Quebec: McGill-Queen's University Press, 1983).

Brady, C., *Guardians of the Peace* (Dublin: Gill and Macmillan, 1974).

Breathnach, S., *The Irish Police: From Earliest Times to the Present Day* (Dublin: Anvil Books, 1970).

Brenan, Rev M., *Schools of Kildare and Leighlin AD 1775–1835* (Dublin: M.H. Gill & Son, 1935).

Brown, T., *Ireland: A Social and Cultural History, 1922–85* (London: Fontana, 1985).

Burke Savage, R., *A Valiant Dublin Woman: The Story of George's Hill (1766–1940)* (Dublin: M.H. Gill and Son, 1940).

Byrne, K.R., 'Mechanics' Institutes in Ireland, 1825–1850', in *Proceedings of the Educational Studies of Ireland Conference: Dublin, 1979* (Galway: Officinia Typographica / Galway University Press, 1979).

Clear, C., *Nuns in Nineteenth Century Ireland* (Dublin: Gill and Macmillan; Washington, D.C.: The Catholic University of America Press, 1987).

Connolly, S., *Priests and People in Pre-Famine Ireland 1780–1845* (Dublin: Four Courts Press, 2001).

Coolahan, J., *Irish Education: History and Structure* (Dublin: Institute of Public Administration, 1981).

_____ *The ASTI and Post-Primary Education in Ireland 1909–84* (Dublin: Cumann na Meánmhúinteoirí, Éire, 1984).

Cooney, J., *John Charles McQuaid: Ruler of Catholic Ireland* (Dublin: O'Brien Press, 1999).

Corcoran, T., *State Policy in Irish Education, 1513–1816, Selected Texts* (Dublin: Fallon, Longmans, Green, 1916).

_____ *Education Systems in Ireland from the Close of the Middle Ages* (Dublin: UCD, 1928).

Corish, PJ., *The Irish Catholic Experience, A Historical Survey* (Dublin: Gill and Macmillan, 1985).

Cullen, C., '"Laurels for fair as well as manly brows": Women at Dublin's Museum of Irish Industry, 1854–1867', in M. Mulvihill (ed.), *Lab Coats and Lace* (Dublin: WITS, 2009).

_____ '"A pure school of science": the Royal College of Science for Ireland and scientific education in Victorian Ireland', in J. Adelman and É. Agnew (eds), *Science and Technology in Nineteenth-Century Ireland* (Dublin: Four Courts Press, 2011).

Cullen, M. (ed.), *Girls Don't Do Honours: Irish Women in Education in the Nineteenth and Twentieth Centuries* (Dublin: Women's Education Bureau, 1987).

Cullen, M. and M. Luddy, *Women, Power and Consciousness in Nineteenth-Century Ireland* (Dublin: Attic Press, 1995).

Curtis, S. and M. Boultwood, *An Introductory History of English Education Since 1800* (London: University Tutorial Press, 1960).

Crone, R. and J. Malone, *The Human Curriculum: The Experience of the Northern Ireland Schools Support Service 1978-1982* (Belfast: Farset Co-operative Press, 1983).

Daly, M.E., 'The Development of the national school system 1831-40', in Cosgrave, A. and J. Darby, 'Divisiveness in Education', *The Northern Teacher*, 11.1 (Winter 1973).

Donnelly, J.S. and A. Kerby (eds), *Irish Popular Culture 1650–1850* (Dublin: Irish Academic Press, 1998).

Dowling, PJ., *The Hedge Schools of Ireland* (Dublin: Talbot Press, 1935, reprinted by Cork: Mercier Press, 1968).

_____ *A History of Irish Education: A Study in Conflicting Loyalties* (Cork: Mercier Press, 1971).

Drudy, S. and K. Lynch, *Schools and Society in Ireland* (Dublin: Gill and Macmillan, 1993).

Duffy, E. (ed.), *Catholic Primary Education: Facing New Challenges* (Dublin: The Columba Press, 2012).

Durcan, T.J., *History of Irish Education from 1800 with Special Reference to Manual Instruction* (Bala, North Wales: Dragon Books, 1972).

Farren, S., *The Politics of Irish Education 1920-65* (Belfast: Institute of Irish Studies, Queen's University Belfast, 1995).

Fischer, K., 'University historians and their role in the development of a "shared history" in Northern Ireland schools, 1960s-1980s: an illustration of the ambiguous social function of historians', *History of Education*, 40.2 (March 2011).

Fitzpatrick, G., *St Andrew's College, 1894–1994* (Dublin: St Andrew's College, 1994).

Gallagher, C., 'The Contribution of History to Education for Mutual Understanding', *Network: the Journal of the Association of Teachers of Cultural and Social Studies*, 6 (October 1983).

Gillespie, R., 'Church, State and Early Education in Early Modern Ireland', in O' Connell, M., *Daniel O'Connell, Education, Church and State: Proceedings of the Annual Daniel O'Connell Workshop* (Dublin: Institute of Public Administration, 1992).

Girvin, B., *Between Two Worlds: Politics and Economy in Independent Ireland* (Dublin: Gill and Macmillan, 1989).

Hayes, M., *Minority Verdict – Experiences of a Catholic Public Servant* (Belfast: Blackstaff Press, 1995).

Hyland, Á. and K. Milne (eds), *Irish Educational Documents, volume I* (Dublin: CICE, 1987).

_____ *Irish Educational Documents volume II* (Dublin: CICE, 1992).

Jones, V., *A Gaelic Experiment: the Preparatory System 1926-61 and Colaiste Moibhi* (Dublin: Woodfield Press, 2006).

Kelly, A., *Compulsory Irish – Language and Education in Ireland 1870s-1970s* (Dublin: Irish Academic Press, 2002).

Keogh, D., *Edmund Rice* (Dublin: Four Courts Press, 1996).

_____ *Edmund Rice and the First Christian Brothers* (Dublin: Four Courts Press, 2008).

Keogh, D. and M.H. Haltzel (eds), *Northern Ireland and the Politics of Reconciliation* (Cambridge, MA: Cambridge University Press, 1993).

Kingsmill Moore, H., *An Unwritten Chapter in the History of Education, Being the History of the Society for the Education of the Poor of Ireland, generally known as the Kildare Place Society 1811–1831* (London: Macmillan and Company, 1904. Reprinted by Nabu Public Domain Reprints, Breingsville, PA, USA, 2010).

Kogan, M. (assisted by K. Bowden), *Educational Policy-Making: A Study of Interest Groups and Parliament* (London: Allen and Unwin, 1975).

Lecky, W., *History of Ireland in the Eighteenth Century* (London: Longmans Green, 1913).

Lee, J., *Ireland 1945–70* (Dublin: Gill and Macmillan, 1979).

_____ *Ireland 1912–1985, Politics and Society* (Cambridge: Cambridge University Press, 1989).

_____*The Modernisation of Irish Society 1848–1918* (Dublin: Gill and Macmillan, 1973).

Logan, J. (ed), *Teachers' Union: The TUI and its Forerunners 1899-1994* (Dublin: A. & A. Farmar, 1999).

Luddy, M., *Women and Philanthropy in Nineteenth-Century Ireland* (Cambridge: Cambridge University Press, 1995).

_____*Women in Ireland, 1800–1918 – A Documentary History* (Cork: Cork University Press, 1995).

Luddy, M. and C. Murphy, *Women Surviving: Studies in Irish Women's History in the Nineteenth and Twentieth Centuries* (Dublin: Poolbeg Press, 1989).

Lynch, P., 'Societal Change and Education: Investment in Education Revisited', in Farrell, B., *Issues in Education: Changing Education, Changing Society* (Dublin: ASTI Journal, 1999).

Lyons, T., *The Education Work of Richard Lovell Edgeworth, Irish Educator and Inventor, 1744-1817* (New Jersey: Mellen Press, 2003).

Magee, J., *The Teaching of Irish History in Irish Schools* (Belfast: The Northern Ireland Community Relations Commission, 1971).

McCormack, C., '"Straw bonnets" to superior schooling: the "failure" of the charity school movement in the context of nineteenth-century Ireland: a reappraisal'. *Paedagogica Historica: International Journal of the History of Education*, 48, 5 (2012).

McDowell, R.B. (ed.), *Social Life in Ireland 1800–45* (Cork: Mercier Press, 1976).

McDowell, R.B. and D.A. Webb, *Trinity College Dublin, 1592–1952: An Academic History.* (Cambridge: Cambridge University Press, 1982).

Mc Elligott, T.J., *Secondary Education in Ireland 1870–1921* (Dublin: Irish Academic Press, 1981).

McGlynn, C., 'Integrated and Faith-Based Schooling in Northern Ireland', *The Irish Journal of Education*, 36 (2005).

McGrath, T., *Politics, Interdenominational Relations and Education* (Dublin: Four Courts Press, 1999).

McManus, A., *The Irish Hedge School and Its Books, 1695–1831* (Dublin: Four Courts Press, 2002).

McNiffe, L., *A History of the Garda Síochána* (Dublin: Wolfhound Press, 1997).

Milne, K., *The Irish Charter Schools, 1730–1830* (Dublin: Four Courts Press, 1997).

Moffat, C., (ed.), *Education Together for a Change: Integrated Education and Community Relations in Northern Ireland* (Belfast: Fortnight Educational Trust, 1993).

Moody, T.W. and J.C. Beckett, *Queen's, Belfast 1845–1949: The History of a University* (2 vols), (London: Faber and Faber for QUB, 1959).

Murray, D., *Worlds Apart: Segregated Schools in Northern Ireland* (Belfast: Appletree Press, 1985).

Neuburg, V.E., *Popular Education in Eighteenth Century England* (London: Woburn Books, 1971).

Ó Buachalla, S., *Education Policy in Twentieth Century Ireland* (Dublin: Wolfhound Press, 1988).

O'Callaghan, J., *Teaching Irish Independence: History in Irish Schools* (Cambridge Scholars' Publishing, 2009).

Ó Canainn, S., 'The Education Inquiry 1824-26 in its Social and Political Context', *Irish Educational Studies*, 3, 2 (1983).

O' Connell, M., (ed.), *Daniel O'Connell, Education, Church and State: Proceedings of the*

Annual Daniel O'Connell Workshop (Dublin: Institute of Public Administration, 1992).

O'Connell, P., *The Schools and Scholars of Breiffne* (Dublin: Browne and Nolan, 1942).

O'Connor, A.V. and S.M. Parkes, *Gladly Learn and Gladly Teach: Alexandra College and School 1866-1966* (Dublin: Blackwater Press, 1983).

O'Connor, M., *The Development of Infant Education in Ireland, 1838–1948* (Oxford: Peter Lang, 2010).

O'Connor, S., *A Troubled Sky: Reflections on the Irish Educational Scene* (Dublin: Educational Research Centre, 1986).

O'Donoghue, T.A., *The Catholic Church and the Secondary School Curriculum in Ireland, 1922-1962* (New York: Peter Lang, 1999).

Osborne, R., R. Cormack, Anthony Gallagher (eds), *After the Reforms: Education and Policy in Northern Ireland* (Aldershot, UK: Avebury, 1993).

O'Sullivan, D., *Cultural Politics and Irish Education Since the 1950s: Policy, Paradigms and Power* (Dublin: Institute of Public Administration, 2005).

Parkes, S.M., *A Guide to Sources for the History of Irish Education, 1780–1922* (Dublin: Four Courts Press, 2010).

_____ *Kildare Place: A History of the Church of Ireland Training College and College of Education 1811–2010* (Dublin: CICE, 2011).

_____ *Kildare Place: A History of the Church of Ireland Training College 1811–1969* (Dublin: CICE, 1984).

Paz, D.G., *The Politics of Working-Class Education in Britain 1830–50* (Manchester: Manchester University Press, 1980).

Peckham Magray, M., *The Transforming Power of the Nuns. Women, Religion, and Cultural Change in Ireland, 1750–1900* (Oxford: Oxford University Press, 1985).

Raftery, D., 'Teaching as a profession for first-generation women graduates: a comparison of sources from Ireland, England and North America', *Irish Educational Studies*, 16 (1997).

_____ '"Je suis d'aucune nation": the recruitment and identity of Irish women religious in the international mission field, c. 1840–1940', *Paedagogica Historica: International Journal of the History of Education*, 49, 4 (2013).

Raftery, D. and S.M. Parkes, *Female Education in Ireland, 1700–1900: Minerva or Madonna?* (Dublin and Portland, OR: Irish Academic Press, 2007).

Randles, E., *Post-Primary Education in Ireland 1957–1970* (Dublin: Veritas, 1975).

Relihan, M., 'The Nineteenth-Century National School System in Ireland: An Egalitarian Concept?', *History of Education Researcher*, 78 (2006).

Richardson, N. and T. Gallagher (eds), *Education for Diversity and Mutual Understanding: The Experience of Northern Ireland* (Bern: Peter Lang, 2011).

Robins, J., *The Lost Children: A Study of Charity Children in Ireland, 1700–1900* (Dublin: Institute of Public Administration, 1980).

Smith, A. and A. Robinson, *Education for Mutual Understanding, The Initial Statutory Years* (Coleraine: University of Ulster, 1996).

Smith, M., *Reckoning with the Past: Teaching History in Northern Ireland* (Lanham, Maryland: Lexington Books, 2005).

Wallace, W.J.R., *Faithful to Our Trust : A History of the Erasmus Smith Trust and the High School Dublin* (Dublin: Columba Press, 2004).

Walsh, B., *Roman Catholic Nuns in England and Wales, 1800–1937: A Social History* (Dublin: Irish Academic Press, 2002).

Walsh, J., *The Politics of Expansion: the Transformation of Educational Policy in the Republic of Ireland, 1957–72* (Manchester and New York: Manchester University Press, 2009).

Walsh, T.J., *Nano Nagle and the Presentation Sisters* (Dublin: M.H. Gill & Son, 1959).

Whelan, B. (ed.), *Women and Paid Work in Ireland, 1500–1930* (Dublin: Four Courts Press, 2000).

UNPUBLISHED DISSERTATIONS AND THESES

Bradley, W.J., 'Sir Thomas Wyse, Irish Pioneer in Education Reform' (Unpublished PhD thesis, University of Dublin, Trinity College, 1945).

Clarke, M., 'Vocational Education in a local context 1930–1998' (Unpublished PhD thesis, University College Dublin, 1999).

Clayton, H.R., 'Societies Formed to Educate the Poor in Ireland in the Late Eighteenth and Early Nineteenth Centuries' (Unpublished PhD thesis, University of Dublin, Trinity College, 1980).

Cosgrove, J., 'The Educational Aims and Activities of Sir Thomas Wyse 1791–1862' (Unpublished PhD thesis, University of Manchester, 1975).

Fahey, A., 'Female Asceticism in the Catholic Church: A Case Study of Nuns in Ireland in the Nineteenth Century' (Unpublished PhD thesis, University of Illinois, 1982).

Fischer, K., 'L'histoire irlandaise à l'école en Irlande 1922-1996' (Unpublished PhD thesis, University of Caen, 2000).

Hislop, H., 'The Kildare Place Society, 1811–1831. An Irish Experiment in Popular Education' (Unpublished PhD thesis, University of Dublin, Trinity College, 1990).

Jones, V., 'Recruitment and Formation of Students into the Church of Ireland Training College 1922-1961' (Unpublished MLitt. thesis, University of Dublin, Trinity College, 1989).

McCormack, C.F., 'The Endowed Schools Commissions 1791–1894 as mediators of superior schooling in Ireland' (Unpublished PhD thesis, University College Dublin, 2010).

O'Connell, P.J., 'Thomas Sheridan and the Education of Young Gentlemen in the Eighteenth Century: with Particular Reference to Ireland' (Unpublished MEd thesis, University College Dublin, 1994).

O'Sullivan, E., 'The Training of Women Teachers in Ireland, 1824–1919, with special reference to Mary Immaculate College and Limerick' (Unpublished MA thesis, Mary Immaculate College, University of Limerick, 1998).

Relihan, M., 'The Church of Ireland and its Relationship with the Irish Education System, 1922-1950 with Particular Reference to the Irish Language and Gaelic Culture' (Unpublished PhD thesis, University College Dublin, 2008).

Revington, C., 'The Kildare Place Society: Its Principles and Policy' (Unpublished MEd thesis, University of Dublin, Trinity College, 1981).

Smyth, W., 'Irish History in Secondary Intermediate Schools in Northern Ireland – A Survey of Extent, Teaching Methods, Qualifications of Teachers and Pupil Attitudes' (Unpublished MA thesis, Queen's University, Belfast, 1974).

INDEX